The BONNIE BUNCH of ROSES

by Dan Milner
Music transcribed by Paul Kaplan

OAK PUBLICATIONS
New York • London • Sydney

Cover design by Nina Clayton
Edited by Patricia Ann Neely, Peter Pickow, and Steven Rosenhaus

Order No. OK 63883
International Standard Book Number: 0.8256.0256.4
Library of Congress Catalog Card Number: 80-83112

Exclusive Distributors:
Music Sales Corporation
257 Park Avenue South, New York, NY 10010 USA
Music Sales Limited
8/9 Frith Street, London W1V 5TZ England
Music Sales Pty. Limited
120 Rothschild Street, Rosebery, Sydney, NSW 2018, Australia

Printed in the United States of America by
Vicks Lithograph and Printing Corporation

To my father, Bill Milner.
He started me singing.

Contents

Introduction

I grew up singing in a singing family—at first in Birmingham and Ballybunion, later on in the immigrant surroundings of Toronto, Boston, and Brooklyn. My father had a few of the old songs: **The Wild Rover, I Wish They'd Do It Now, McCaffery, Early One Morning, Barbara Allen**—plus a host of sentimental Irish songs. Even my mother's side, the relatively non-musical Kerry Cremins, have kinship to "The Weaver," Denis Murphy of Gneeveguilla. So it is out of a long love for traditional music and a matchmaker's zeal to see others wooed with its beauty that I thought to put together this sampler.

Here is a book of songs for singers. A mixed bag of tenderness, sly humor, sheer horror, compelling lust, history and pseudo-history, repeated thoughtless stupidity, a few lies, great heroic effort, sublime devotion, and just damn bad luck. They are songs from England, Ireland, and Scotland: Irish songs from Hampshire and Scots ones from Galway, set with altogether further-fetched mutations.

No one in his right mind would wish to learn all of these songs, though every one is suitable for many people. They run the gamut from very popular to totally obscure. There is great breadth here, but no attempt was made to be fully representative; the magnificent old Gaelic music is not ignored, simply not dealt with. I hope that experienced singers—those who sing often and sing well—will enjoy the selection and that novices—those still learning the subtleties of folksong—will move smoothly from best known to unknown pieces to the bibliography and on again. I offer them some advice . . . advice passed on to me by some truly brilliant singers:

1. Have no special favorite. Listen to as many singers and songs as you can. Listen to instrumental music, the relationship is very important.

2. Not every song suits every singer.

3. Sing naturally. Mean what you sing. Sincerity cannot take a backseat to technique. Ennunciate well.

4. Sing only martial music to the hard beat. Sing everything else to the pulse, singing within and around the rhythm as skill increases.

Singers come in three categories: those who tell the tale precisely as they heard it, those who would only occasionally alter certain details to clarify the message, and those very individualistic singers who stamp much of their repertoire with their own trademark. In preparing this book, we have noted songs which come directly from other singers as precisely as possible. Transcriptions from my singing, naturally, are not identical to my sources' singing. Texts taken from broadsides and earlier collections have received treatment varying from exact reproduction to collation, while certain tunes, as noted, have been adapted or newly composed. There is a real mixture.

Loosely defined, all here are folk songs inasmuch as they are or have been a representative expression of a community. In most cases, the composer is unknown and, likely, text and melody have altered over the years as successive performers have both consciously and unconsciously reshaped the song. Intrinsic to this process is the type of aural transmission which allows for flexible performance. There is no definitive version of any real folk song— here or elsewhere.

On the way through this book I have commented on each of the songs, sometimes factually, sometimes humorously—at least either to be factual or humorous was my intention. I defer to serious students of folklore and ethnomusicology on matters of information and to persons of true natural charm on matters of wit. "They know their onions," as my father would have said. I only claim to be a singer. The songs stand well enough by themselves.

I was helped on this project by many, immensely talented persons. Indeed, it was they who inspired me in the first place. Having got to know each of them better is the greatest reward this book will bring. To whatever degree this selection of ballads and lyrical songs succeeds—esthetically or popularly —it is because of them. The flaws are mine.

First, thanks to everyone who gave me a song. No finer group could be assembled. They are Frankie Armstrong, Joe Heaney, Dáithí Sproule, Martin Carthy, Dave Surman, Tony Barrand, Donál Maguire, Cilla Fisher and Artie Trezise, Seamus Walker, Louie Killen, Patsy Lane, Séan Cannon, Johnny Beggan, John Roberts, Tony Callanan, Declan Hunt, Cathal McConnell, Margaret Barry, Allan Carr, Father Charlie Coen, Mick Moloney, the Waterson family, Charles O'Hegarty, David Jones, Peter Bellamy, Roy Harris, and Ewan MacColl. Great singers make everyone sing better. Thanks also to Jean Ritchie and George Pickow who have allowed me to use items from their British Isles field recordings.

Maddy DeLeon and Joe Heaney suggested a title both evocative and descriptive. Ed Haber and Bob Rodriguez, record collectors, supplied some discographical information. Lisa Null and Frank Woerner let me look through their fine libraries. Susan Veasey both typed while I cooked and cooked while I typed, thereby allowing some variety in my life. Roy Harris and Mick Moloney read the manuscript and strengthened it with their suggestions. The interest shown by Peter Pickow and Jason Shulman of Oak Publications has been rivaled only by their patience. Thank you all.

I could have had no finer collaborator than Paul Kaplan. A gentle nature allows great sympathy.

A Note from the Transcriber

Musical notation of folk songs in a publication such as this must involve a certain amount of compromise. The highly personal nature of folk song performance can produce extremely subtle variations in rhythm, tempo, and melody which, if faithfully transcribed, would leave all but a select group of scholarly readers hopelessly bewildered. However, the reader who is able to (and chooses to) decipher the various grace notes, scooped notes, fermatas and tempo changes which have been set down will be able to recreate the original performance fairly accurately. In some instances, more accurate versions of particular measures are offered at the bottom of the page.

In general, an effort has been made to retain each singer's individual style in the transcriptions. Since only the first verse has been notated, the reader is advised to retain the feeling of the first verse when singing subsequent verses, even if this means deviating from the given rhythms, melody notes, etc.

Finally, it cannot be stressed enough how important it is to hear the singing of people such as those included in this book. The more familiar the reader is with the styles of these folksingers, the easier it will be to bring to life the songs in this collection, using the transcriptions. Folk music is by definition an oral tradition; it is in these singers, and those who learn from them, that the tradition lives.

About the Accompaniments

The songs have been notated wherever possible in keys that keep the melody within the vocal range of the average singer, at the same time generating chords which will present minimal difficulty for the beginning to intermediate instrumentalist. Occasionally, alternate chords have been included in parentheses for the more adventuresome musician.

A few songs have all the chords in parentheses. In these cases the transcribed performance was *a cappella*, and no chords could be found that would not intrude upon the pure vocal beauty. Chords are offered for chord fanatics, on the condition that they recognize that they will be altering the nature of the song by using chords.

In cases where no chordal accompaniment was provided by the singer, and it seemed appropriate to invent one, the approach has been conservative. This means that, in general, chords have not been suggested which include chromatic notes, unless they appear in the melody. For instance, songs in the key of A minor use the chord E minor, which includes the note G, rather than the chord E major, which includes the note G♯, unless G♯ is used in the melody.

About the Modes

Some of the songs have a notation in the upper left-hand corner indicating that they are in a particular "mode," such as Mixolydian or Dorian. These are songs using scales which differ from the normal major and minor scales, thus achieving a richness that must be a major factor in their survival (in some cases, for centuries).

Actually, songs that are in modes do use the major scale, but the tonal center ("home base") is not where we expect it to be. For instance, if a song uses the scale of C major, but sets up the note D as the tonal center, then the song is said to be in the "Dorian mode." The Dorian scale of D, then, is DEFGABCD, which is neither major nor minor (although it has a distinctly minor feel).

D   E   F   G   A   B   C   D

If the tonal center is G, using the C major scale produces what sounds like the key of G major, only the seventh step is flatted (F♮ instead of F♯). The scale thus produced is called the "Mixolydian mode." So in **Thomas o' Winesberrie**, which is in the Mixolydian of A, the key signature has two sharps, F♯ and C♯. The scale of A major has a third sharp, G♯, but here it has been flatted to G♮ to produce the Mixolydian of A.

A   B   C   D   E   F   G   A

Of course, the major and natural minor scales (which, strictly speaking, are also modes) are also used. In certain instances, one of these is used together with one of the modes mentioned above to form a "combined mode." In these cases the major scale is identified as the "Ionian mode" and the natural minor is called the "Aeolian mode."

Finally, certain songs are labeled as "pentatonic." The five notes of the pentatonic scale can be outlined by playing the black keys on the piano, or by playing a major scale minus the fourth and seventh steps. Any one of the five notes in the pentatonic scale can be used as the tonic note, so that some pentatonic songs will sound major and others minor.

9

Guitar Chords Used in this Book

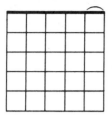 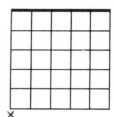

These are bar chords. The first finger covers all of the indicated strings simultaneously.

The arrow points to the root of the chord. This is the note that gives the chord its name, and is the preferred bass note.

× marks a string that should not be sounded in the chord.

(▲) This is not the root of the chord, but is the best available bass note.

B7
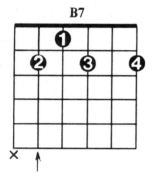
× ↑

Bm
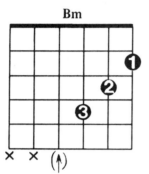
× × (↑)

or

Bm
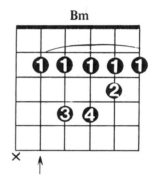
× ↑

E
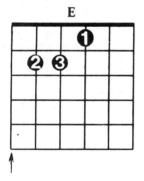
↑

E7
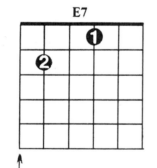
↑

or

E7
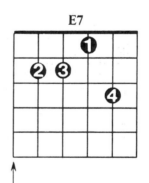
↑

Em
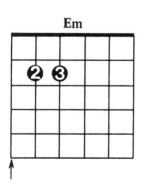
↑

or

Em
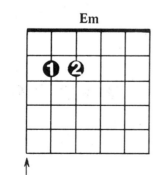
↑

A
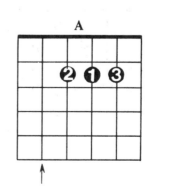
↑

or

A
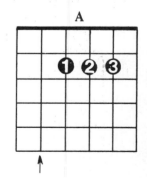
↑

A7 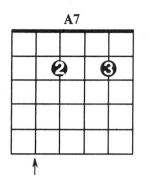 or **A7** 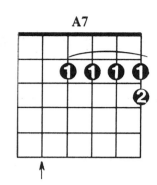 **Am** 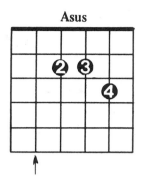 **Asus**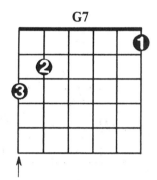

D 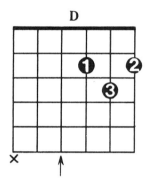 **D7** 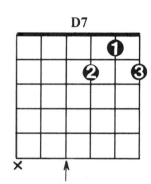 **Dm** 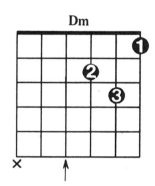 **G7**

G 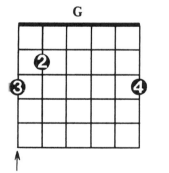 or **G** 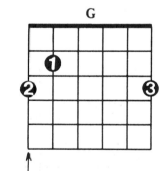 **Gm** 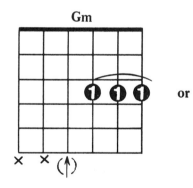 or **Gm**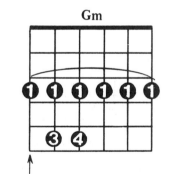

C 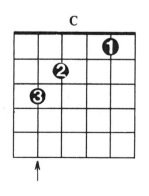 **C#m** 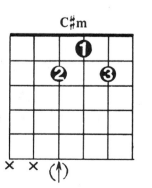 or **C#m**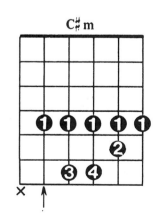

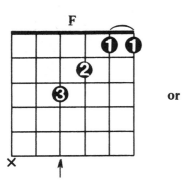

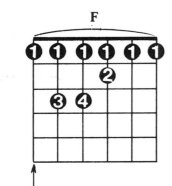

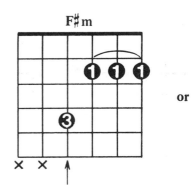

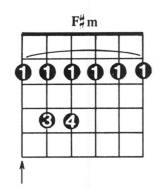

or

or

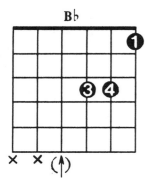

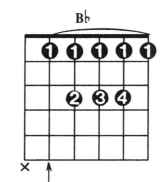

or

Guitar Tunings

All of the songs can be played on the guitar as it is normally tuned, that is,

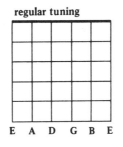

regular tuning

E A D G B E

EADGBE. But for some of the songs, alternate tunings can make the accompaniment more expressive. The most common of these are the so-called "modal tunings," in which the all-important "3rd" is missing from the tonic chord, leaving it ambiguous in nature, neither major nor minor. Two simple modal tunings are given below, along with a listing of songs for which they may be used. When these tunings are used, some chords are fingered in the normal way and others are not. New fingerings are diagrammed for each tuning.

12

A modal tuning:

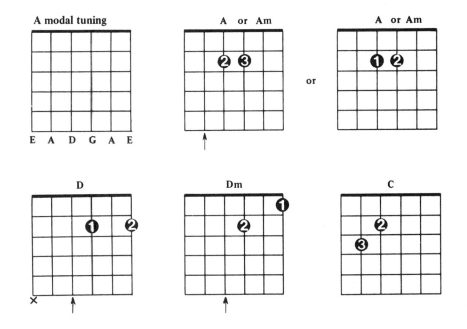

Thomas o' Winesberrie, The Saucy Bold Robber, James McDonald, The Green Fields of America, The May Morning Dew, The Flower of Sweet Strabane, Heather on the Moor, The Little Ball of Yarn, The Buxom Lass.

D modal tuning:

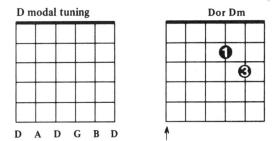

The Maid and the Soldier, The Rocky Road to Dublin, Poor Murdered Woman, The Banks of the Nile, The Wings of a Gull, I Am a Maid that Sleeps in Love, The Woods of Trugh.

Some guitarists alter the standard tuning even further. One interesting tuning is a combination of the D and A modal tunings, known as DADGAD. This is used by Dáithí Sproule, who gave us The Death of Queen Jane and Johnny of Hazelgreen.

DADGAD tuning:

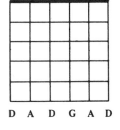

Of course, there are hundreds of other possible tunings, many of which haven't been invented yet. Go to it!

Older Ballads

Binnorie

Certain of the ballads are thought to have been sung while dancing, **Binnorie** (or **The Two Sisters**) amongst them. This tradition is, incidentally, still to be seen in certain parts of Appalachia in what's called the play-party.

Most interesting about this version, a Northumbrian one, is the "recycling" of the younger sister, as her breastbone becomes a harp. There is a type of logic in this continuation of beauty from the visual to the aural that is somewhat lost to the modern sensibility.

Source: J. C. Bruce and J. Stokoe, *Northumbrian Minstrelsy.*

Recording: Ewan MacColl, *The English and Scottish Popular Ballads (The Child Ballads),* Washington 715.

(Child 10)

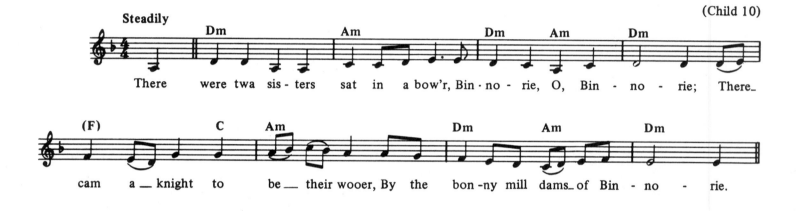

There were twa sisters sat in a bow'r, Binnorie, O, Binnorie; There cam a knight to be their wooer, By the bonny mill dams of Binnorie.

There were twa sisters sat in a bow'r
Binnorie, O, Binnorie;
There cam a knight to be their wooer,
By the bonny mill dams of Binnorie.

He courted the eldest wi' glove and ring,
Binnorie, O, Binnorie;
But he lo'ed the youngest aboon a' thing.
By the bonny mill dams of Binnorie.

He courted the eldest wi' broach and knife,
But he lo'ed the youngest aboon his life.

The eldest she was vexed sair,
And sore envied her sister fair.

The eldest said to the youngest ane:
"Will you go and see our father's ships come in."

She's ta'en her by the lily hand,
And led her down to the river strand.

The youngest stude upon a stane,
The eldest cam and pushed her in.

She took her by the middle sma',
And dashed her bonny back to the jaw.

"O sister, sister, reach your hand,
And ye shall be heir to half my land."

"O sister, I'll not reach my hand,
And I'll be heir of all your land."

"Shame fa' the hand that I should take,
It's twined me, and my world's make."

"O sister, reach me but your glove,
And sweet William shall be your love."

"Sink on, nor hope for hand or glove,
And sweet William shall better be my love.

"Your cherry cheeks and your yellow hair
Garr'd me gang maiden ever mair."

Sometimes she sunk, sometimes she swam,
Until she cam to the miller's dam.

The miller's daughter was baking bread,
And gaed for water as she had need.

"O father, father, draw your dam!
There's either a mermaid or a milk-white swan."

The miller hasted and drew his dam,
And there he found a drown'd woman.

Ye couldna see her yellow hair
For gawd and pearls that were sae rare.

Ye couldna see her middle sma',
Her gowden girdle was sae braw.

Ye couldna see her lily free,
Her gowden fringes were sae deep.

A famous harper passing by,
The sweet pale face he chanced to spy;

And when he looked that lady on,
He sighed and made a heavy moan.

"Sair will they be, whate'er they be,
The hearts that live to weep for thee."

He made a harp o' her breast bone,
Whose sounds would melt a heart of stone;

The strings he framed of her yellow hair
Their notes made sade the listening ear.

He brought it to her father's ha',
There was the court assembled a'.

He laid the harp upon a stane,
And straight it began to play alane—

"O yonder sits my father, the king,
And yonder sits my mother, the queen;

"And yonder stands my brother Hugh,
And by him my William, sweet and true."

But the last tune that the harp played then
Was-"Woe to my sister, false Helen!"

16

My Boy Tommy, O!

Better known as **Billy Boy**, this ballad is regarded as a parady of the older **Lord Randal**, in which the young man is poisoned by his lover. This Irish version has him treated very well indeed, an older woman seeing to his every need. The story is ancient and spread throughout Europe.

I've changed this song slightly over the years, I know. The original was collected in 1921 from Bat Riordan of Kilnanare, Co. Kerry.

Source: Adapted from the *Journal of the Irish Folk Song Society*, XVIII.

Recordings: Five versions, *The Child Ballads*, Caedmon TC 1145. Martin Carthy, *Sweet Wivelsfield*, Rounder 3020.

Combined Dorian and Aeolian of A

(Child 12)

"Where have you been all the day,— My boy Tom-my, O? — Where have you been all the day,- My bon - ny blue - eyed Tom?" "I've been rol - ling in— the hay, With a las - sie young and gay." "Was - n't she the fine — one's late - ly left— her mam - my, O?"

"Where have you been all the day,
My boy Tommy, O?
Where have you been all the day,
My bonny blue-eyed Tom?"
"I've been rolling in the hay,
With a lassie young and gay."
*"Wasn't she the fine one's
Lately left her mammy, O?"*

"What did she give you to eat,
My boy Tommy, O?
What did she give you to eat,
My bonny blue-eyed Tom?"
"She gave me bread, she gave me meat,
And that's what she gave me to eat."
*"Wasn't she the fine one's
Lately left her mammy, O?"*

"What did she give you to drink,
My boy Tommy, O?
What did she give you to drink,
My bonny blue-eyed Tom?"
"She gave me wine as black as ink,
And that's what she gave me to drink."
*"Wasn't she the fine one's
Lately left her mammy, O?"*

"Can she mend and can she make,
My boy Tommy, O?
Can she mend and can she make,
My bonny blue-eyed Tom?"
"She can mend and she can make,
She can give and she can take."
*"Wasn't she the fine one's
Lately left her mammy, O?"*

"Can she bake a corn-cake,
My boy Tommy, O?
Can she bake a corn-cake,
My bonny blue-eyed Tom?"
She can bake a corn-cake
Fit for any man to eat."
*"Wasn't she the fine one's
Lately left her mammy, O?"*

"Can she make a feather bed,
My boy Tommy, O?
Can she make a feather bed,
My bonny blue-eyed Tom?"
"She can make a feather bed
Fit for any man to rest."
*"Wasn't she the fine one's
Lately left her mammy, O?"*

"What age is this young thing,
My boy Tommy, O?
What age is this young thing,
My bonny blue-eyed Tom?"
"Twice two and twice four,
Twice seven and eleven more."
*"Wasn't she the fine one's
Lately left her mammy, O?"*

Hind Horn

In his notes to **Hind Horn,** Professor Child cites three related medieval romances from which the present ballad may have been fragmented and condensed. They are written in early English, and the oldest of these dates from about 1250. **Horn et Rymenhild,** the longest of the romances, has over five thousand verses!

Both the melody and the story of this ballad are very compelling. It's a rather long song, however, and I suggest it be saved for those occasions when time is of no consequence and the tale can be told slowly and beautifully.

Source: Text collated from various sources; tune from G. Greig and A. Keith, *Last Leaves of the Traditional Ballads and Ballad Airs.*

Recording: Ewan MacColl, *The English and Scottish Popular Ballads (The Child Ballads)*, Washington 715.

Near Edinburgh town was a young child born,
With a high loo low and a high loo land.
His name was called young Hind Horn
And the birk and the broom blooms bonnie-o.

Seven years he served the King,
With a high loo low and a high loo land.
All for the sake of his daughter Jean.
And the birk and the broom blooms bonnie-o

The King an angry man was he
And he sent young Hind Horn to the sea.

She's given to him a golden ring
With seven diamonds set therein.

When this ring grows pale and wan
You may know by it that my love is gone.

One day he looked his ring upon
And he knew she loved another man.

He's left the sea and come to the land
And there's he's met an old beggar man.

"What's news, what news doth thee betide?"
"No news but the Princess Jean's a bride."

"Will you give to me thy begging tweed
And I'll give to you my riding steed?"

The beggar he was bound for to ride
And Hind Horn he was bound for the bride.

When he came to the King's own gate
He sought a drink for Hind Horn's sake.

He drank out the wine and dropped in the ring
And bade them take it to the Princess Jean.

"Got you this ring by sea or land,
Or got you this from a dead man's hand?"

"Not from sea and not from land.
But I got it from thy milk-white hand."

"I'll cast off my gown of brown
And I'll follow you from town to town."

"You needn't cast off your gowns of brown,
For I'll make you the lady of many a town."

"I'll cast off my dress of red
And I'll follow you and beg my bread."

"You needn't cast off your dress of red,
For I'll maintain you with wine and bread.

The bridegroom had the bride first wed,
But young Hind Horn took her first to bed.

18

Down by the Greenwood Sidey

This ballad has had greater popularity in America than in the Isles over the last 150 years, though there is no shortage of excellent versions as a result. Occasionally the mother meets three children, the third being Jesus Christ:

As she went on her homeward way
She met three children a-playing ball.

One was dressed in silks so fine,
The other two were dressed as naked as born.

Child prints a number of texts, one Scottish and having the title **The Minister's Daughter of New York**. He also quotes a similar Danish ballad:

She spread her cloak down on the earth
And on it to two little twins gave birth.

She laid them under so broad a stone
Suffered sorrow nor harm for what she had done.

Source: Collated from various sources; tune from *Journal of the Folk Song Society*, III.

Recording: Jean Redpath, *Skipping Barefoot Through the Heather*, Prestige International 13041. Dominic Behan, *The Singing Streets*, Folkways FW 8501.

(Child 20)

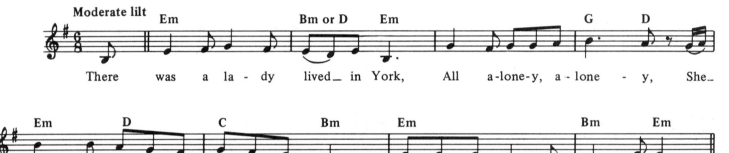

There was a lady lived in York,
 All aloney, aloney,
She fell in love with her father's clerk,
 Down by the greenwood sidey.

He courted her a year and a day,
 All aloney, aloney
And then he did that girl betray.
 Down by the greenwood sidey.

She leaned her back against a thorn,
And there she had two pretty babes born.

She had a penknife long and sharp
She pierced those tender babies' hearts.

She washed the knife clean in the flood,
She turned the river all to blood.

She buried them under a marble stone,
And then she turned her face toward home.

As she came by her father's hall,
She saw two pretty babes playing at ball.

"Oh babes! Oh babes! If you were mine,
I'd dress you up in silks so fine."

"Oh mother! Oh mother! We once were thine,
You did not prove to us so kind.

"Seven years, seven years you shall burn in Hell,
Seven years and you won't see heaven until."

19

The Well Below the Valley

Long thought extinct in oral tradition, this ballad was recorded by Tom Munnelly, for the first time in Ireland, from the singing of the late John Reilly, an Irish traveler who died under pathetic circumstances in 1966 at Boyle, Co. Roscommon; the musical transcription used here is a simplified one. More detailed information on Reilly and his songs can be found in the recording *The Bonny Green Tree*. Incidentally, the royalties from the record go to a travelers' workshop in Ireland. Oak has also made a small donation in John Reilly's name.

Source: Adapted from B. H. Bronson, *The Singing Tradition of Child's Popular Ballads.*

Recordings: John Reilly, *The Bonny Green Tree*, Topic 12T359. Planxty, *Planxty*, Polydor 2383 186.

Combined Dorian and Aeolian of D

(Child 21)

A gentleman was passing by;
He asked for a drink, he was dry
At the well below the valley O,
Green grows the lily O
Right among the bushes O.

"My cup it is in overflow
And if I do stoop I may fall in
At the well below the valley O."
Green grows the lily O
Right among the bushes O.

"Well if your true love was passing by
You'd fill him a drink if he got dry
At the well below the valley O."

She swore by grass and swore by corn
That her true love was never born.
"I say, fair maiden, you've swore in wrong
At the well below the valley O."

"Well if you're a man of that noble fame
You'll tell to me the father o' them
At the well below the valley O."

"Two o' them by your father dear
At the well below the valley O."

"Two more o' them came by your uncle Dan
At the well below the valley O."

"Another one by your brother John
At the well below the valley O."

"Well if you're a man of the noble fame
You'll tell to me what happened then
At the well below the valley O."

"There was two o' them buried by the kitchen fire
At the well below the valley O."

"Two more o' them buried by the stable door
At the well below the valley O."

The other was buried by the well
At the well below the valley O."

"Well if you're a man of the noble fame
You'll tell to me what will happen myself
At the well below the valley O."

"You'll be seven long years a-ringin' a bell
At the well below the valley O."

You'll be seven more a-porin' in Hell
At the well below the valley O."

"I'll be seven long years a-ringin' the bell
But the Lord above might save my soul
From portin' in Hell
At the well below the valley O."

Thomas the Rhymer

Thomas of Erceldoune, **Thomas the Rhymer**, was a real man. From before his death in the late thirteenth century until the turn of the last century, he was venerated in Scotland as a "seer." Many of his sayings or prophecies were passed from generation to generation. This ballad tells the story of how Thomas received his power, which was a gift from the Queen of Elfland.

Source: Adapted from Sir Walter Scott, *Minstrelsy of the Scottish Border.*

Recording: Ewan MacColl, *The English and Scottish Popular Ballads (Child Ballads)*, Folkways FG 3509.

(Child 37)

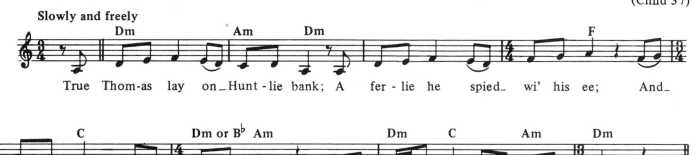

21

True Thomas lay on Huntlie bank;
A ferlie he spied wi' his ee;
And there he saw a ladye bright,
Come riding down by the Eildon Tree.

Her shirt was o' the grass-green silk,
Her mantle o' the velvet fyne;
At ilka tett of her horse's mane,
Hung fifty siller bells and nine.

True Thomas, he pull'd aff his cap,
And louted low down to his knee,
"All hail, thou mighty Queen of Heaven!
For thy peer on earth I never did see."

"O no, O no, Thomas," she said,
"That name does not belang to me;
I am but the Queen of fair Elfland,
That am hither come to visit thee.

"Harp and carp, Thomas," she said;
"Harp and carp along wi' me;
And if ye dare to kiss my lips,
Sure of your bodie I will be."

"Betide me weal, betide me woe,
That weird shall never daunton me."
Syne he has kissed her rosy lips,
All underneath the Eildon Tree.

"Now, ye maun go wi' me," she said;
"True Thomas, ye maun go wi' me;
And ye maun serve me seven years,
Thro' weal or woe as may chance to be."

She mounted on her milk-white steed;
She's ta'en true Thomas up behind:
And aye, whene'er her bridle rung,
The steed flew swifter than the wind.

O they rade on, and farther on;
The steed gaed swifter than the wind;
Until they reach'd a desert wide,
And living land was left behind.

"Light down, light down, now, true Thomas,
And lean your head upon my knee;
Abide and rest a little space,
And I will shew you ferlies three."

"O see ye not yon narrow road,
So thick beset with thorns and briers?
That is the path of righteousness,
Though after it but few enquires."

"And see ye not that braid braid road,
That lies across that lily leven?
That is the path of wickedness,
Though some call it the road to heaven."

"And see not ye that bonny road,
That winds about the fernie brae?
That is the road to fair Elfland,
Where thou and I this night maun gae."

"But Thomas, ye maun hold your tongue,
Whatever ye may hear or see;
For, if you speak in Elflyn land,
Ye'll ne'er get back to your ain countrie."

O they rade on, and farther on,
And they waded through rivers aboon the knee,
And they saw neither sun nor moon,
But they heard the roaring of the sea.

It was mirk mirk, night and there was nae stern light,
And they waded through red blude to the knee;
For a' the blude that's shed on earth
Rins through the springs o' that countrie.

Syne they came on to a garden green,
And she pu'd an apple frae a tree.
"Take this for thy wages, true Thomas;
It will give thee the tongue that can never lie."

"My tongue is mine ain," true Thomas said;
"A gudely gift ye wad gie to me!
I neighter dought to buy nor sell,
At fair or tryst where I may be."

"I dought neither speak to prince or peer,
Nor ask of grace from fair ladye."
"Now hold thy peace!" the lady said,
"For as I say, so must it be."

He has gotten a coat of the even cloth,
And a pair of shoes of velvet green;
And till seven years were gane and past,
True Thomas on earth was never seen.

Tomlin

Sir Walter Scott is quoted in Child's introduction: "The wife of a farmer in Lothian had been carried off by the fairies, and, during the year of probation, repeatedly appeared on Sunday, in the midst of her children, combing their hair. On one of these occasions she was accosted by her husband; when she related to him the unfortunate event which had separated them [and] instructed him by what means he might win her ... the farmer, who ardently loved his wife, set out at Halloween, and, in the midst of a plot of furze, waited impatiently for the procession of fairies. At the ringing of the fairy bridles, and the wild, unearthly sound which accompanied the cavalcade, his heart failed him and he suffered the ghostly train to pass by without interruption. When the last rode past, the whole troop vanished, with loud shouts of laughter and exultation, among which he plainly discovered the voice of his wife, lamenting that he had lost her forever."

The words come from a small ballad book privately printed in Edinburgh in 1885, and said to be taken down from the recitation of an old woman. It was evidently "improved" a mite in the process, and this, of course, has had a good and a bad effect.

Source: Text from J. Maidment, *A New Book of Old Ballads*; tune is mine.

Recording: Frankie Armstrong, *Here's a Health to the Man and the Maid*, Living Folk LFR 103.

(Child 39)

Moderately fast

O! — All you la-dies young and — gay, Who are so sweet — and fair; Do — not go in-to — Chas-ter's — wood, For — Tom-lin will — be there.

O! all you ladies young and gay,
Who are so sweet and fair;
Do not go into Chaster's wood,
For Tomlin will be there.

Fair Margaret sat in her bonny bower,
Sewing her silken seam:
And wished to be in Chaster's wood,
Among the leaves so green.

She let the seam fall to her foot,
The needle to her toe;
And she has gone to Chater's wood
As Fast as she could go.

When she began to pull the flowers,
She pull'd both red and green;
They by did come, and by did go,
Said "Fair maid let abene.

"O! why pluck you the flowers, lady,
Or why climb you the tree;
Or why come ye to Chaster's wood
Without the leave of me?"

"O! I will pull the flowers," she said,
"Or I will break the tree,
For Chaster's wood it is my own;
I'll ask no leave at thee."

He took her by the milk-white hand,
And by the grass-green sleeve;
And laid her down upon the flowers,
At her he ask'd no leave.

The lady blush'd and sourly frown'd,
And she did think great shame;
Says, "If you are a gentleman,
You will tell me your name."

"First they did call me, Jack," he said,
"And then they call'd me John;
But since I liv'd in the fairy court,
Tomlin has always been my name.

"So do not pluck that flower, lady,
That has these pimples gray;
They would destroy the bonny babe
That we've gotten in our play."

"O! tell to me, Tomlin," she said,
"And tell it to me soon:
Was you ever at a good church door,
Or got you Christendom?"

"O! I have been at a good church door,
And *oft her* yetts within;
I was the laird of Foulis's son,
The heir of all his land.

"But it fell once upon a day,
As hunting I did ride;
As I rode east and west yon hill,
There woe did me betide.

"O! drowsy, drowsy as I was,
Dead sleep upon me fell;
The Queen of fairies she was there,
And took me to hersel'.

"The morn at even is Hallowe'en,
Our fairy court will ride
Through England and Scotland both.
Through all the world wide;
And if that ye would me borrow,
At Rides Cross ye may bide.

"You may go into the Miles Moss,
Between twelve hours and one;
Take holy water in your hand,
And cast a compass round.

"The first court that comes along,
You'll let them all pass by;
The next court that comes along,
Salute them reverently.

"The next court that comes along,
Is clad in robes of green;
And its the head court of them all,
For in it rides the Queen.

"And I upon a milk-white steed;
With a gold star in my crown;
Because I am an earthly man,
I'm next the Queen in renown.

"Then seize upon me with a spring,
Then to the ground I'll fa';
And then you'll hear a rueful cry,
That Tomlin is awa'.

"Then I'll grow in your arms two,
Like to a savage wild;
But hold me fast, let me not go,
I'm father of your child.

"I'll grow into your arms two,
Like an adder, or a snake;
But hold me fast, let me not go,
I'll be your earthly maik.

"I'll grow into your arms two,
Like ice on frozen lake;
But hold me fast, let me not go,
Or from your goupen break.

"I'll grow into your arms two,
Like iron in strong fire;
But hold me fast, let me not go,
Then you'll have your desire."

And its next night into Miles Moss,
Fair Margaret has gone;
When lo she stands beside Rides Cross,
Between twelve hours and one.

There's holy water in her hand,
She casts a compass round:
And presently a fairy band
Comes riding o'er the mound.

Captain Wedderburn's Courtship

It's generally thought that the riddle portion of this one is older than the entire ballad; certainly the custom goes back for ages. **Captain Wedderburn's Courtship** is most often heard in Ireland today, although related songs like **I Gave My Love a Cherry** (or **Apple**) are common in America.

Source: Text is a collation; tune is very common, also used for **Paddy West** and **Come A' Ye Tramps an' Hawkers** (#38).

Recordings: Seamus Ennis, *The Child Ballads*, Caedmon TC 1145. Ewan MacColl, *The English and Scottish Popular Ballads (Child Ballads)*, Folkways FG 3510. Frank Donnelly, *Singing Men of Ulster*, Green Linnet SIF 1005.

Pentatonic

(Child 46)

A gen - tle man's fair daugh - ter walked down a nar - row lane. She met with Cap - tain Wed - der - burn, the keep - er of the game. He said un - to his serv - ant man, "If it was-n't for the law I'd have that maid in bed with me and she'd lie next to the wall."

A gentleman's fair daughter walked down a narrow lane.
She met with Captain Wedderburn, the keeper of the game.
He said unto his servant man, "If it wasn't for the law,
I'd have that maid in bed with me and she'd lie next to the wall."

"Oh, go your way, young man," she says, "and do not bother me.
Before you'll lie one night with me, you must answer questions
   three.
Three questions you must answer me and I'll set forth them all,
Before you lie one night with me and I lie next the wall.

"Oh, for my breakfast you must get me a cherry without a stone
And for my dinner you must get me a bird without a bone
And for my supper you must get me a bird without a gall,
Ere you and I in one bed lie and I lie next the wall."

"Well, when the cherry's in blossom it surely has no stone
And when the bird is in the egg it surely has no bone.
The dove it is a gentle bird, it flies without a gall.
Now you and I in one bed'll lie and you'll lie next the wall."

"Oh, go your way, young man," she says, "and do not me perplex.
Before you'll lie one night with me, you must answer questions six.
Six questions you must answer me and I'll set forth them all,
Before you lie one night with me and I lie next the wall.

"What is rounder than a ring? What's higher than a tree?
What is worse than a woman's wrath? What's deeper than the sea?
What bird sings best? What tree buds first and on it the dew first
   falls,
Ere you and I in one bed lie and I lie next the wall?"

"The world is rounder than a ring. Heaven's higher than a tree.
The Devil's worse than a woman's wrath. Hell's deeper than the sea.
The lark sings best. The oak buds first and on it the dew first falls.
Now you and I in one bed lie and you'll lie next the wall."

"First you must get me Winter fruit that in December grew.
You must get for me a silk mantle that weft nor warp went through,
A sparrow's horn and a priest unborn to bind us both in twa,
Ere you and I in one bed lie and I lie next the wall."

"My father had some Winter fruit that in December grew.
My mother had a silk mantle that weft nor warp went through.
A sparrow's horn is easy found; there's one in every claw
And Melkisitik was a priest unborn and you'll lie next the wall."

Lord Bateman

Based on or heavily influenced by the romance of Gilbert, father of Thomas à Becket, **Lord Bateman**'s origins are a minimum of seven hundred years old . . . and the tale is simply fantastic.

Gilbert was on a pilgrimage to the Holy Land when captured by the Saracen prince Admiraud. After considerable hardship as a prisoner, he was given the privilege of serving the prince at meals, chained as he still was. Gilbert's answering of the prince's questions on England and Catholicism drew the attention of Admiraud's sister, and she, of course, fell in love with Gilbert.

The princess told him that because of her love for him and his devotion to Christ she would marry him and take his religion. Gilbert suspected some sort of trap and asked for time to consider her proposal. Necessity is the mother of invention, as they say, and sometime afterwards Gilbert and a group of other Christians escaped. I suppose men were totally unequipped to deal with forward females at the time.

The princess followed after. Eventually reaching London, she roamed the streets, "followed by a noisy and jeering crowd of wild boys and whatnot," searching for Gilbert. And he still couldn't make up his mind!

At the same time, there was a conference of bishops; Gilbert went to St. Paul's, told them his story, and asked their advice. Prophetically, one of them received a divine indication that Gilbert and the princess were to be married.

Our setting for this song is simplified, based only on the first verse. Singing this song in proper style requires fitting the melody to the sense and cadence of each line, making musical variations to accommodate the uneven length of lines from verse to verse.

Source: Text is a collation; tune is adapted from F. Kidson, *Journal of the Folk Song Society*, I.

Recordings: John Reilly, *The Bonny Green Tree*, Topic 12-T359. Frankie Armstrong, *Out of Love, Hope and Suffering*, Bay 206.

(Child 53)

Lord Bateman was a noble Lord,
A noble Lord of high degree.
He lived uneasy and discontented.
Some foreign country for to see.

He sailed East and he sailed Westward.
He sailed till he came to the Turkish shore.
The Turk he caught him and sadly used him
Until his life he would give o'er.

The Turk he had an only daughter,
The fairest creature e'er my eyes did see.
She stole the keys to her father's prison
And vowed Lord Bateman she would go see.

"Have you got gold? Have you got silver?
Have you got lands of high degree?
What would you give to the fair young lady
That out of prison would set you free?"

"I've got gold and I've got silver,
Half Northumberland belongs to me.
I'll give it all to the fair young lady
That out of prison would set me free!"

She took him to her father's hall,
And gave to him the best of wine,
And every health she drank unto him,
Said, "I wish, Lord Bateman, you were mine."

"For seven years I'll make a vow, Love,
For seven years and I'll keep it strong,
If you will wed no other woman,
Then I will wed no other man."

She took him to her father's harbour
And gave to him a ship of fame.
"Farewell, farewell, my dear Lord Bateman,
I'm afraid I ne'er shall see you again."

When seven years were gone and past
And fourteen days well known to me,
She packed up all her gayest clothing
And swore Lord Bateman she'd go see.

When she came to Lord Bateman's castle
So boldly she did ring the bell.
"Who's there? Who's there?" cried the proud young porter,
"Who's there, now come unto me tell."

"Oh is this Lord Bateman's castle?
And is his Lordship here within?"
"Oh yes, oh yes," cried the proud young porter,
"He's just taken his new bride in."

"Then tell him to send me a slice of bread
And a bottle of his very best wine
And not to forget the fair young lady
That did release him when close confined."

Away, away went this proud young porter,
Away, away and away went he
Until he came to Lord Bateman's chamber,
Then down on bended knees fell he.

"What news, what news, my proud young porter?
What news, what news have you brought to me?
"Oh, there is the fairest of all young ladies
That ever my two eyes did see.

She has got rings on every finger
And round the one she has got three.
There's as much gold hangs around her middle
As would buy all Northumberland for thee."

Lord Bateman flew into a passion.
He broke his sword in splinters three,
Saying, "I would give all my father's riches,
If that Sophia has crossed the sea."

Then up spoke the young bride's mother,
Who was never known to speak so free,
"You'll not forget my only daughter,
This very day has wedded thee."

"I own I made a bride of your daughter.
She's neither the better nor the worst for me.
She came to me with a horse and saddle;
She may go home with a coach and three."

The Carnal and the Crane

No text for this religious ballad has been found dating from before the eighteenth century, though it is certainly older. No text for this religious ballad has been found dating from before the eighteenth century, though it is certainly older. Our text is from Child, who had it in turn from an 1883 collection, *Christmas Carols*, published by Sandys. The tune was collected by Lucy Broadwood in 1893 from the Goby family, "well-known Gypsy tramps in the neighborhood of Horsham and Dorking."

The story revolves around a catechism lesson administered by a crane to a crow (or carnal, after the French: *corneille*)

and concerns the early days of Jesus, some events from the approved Gospel and some apocryphal in nature.

Source: Text from F. J. Child, *The English and Scottish Popular Ballads*; tune from L. E. Broadwood, *English Traditional Songs and Carols*.

Recordings: Peter Bellamy, *The Fox Jumps Over the Parson's Gate*, Topic 12T200. The Watersons, *For Pence and Spicy Ale*, Topic 12TS265.

The Carnal and the Crane

As — I passed by the — riv - er side, And there as I did — reign. In ar - gu - ment — I — chanced to — hear a Car - nal and a — Crane.

As I passed by the river side,
And there as I did reign,
In argument I chanced to hear
A Carnal and a Crane.

The Carnal said unto the Crane,
If all the world should turn,
Before we had the Father,
But now we have the Son!

'From whence does the Son come,
From where and from what place?'
He said, "In a manger,
Between an ox and ass."

'I pray thee," said the Carnal,
'Tell me before thou go,
Was not the mother of Jesus
Conceived by the Holy Ghost?'

She was the purest virgin,
And the cleanest from sin;
She was the handmaid of our Lord
And mother of our king.

'Where is the golden cradle
That Christ was rocked in?
Where are the silken sheets
That Jesus was wrapt in?'

A manger was the cradle
That Christ was rocked in:
The provender the asses left
So sweetly he slept on.

There was a star in the east land,
So bright it did appear,
Into King Herod's chamber,
And where King Herod were.

The Wise Men soon espied it,
And told the king on high
A princely babe was born that night
No king could eer destroy.

'If this be true,'King Herod said,
'As thou tellest unto me,
This roasted cock that lies in the dish
Shall crow full fences three."

The cock soon freshly feathered was,
By the work of God's own hand,
And then three fences crowed he,
In the dish where he did stand.

'Rise up, rise up, you merry men all,
See that you ready be;
All children under two years old
Now slain they all shall be.'

Then Jesus, ah, and Joseph,
And Mary, that was so pure,
They travelled into Egypt,
As you shall find it sure.

And when they came to Egypt's land,
Amongst those fierce wild beats,
Mary, she being weary,
Must needs sit down to rest.

'Come sit thee down,' says Jesus,
'Come sit thee down by me,
And thou shalt see how these wild beasts
Do come and worship me.'

First came the lovely lion,
Which Jesus's grace did bring,
And of the wild beasts in the field
The lion shall be king.

We'll choose our virtuous princes
Of birth and high degree,
In every sundry nation,
Whereer we come and see.

Then Jesus, ah, and Joseph,
And Mary, that was unknown,
They travelled by a husbandman,
Just while his seed was sown.

'God speed thee, man,' said Jesus,
'Go fetch thy ox and wain,
And carry home they corn again
Which thou this day hast sown.'

The husbandman fell on his knees,
Even upon his face:
'Long time hast thou been looked for,
But now thout art come at last.

'And I myself do now believe
Thy name is Jesus called;
Redeemer of mankind thou art,
Though undeserving all.'

'The truth, man, thou hast spoken,
Of it thou mayst be sure,
For I must lose my precious blood
For thee and thousands more.

'If any one should come this way,
And enquire for me alone,
Tell them that Jesus passed by
As thou thy seed did sow.'

After that there came King Herod,
With his train so furiously,
Enquiring of the husbandman
Whether Jesus passed by.

'Why, the truth it must be spoke,
And the truth it must be known;
For Jesus passed by this way
When my seed was sown.

'But now I have it reapen,
And some laid on my wain,
Ready to fetch and carry
Into my barn again.'

'Turn back,' says the captain,
'Your labor and mine's in vain;
It's full three quarters of a year
Since he his seed has sown.'

So Herod was deceived,
By the work of God's own hand,
And further he proceeded
Into the Holy Land.

There's thousands of children young
Which for his sake did die;
Do not forbid those little ones,
And do not them deny.

The truth now I have spoken,
And the truth now I have shown;
Even the Blessed Virgin
She's now brought forth a son.

Diverus and Lazarus

The earliest record Child found of Diverus and Lazarus was the 1557 licensing of "a ballet of the Ryche man and poor Lazarus . . . to Master John Wallye and Mistress Toye." The piece has been found in tradition several times during this century. No doubt its popularity among poor folk has had a great deal to do with the "just desserts" moral.

Our text is compiled from many others, our melody being adapted from one collected from a mole catcher's widow, Mrs. Harris of Eardisley, Herefordshire, in 1905. The base melody is very old and has supported many other songs, including a hymn of similar spirit, **Come All You Worthy Christian Men.**

Source: Text is a collation; tune adapted from *Journal of the Folk Song Society,* II.

Recording: Tony Barrand and John Roberts, *Nowell Sing We Clear*, Front Hall FHR-013.

(Child 56)

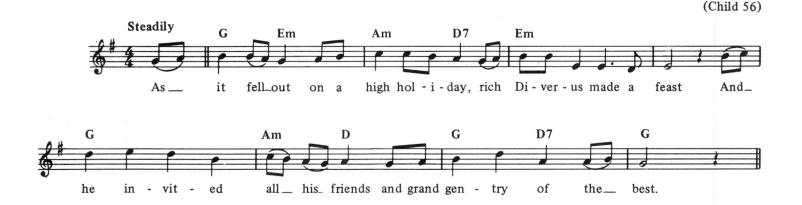

As it fell out on a high holiday, rich Diverus made a feast
And he invited all his friends and grand gentry of the best.

Then Lazarus laid himself down, down and down at Diverus' door
"Some meat, some drink, brother Diverus bestow upon the poor!"

"Thou art none of my bretheren that lies begging at my gate.
No meat or drink will I give to thee for Jesus Christ's own sake."

Then Diverus sent out his hungry dogs to drive poor Lazarus away.
They had no power to bite at all but they licked his wounds away.

Then Diverus sent out his two merry men to whip poor Lazarus away.
They had no power to strike at all but they threw their whips away.

As it fell out upon one day, poor Lazarus sickened and died.
There came two angels out of heaven his soul therein to guide.

"Rise up, rise up, brother Lazarus, and come along with me,
For there is a place prepared in heaven to sit on an angel's knee."

And it fell out upon one day, rich Diverus sickened and died.
There came two serpents out of hell his soul therein to guide.

"Rise up, rise up, brother Diverus, and come along with me,
For there's a place prepared in hell from which thou can'st not flee."

Then Diverus lifted up his eyes and he saw poor Lazarus blest,
"A drop of water, brother Lazarus, for to quench my flaming thirst!"

Oh, hell is dark and hell is deep! Oh, hell is full of fire.
It is a pity any poor sinful soul should not our Lord admire.

And now my carol's ended, no longer can I stay here.
God bless you all, both great and small, and send you a happy New Year.

Fair Annie

The exquisite English folksinger Frankie Armstrong is particularly interested in feminist songs. Little wonder this old ballad, concerning an unmarried "wife" about to be pushed aside on the arrival of a woman who brings a large dowry, should appeal to her. Sisterhood in this case was much more than figurative in nature.

Frankie has collated from Child's texts, Anglicizing the final version somewhat to suit her own speech.

There is a Northern Ireland version in Sam Henry's *Songs of the People* series.

Source: Frankie Armstrong.

Recording: Ewan MacColl, *Blood and Roses*, Blackthorne ESB 79.

Frankie Armstrong Photo by author

(Child 62)

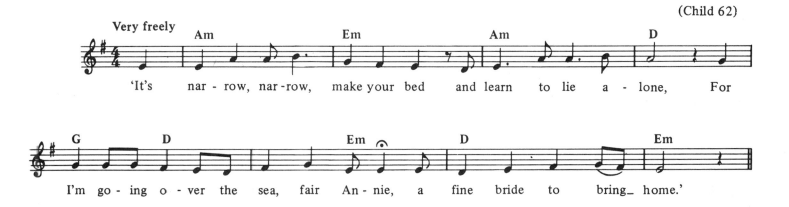

'It's narrow, narrow, make your bed and learn to lie alone, For I'm going over the sea, fair Annie, a fine bride to bring home.'

'It's narrow, narrow, make your bed and learn to lie alone,
For I'm going over the sea, fair Annie, a fine bride to bring home.

With her I'll get both gold and gear, with you I ne'er got none,
I took you as a waif woman, I'll leave you as the same.

But who will bake my bridal bread, who'll brew my bridal ale,
And who will welcome my brisk bride, that I bring o'er the dale?'

'It's I will bake your bridal bread, and I'll brew your bridal ale,
And I will welcome your brisk bride, that you bring o'er the dale.'

'But she that welcomes my brisk bride must go like a maiden fair,
And she must lace her middle so neat and braid her yellow hair.'

'But how can I go maiden-like when maiden I am none?
For I have borne seven sons by thee and am with child again.'

She's taken her young son in her arms, another in her hand,
And she is up to the higest tower, to see him come to land.

'Come up, come up, my eldest son, and look o'er yon sea strand,
And see your father's new-come bride, before she come to land.'

'Come down, come down, my mother dear, come from the castle wall,
I fear if long that you stand there you'll let yourself down fall.'

And she got down and further down, her love's fine ship to see,
And the top mast and the main mast they shone like silver free.

And she's gone down and further down the bride's ship to behold,
And the top mast and the main mast they shone like burning gold.

She took her seven sons in her hand, and O she did not fail,
She met Lord Thomas and his bride as they come o'er the dale.

'You're welcome to your house, Lord Thomas, you're welcome to your land,
You're welcome with your fair lady that you lead by the hand.

You're welcome to your halls, lady, you're welcome to your bowers
You're welcome to your home, lady, for all that's here is yours.'

'I thank thee Annie, I thank thee Annie, so dearly I thank thee,
You're the likest to my sister, Annie, that ever I did see.

There came a knight from over the sea and stole my sister away,
O shame on him and his company and the land where'er he stay.'

And aye she served the long tables with white bread and white wine,
And aye she drank the wan water to hold her colour fine.

And aye she served the long tables with white bread and with brown,
And aye she turned her round about so fast the tears fell down.

When bells were rung and mass was sung and all were bound for bed,
Lord Thomas and his new-come bride to their chamber they were led.

She took her harp all in her hands to harp these two to sleep,
And as she harped and as she sang full sorely she did weep.

29

If my seven sons were seven young rats running on the castle wall,
And I were a grey cat myself, I soon should worry them all.

If my seven sons were seven young hares running on yon lily lea,
And I were a greyhound myself soon worried they should be.'

'My gown is on', said the new-come bride. 'My shoes are on my
  feet,
And I will to fair Annie's chamber and see what makes her greet.

What ails, what ails thee, fair Annie, that you make such a moan?
Have your wine barrels cast their girds or is your white bread gone?

O who was your father, Annie, and who was your mother?
And had you any sisters, Annie, and had you any brother?'

'King Easter is my father dear, the queen my mother was,
John Armstrong from the western lands, my eldest brother is.'

'If King Easter is your father dear, then also is he mine,
And it shall not be for lack of gold that you your love shall tyne.

For I have seven ships of my own a-loaded to the brim,
And I will give them all to you and four to your eldest son,
And thanks to all the powers in heaven that I go a maiden home.'

Fair William and Lady Maisry

I was so enamored of A. L. Lloyd's **Jack Orion**, a reworking
of **Glasgerion** (Child 67), that I decided to try for myself
this idea of taking an unsung relic ballad and breathing new
life into it. **Fair William and Lady Maisry** is an adaptation
of **Willie and Lady Maisry** (Child 70); I changed the title
because Willie seemed a bit common a name for the son of
an Earl.

Source: Text adapted from F. J. Child. *The English and
Scottish Popular Ballads*; tune is an adaptation of the *Gill
Morice* air in G. Greig and A. Keith, *The Last Leaves of the
Traditional Ballads and Ballad Airs.*

Pentatonic

(Child 70)

Moderately fast

Fair Wil-li-am was an Earl's— son and lived down by the strand. La-dy Mais-ry was the King's one daugh-ter and lived on up-per land. La-dy Mais-ry was the first— wo-man to drink with him the wine And, as the healths went 'round and 'round, says, "Wil-li-am, you'll be mine."

Fair William was an Earl's son and lived down by the strand.
Lady Maisry was the King's one daughter and lived on upper land.
Lady Maisry was the first woman to drink with him the wine
And, as the healths went 'round and 'round, says, "William, you'll
  be mine."

"Oh, you must come to my bower, Willie, when the evening bells
  are rung
And you must come to me bower, Willie, when the evening mass is
  sung."
Well, he has mounted his chestnut steed and ridden to the King's
  own hall.
He's tied him there and climbed the rock and walked upon the wall.

The King's life guards they heard the noise and towards him they
  have ran,
But he's took his sword from out his sheath and killed them to a
  man.
Now he is on to Maisry's bower so softly cross the floor.
He's cannily knocked the wood thereat and said, "Unlatch the door."

With feet as white as driven snow, she's walked her bower within
And with her fingers fine and long she's let Fair William in.
She's leaned down low, down to her toe, to loose her lover's shoes,
But cold, cold were the drops of blood that fell from off his sword.

"What a frightful sight to see, my love. What a frightful sight to see.
How come this blood upon your sword, my true love, tell to me?"
"As I came by the woods this night, the wolf stalked after me.
Should I have killed the wolf, my love, or let the wolf slay me?"

They hadn't kissed not once, not once, as lovers when they meet,
When up he woke the King himself from out his drowsy sleep.
"Where are my guards led by my son, my son and only heir?
I hear a din inside my hall. A stranger, he lies near."

In then he came, her father dear, with a broad sword by his side.
He's struck a blow to Fair William that's wounded deep and wide.
"Woe be to you, father," she said, "and an ill death may you see,
For you have killed Fair William, who would have married me."

"This night he's slain my own house guards, a dozen stout, bold men.
Likewise he's slain your brother, John, to me worth all of them."
"If William's killed my own brother, I'm sure he's not to blame,
For, just this night, he a plot contrived, to have Fair William slain."

She's rung her hands and tore her hair, so sorely felt she sad
And through the woods and fields she's run. Sweet Maisry has gone
  mad.

Lord Gregory

Lord Gregory has left his lover pregnant. When the girl comes to find him, Gregory is sleeping and she meets his mother instead. The mother says he is away in Scotland, bringing home a bride, and advises her to drown herself, to hide her shame in the sea. Gregory wakes later, having dreamt of the goings-on, and sets out to find the girl, though it is almost definitely too late. The last couplet echoes the mother's malison. The famous Irish (old-style) singer Joe Heaney is often requested to sing **Lord Gregory**. He calls it "a song you can't do justice to and a song you can't run away with . . . just treat it as it comes."

Though Joe sings a number of light and regular songs, (**The Banks of the Roses** and **Cunnla** are two examples), his reputation is built on the heavy mettle of the big ballads. Joe's genius lies in his superb technical ability, coupled with tremendous commitment—a commitment so strong that, emotionally, he becomes an eyewitness to the events of a ballad, indeed a participant at times! This same commit-

ment transcends the mechanical aspects of a song as well; meter and melody. Time is measured by the pulse of a song. Certain notes, words, phrases are held longer or sung more abruptly than the norm because they are more important and require greater impact, but the throb is always there.

While the essential tune of **Lord Gregory** is very simple, Joe's rendition is virtually impossible to transcribe exactly. His use of melodic variation is such that no verse is ornamented the same and no two performances are identical. Paul Kaplan's setting of **Lord Gregory** shows types of ornamentation Joe is likely to employ.

Source: Joe Heaney.

Recordings: Elizabeth Cronin, *The Child Ballads*, Caedmon TC 1145. Ewan MacColl, *The English and Scottish Popular Ballads (Child Ballads)*, Folkways FG 3510.

(Child 76)

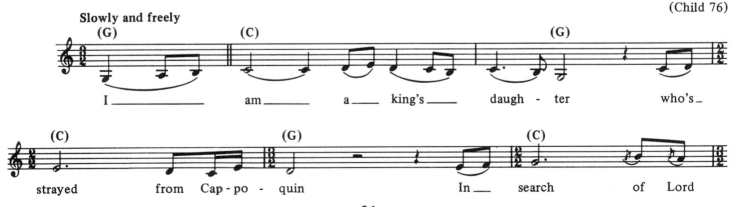

Slowly and freely

I am a king's daugh-ter who's strayed from Cap-po-quin In search of Lord

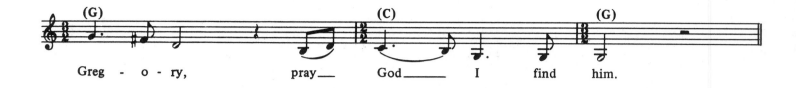

Greg - o - ry, pray__ God__ I find him.

m 2

daugh - ter who's__

m 6

Greg - o - ry, pray -

m 7

God_____ I find

I am a king's daughter who's strayed from Cappoquin
In search of Lord Gregory, pray God I find him.

"The rain beats at my yellow locks, the dew wets my skin,
My babe is cold in my arms; Lord Gregory let me in."

"Lord Gregory's not home my dear, henceforth he can't be seen.
He's gone to bonny Scotland to bring home a new queen.

"So leave you these windows and likewise this hall
For it's deep in the ocean you must hide your downfall."

"Who'll shoe my babe's little feet, who'll put gloves on her hand,
"Who'll tie my babe's middle with a long and green band?

"Who'll comb my babe's yellow locks with an ivory comb.
Who'll be my babe's father till Lord Gregory comes home?"

"I'll shoe your babe's little feet, I'll put gloves on her hand,
I'll tie your babe's middle with a long and green band.

"I'll comb your babe's yellow locks with an ivory comb,
I'll be your babe's father till Lord Gregory comes home.

"So leave you these windows and likewise this hall
For it's deep in the ocean you must hide your downfall."

"You remember Lord Gregory that night in Cappoquin
We changed silken handkerhiefs and all against my will.

"Yours were of fine linen, love, and mine was all cloth;
Yours cost one guinea, love, and mine none at all.

"You remember Lord Gregory that night in my father's hall
We changed rings on our fingers and that was worse than all.

"Yours were of fine silver, love, and mine was old tin;
Yours cost one guinea, love, and mine just one cent."

"But leave you these windows and likewise this hall
For it's deep in the ocean you must hide your downfall."

"My curse on you mother and sister also,
Tonight the lass of Aughrim came knocking at my door."

"Lie down my little son, lie down and sleep,
Tonight the lass of Aughrim lies sleeping in the deep."

"Saddle me the brown horse, the black or the grey,
But saddle me the best horse in my stable this day."

"And I'll roam over the valleys and the mountains so wild
Till I find the lass of Aughrim and lie by her side."

"Oh, leave you these windows and likewise this hall
For it's deep in the ocean you must hide your downfall."

Cold Blows the Wind

From Roman times till the present, various peoples have thought that continued or excessive grieving for the dead prevents repose in afterlife. Child gives many examples, including one from the Scottish Highlands in which a man returns from the grave to tell his sister "every tear thou sheddest falls on this dark shroud without drying, and every night thy tears still more chill and encumber me."

Source: Text from C. S. Burne, *Shropshire Folk-Lore:* tune adapted from same.

Recording: A. L. Lloyd, *The English and Scottish Popular Ballads (The Child Ballads)*, Washington 715. John Kirkpatrick and Sue Harris, *Among the Many Attractions . . .* Topic 12TS295.

(Child 78)

'Cold blows the wind o'er my true love, Cold blow the drops of rain; I never had but one true love, And in Camvile he was slain. I'll do as much for my true love As any young girl may, I'll sit and weep down by his grave For twelve months and one day.'

'Cold blows the wind over my true love,
Cold blow the drops of rain;
I never had but one true love,
And in Camvile he was slain.'

'I'll do as much for my true love
As any young girl may,
I'll sit and weep down by his grave
For twelve months and one day.'

But when twelve months were come and gone,
This young man he arose.
'What makes you weep down by my grave?
I can't take my repose.'

'One kiss, one kiss, of your lily-white lips,
One kiss is all I crave;
One kiss, one kiss, of your lily-white lips,
And return back to your grave!'

'My lips they are as cold as my clay,
My breath is heavy and strong,
If thou wast to kiss my lily-white lips
Thy days would not be long!'

'O don't you remember the garden grove
Where we was used to walk?
Pluck the finest flower of them all,
'Twill wither to a stalk!'

'Go fetch me a nut from a dungeon deep,
And water from a stone,
And white milk from a maiden's breast
That babe bare never none.'

'Go did me a grave both long, wide, and deep,
As quickly as you may
I will lie down in it and take one sleep,
For a twelvemonth and one day!'

33

Barbara Allen

The best-known—"popular," if you like— of the Popular Ballads. I first heard my father sing **Barbara Allen**. He'd learned it at school, I believe. The tune and some of the words are from him, and the harmony line was set by Paul Kaplan.

Source: William Milner, with additional verses from printed sources.

Recordings: Various singers, *The Child Ballads*, Caedmon TC 1145. Mairéad Ní Dhomhnaill, *Sailing into Walpole's Marsh*, Green Linnet SIF 1004.

(Child 84)

In Scar-let Town, where I__ was born, There was a fair maid dwell-ing. Made

ev-'ry youth cry_well-a-day. Her name_ was_ Bar - bara Al - len.____

Melody: m1

Town, where I __ was

m6

Bar - bara -

Harmony: m7, last time only

Al - len.__

34

In Scarlet Town, where I was born,
There was a fair maid dwelling.
Made ev'ry youth cry well-a-day.
Her name was Barbara Allen.

'Twas in the merry month of May
When green buds were a-swelling,
Sweet Jimmy Grove on his death bed lay
For love of Barbara Allen.

He sent his man down through the town
To the place where she was dwelling
Saying, "Master's sick, bids me call for you,
If your name be Barbara Allen."

So slowly, slowly she got up
And slowly she drew nigh him
And all she said when she got there,
"Young man, I think you're dying."

"It's I am sick and very sick
And all for Barbara Allen."
"Oh, the better for me you never shall be,
Though your heart's blood were a-spilling.

"Don't you remember the other night?
You were in the tavern drinking.
You made the healths go 'round and 'round
And you slighted Barbara Allen."

He turned his face unto the wall
And death was with him dealing.
"Adieu, adieu my dear friends all.
Be kind to Barbara Allen."

As she was walking o'er the fields,
She heard the dead bell knelling.
And every stroke did seem to say—
Hard-hearted Barbara Allen."

As she was walking through the groves,
She saw his corpse a-coming.
"Lay down, lay down his corpse," she said,
"That I may gaze upon him."

The more she looked, the more she wept,
Till she burst out a-laughing.
And all her friends cried out to her,
"Hard-hearted Barbara Allen!"

"Oh mother dear, come make my bed,
Make it both long and narrow.
My true love died for me today.
I'll die for him tomorrow."

They buried Barbara in the old church yard.
They buried Jimmy nigh her.
From Jimmy's grave sprung a red, red rose.
From Barbara Allen's a briar.

They grew and grew so very high,
Till they could grow no higher,
And at the top formed a true lovers' knot—
The red rose and the briar.

Thomas O' Winesberrie

This is one of two ballads in this book in which James V of Scotland may have figured; **The Jolly Beggar** is the other.

After disguising himself to view the daughter of the Duke of Vendôme (and rejecting her), he met, fell in love with, and married the daughter of King Francis I; hence a possibility that the disguised James and Winesberrie were the same man.

Source: Text from Child; tune adapted from Child.

Recording: Anne Briggs, *Anne Briggs*, Topic 12T207. Dick Gaughan, *Gaughan*, Topic 12TS384.

Mixolydian of A

(Child 100)

It fell up-on a time when the proud king of France Went a hunt-ing for five months and more, That his doch-ter fell in love wi' Thom-as o' Wines-ber-rie, From Scot-land new-ly come o'er, From Scot-land new-ly come o'er.

It fell upon a time, when the proud king of France
Went a-hunting for five months and more,
That his dochter fell in love wi' Thomas O' Winesberrie,
From Scotland newly come o'er,
From Scotland newly come o'er.

Whan her father cam hame frae hunting the deer,
And his dochter before him cam,
Her belly it was big, and her twa sides round,
And her fair colour was wan.
And her fair colour was wan.

"What ails thee, what ails thee, my dochter Janet,
What makes thee to look sae wan?
Ye've either been sick, and very, very, sick,
Or else ye hae lain wi' a man,
Or else ye hae lain wi' a man."

"Ye're welcome, ye're welcome, dear father," she says,
"Ye're welcome hame to your ain,
For I hae been sick, and very, very sick,
Thinking lang for your coming hame.
Thinking lang for your coming hame.

"O pardon, O pardon, dear father," she says,
"A pardon ye'll grant me."
"Na pardon, na pardon, my dochter," he says,
"Na pardon I'll grant thee,
"Na pardon I'll grant thee.

"O is it to a man of micht,
Or to a man of mean?
Or is it to onie of thae rank robbers,
That I sent hame frae Spain,
That I sent hame frae Spain?"

"It is not to a man of micht,
Nor to a man of mean;
But it is to Thomas o' Winesberrie,
And for him I suffer pain,
And for him I suffer pain."

"If it be to Thomas o' Winesberrie,
As I trust well it be,
Before I either eat or drink,
Hie hangit sall he be,
Hie hangit sall he be."

Whan this bonnie boy was brought afore the king,
His claithing was o' the silk,
His fine yellow hair hang dangling doun,
And his skin was like the milk,
And his skin was like the milk.

"Na wonder, na wonder, Lord Thomas," he says,
"My dochter fell in love wi' thee,
For if I war a woman, as I am a man,
My bed-fellow ye shou'd be!
My bed-fellow ye shou'd be!

"Then will ye marry my dochter Janet,
To be heir to a' my land;
O will ye marry my dochter Janet,
Wi' the truth o' your richt hand,
Wi' the truth o' your richt hand?"

"I will marry your dochter Janet,
Wi' the truth o' my richt hand;
I'll hae nane o' your gowd, nor yet o' your gear,
I've eneuch in fair Scotland,
I've eneuch in fair Scotland.

"But I will marry your dochter Janet,—
I care na for your land,
For she's be a queen, and I a king,
Whan we come to fair Scotland,
Whan we come to fair Scotland."

The Shepherd's Boy

A bird in the bush is worth more than ten in the hand.

Source: Broadside without printer's mark; tune from C. J. Sharp and C. L. Marson, *Folk Songs from Somerset*.

Recording: Sam Larner, *Now Is the Time for Fishing*, Folkways FG 3507

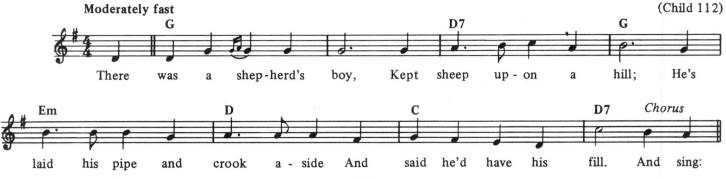

Moderately fast   (Child 112)

There was a shep-herd's boy, Kept sheep up-on a hill; He's
laid his pipe and crook a-side And said he'd have his fill. And sing:

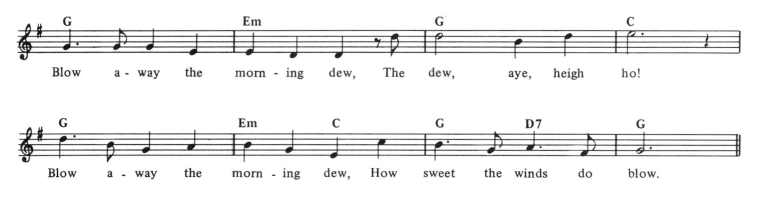

Blow a-way the morn-ing dew, The dew, aye, heigh ho!

Blow a-way the morn-ing dew, How sweet the winds do blow.

There was a shepherd's boy,
Kept sheep upon a hill;
He's laid his pipe and crook aside
And said he'd have his fill.

And sing: Blow away the morning dew,
The dew, aye, heigh ho!
Blow away the morning dew,
How sweet the winds do blow!

He looked high, he looked low,
He gave a wishful look,
And there he saw a pretty maid
Swimming in a brook.

And sing: Blow away the morning dew,
The dew, aye, heigh ho!
Blow away the morning dew,
How sweet the winds do blow!

"Pray, do not touch my mantle,
And let my clothes alone;
You shall have as much bright gold
As you can carry home."

Then he got on a milk-white steed,
And she got on another
And thus they rode along the way,
Like sister and like brother.

And as they went along the road,
They came to cocks of hay,
"This is a pretty place," he said,
"For men and maids to play."

"I'll not get off my horse," she said,
"Till at my father's hall,
Then you shall get my maidenhead
With fifty pounds and all."

When she came to her father's gate,
She pulled at the ring;
And ready was the waiting maid,
To let the lady in.

When the wicket it was open,
So nimbly she jumped in,
Saying, "Sir you are a fool without,
And I'm a maid within."

He bent down, picked up a pin,
Which he put in his sleeve,
Saying, "Cursed be all foolish men
Who do young maids believe."

She bent down, picked up a pin,
And stuck it on her sleeve,
Saying, "Cursed be all foolish men
Who do young maids deceive.

"Down in my father's garden,
There grows a marigold;
So if you would not when you may
You shall not when you would.

"My father he has got a cock,
Which never drove the hen;
But as he crows he claps his wings,
I'm sure you are no man.

"Now pull off your shoes," she said,
"And let your feet go bare;
And if you meet a pretty maid,
Kiss her if you dare."

"I'll not pull off my shoes," he said,
"Nor let my feet go bare;
And if I meet a pretty maid,
Damn me if I spare!"

Robin Hood and Little John

Though Professor Child stated with great finality that Robin Hood was the concoction of ballad poets, other scholars have seen him as an historical and legendary figure and as a carry-over of the pagan forest spirit, the Green Man. He may well be all of the above.

The Robin of the ballads is a yeoman, which places him firmly within the middle class. His manner is quite noble, however. He is manly, remarkably fair and courteous, and exceedingly devout; he is a champion of the poor over the rich, but political in that sense only.

The earliest of the Robin Hood ballads comes from sometime before 1509, possibly one or two hundred years prior. **Robin Hood and Little John** is first mentioned as an entry in the Stationer's Registers on May 14, 1594.

Source: Text is a collation, mostly from Child; the tune, **Jock the Leg**, was collected by Ewan MacColl from Hughie Graham of Galloway.

Robin Hood and Little John

Moderately and steadily

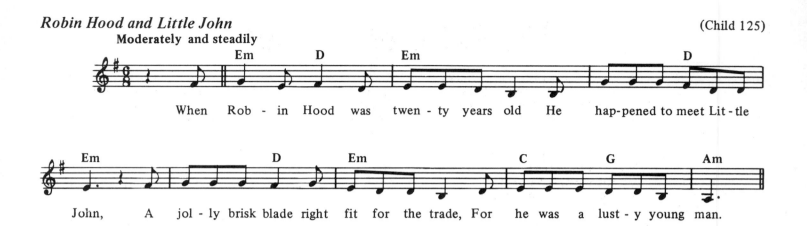

When Rob - in Hood was twen - ty years old He hap-pened to meet Lit - tle

John, A jol - ly brisk blade right fit for the trade, For he was a lust - y young man.

When Robin Hood was twenty years old
He happened to meet Little John,
A young brisk blade right fit for the trade,
For he was a lusty young man.

Well, how they did meet, I'll tell you in brief,
If you'll but listen a while,
For this very jest amongst all the rest
I think it may cause you to smile.

Bold Robin Hood said to his jolly men,
"Pray tarry you here in this grove
And see that you all observe well me call
While through the forest I rove.

Then he shook hands with his merry men all
And bid them at present goodbye,
Then, as near a brook his journey he took,
A stranger he chanced to espy.

They happened to meet on a long narrow bridge
And neither of them would give way.
Said bold Robin Hood and sturdily stood,
"I'll show you right Nottingham play."

"You speak like a coward," the stranger he said,
"As there with your long bow you stand.
How, I protest, could you shoot at me breast
While I have but a staff in me hand."

"The name of a coward," said Robin, "I scorn."
And found him a staff of green oak.
This being done, away he did run
To the stranger and merrily spoke.

"Ah, just see me staff it's lusty and tough,
Now here on the bridge we will play.
Whoever falls in the other shall win
The battle and then we'll away."

Now Robin, he gave the stranger a bang
So hard it made his bones ring.
The stranger he said, "this must be repaid;
I'll give you as good as you bring."

The stranger gave Robin a crack on the crown
Which caused the blood to appear.
Then Robin, enraged, more fiercely engaged
And followed with blows more severe.

O then, in a fury the stranger he flew,
Gave Robin a damnable look,
And with a bold blow that laid him full low
He tumbled him into the brook.

"O, where have you gone and where are you now?"
The stranger he laughed and he cried.
Quoth bold Robin Hood, "I'm here in the flood
And I'm floating along in the tide."

Then Robin he waded all out of the deep
And pulled himself up by a thorn
And just at the last he blew a loud blast
Straightway on his bugle horn.

The hills they did echo, the valleys did ring
Which caused his brave men to appear
All dressed in the green so bold to be seen
Straight up to their master did steer.

"There's no one will harm thee. Be not afraid,
These bowman upon me do wait.
There's three score and nine and if you'll be mine
My livery you can wear right straight."

"O, here is my hand," the stranger replied.
"I'll serve you with all of my heart
My name is John Little, a man of good mettle
Ne're doubt me, I'll play out my part."

"This man's been called John Little," said Robin
"His name shall be changed anon.
The words we'll transpose so wherever he goes
His name shall be called Little John."

A brace of fat deer was quickly brought in,
Good ale and strong liquor likewise;
The feast was so good all in the greenwood
Where this seven-foot babe was baptised.

Then music and dancing did finish the day
At length when the sun waxed low.
Then all the whole from they withdrew
And into their caves they did go.

The Battle of Harlaw

First mention of a ballad, **The Battel of Hayrlau**, comes in a 1549 collection, *The Complaynt of Scotland*, though it is not at all certain that the song referred to has the same root as ours. Child, in fact, thought this song was composed relatively recently.

The encounter took place on July 24, 1411, eighteen miles above Aberdeen. Donald of the Isles, together with ten thousand Highlanders and Islanders, invaded the Lowlands in a territorial dispute over the Earldom of Ross. He was countered by the forces of Mar, Garioch, Angus, and the Mearns. The Lowlanders lost five hundred, and the Celts from the north another nine hundred.

Child mentions that Donald's defeat "was in the interest of civilization against savagery." One should not forget that Civilization is something constantly being redefined. Hitler's savagery, for example, was committed to "enhance" civilization.

Source: G. Greig, *Folk Songs of the North-East*; the tune is very commonly sung.

Recording: The Exiles, *The Hale and the Hanged*, Topic 12T164.

Pentatonic

(Child 163)

As I cam in by Denniedeer
An' doon by Netherha',
There was fifty thousand Hielandmen
A-marchin' to Harlaw.
   *Wi' my dirrum doo dirrum doo daddie
   dirrum dey.*

As I cam on and farther on
And doon and by Balquhain,
It's there I met Sir James the Rose
And wi' him Sir John the Graham.

"Oh cam ye frae the Highlands man,
Oh cam ye a' the wey?
Saw ye McDonald and his men
As they cam in frae Skye?"

"Yes we cam frae the Highlands man
An' we cam a' the wey.
And we saw McDonald and his men
As they cam in frae Skye."

"Oh was ye near McDonald's men?
Did ye their numbers see?
Come tell me Johnnie Hielandman
What micht their numbers be?"

"Yes we was near and near eneuch
And we their numbers saw.
There was fifty thousand Hielandmen
A-marchin' to Harlaw."

"Gin that be true," says Sir James the Rose,
"Will come nae muckle speed.
We'll cry upon our merry men
An' turn oor horses head."

"Oh na. Oh na," says John the Graham,
"That thing can never be.
The gallant Grahams were never beat
We'll try what we can dee."

As I cam on and farther on
And doon and by Harlaw,
They fell fu close on ilka side.
Sic strokes ye never saw.

They fell fu' close on ilka side,
Sic stroked ye never saw,
For ilka sword gaed clash for clash
At the battle o' Harlaw.

The Hielandmen wi' their lang swords
They laid on us fu' sair
And they drove back oor merry men
Three acres breadth and mair.

Braves Forbes to his brother said,
"Oh brither don't ye see.
They've beat us back on ilka side
And we'll be forced to flee."

"Oh na. Oh na," my brother said,
"That thing can never be.
You'll tak your sword into your hand
And ye'll come on wi' me."

Then back to back the brithers twa
Gaed in among the throng
And they laid doon the Hielandmen
Wi' swords baith sharp and lang.

The first ae stroke that Forbes struck,
He gart McDonald reel
And the neist ae stroke that Forbes struck,
The brave McDonald fell.

39

And siccan a Pitlarichie
I'm sure ye never saw,
As was among the Hielandmen
When they saw McDonald fa'.

And when they saw that he was dead,
They turned and ran awa'
And they turned him in Leggart's den
A mile abeen Harlaw.

Some rade, some ran and some did gang
They were o' sma' record,
But Forbes and his merry men
They slew them a' the road.

On Monoday at mornin'
The battle it began,
On Saturday at gloamin'
Ye'd kentna wha had won.

Gin onybody spier at you
For them that cam awa,'
Ye can tell them plain and plain enough,
They're sleepin' at Harlaw.

The Death of Queen Jane

Jane Seymour, who died in 1537, was the third of Henry VIII's amorous sextet. Jane was lady-in-waiting to Ann Boleyn when Henry sent her a purse of gold and the suggestion that she assume a new duty within the royal household—that of mistress. She declined, claiming her honor was of greater wealth. Shortly afterward, Ann was tried and convicted of adultery and beheaded on May 19, 1536. Jane succeeded her immediate predecessor almost without delay.

Although Jane gave birth to Prince Edward (later Edward VI) by natural means, her death twelve days later gave rise to the popular belief that extreme surgery had been required

The text comes from the version collected by Henry Hammond from a Mrs. Russell at Upwey, Dorset, in 1907 and later reprinted in the *Penguin Book of English Folk Songs.*

Source: Dáithí Sproule.

Recording: The Bothy Band, *After Hours*, Mulligan LUN 030.

(Child 170)

Queen Jane lay in labour full nine days or more
Till the women were so tired, they could no longer there,
They could no longer there.

"Good women, good women, good women as you be,
Will you open my right side and find my baby,
And find my baby?"

"Oh no," cried the women, "that never may be.
We will send for King Henry and hear what he may say,
And hear what he may say.

King Henry was sent for. King Henry did come.
"What do ail you, my lady? Your eyes, they look so dim,
Your eyes, they look so dim."

"King Henry, King Henry will you do one thing for me?
That's to open my right side and find my baby,
And find my baby."

"Oh no," cried King Henry, "that's a thing I'll never do,
For if I lose the flower of England, I shall lose the branch too,
I shall lose the branch too."

There was fiddling, aye, and dancing on the day the babe was born,
But poor Queen Jane belovèd lay cold as a stone,
Lay cold as a stone.

Georgy

Georgy may have been anyone, but at least one Scots collector, Kinloch, has pictured him as a sixteenth-century Earl of Huntly—George Gordon. This Georgy was remanded to Edinburgh Castle for failing to catch a Shetland robber he'd received a Royal Commission to apprehend. His enemies wanted him banished, even executed, but in the end he was just fined. High stakes!

Source: Text from a broadside printed by Fortey; the tune is commonly sung.

Recording: June Tabor, *Silly Sisters*, Chrysalis CHR 1101.

(Child 209)

Moderately slow

As I rode o - ver Lon - don Bridge, 'twas in the morn - ing ear - ly, There did I spy a maid - en fair, la - ment - ing for her Geor - gy.

As I rode over London Bridge, 'twas in the morning early,
There did I spy a maiden fair, lamenting for her Georgy.

"Georgy never stole ox or cow, nor calves he never stole any,
Six of the king's white deer he stole, and sold them in Broad Hambury.

"Come saddle me my milk white steed, come saddle it so ready,
Then I will ride to my good Lord Judge, to beg for the life of my Georgy."

But when she came into the hall, where Lords and Ladies plenty,
And down on her bended knees she did fall, "Spare me the life of my Georgy."

"I have got sheep, I have got cows, oxen I have plenty,
And you shall call it your own, spare me the life of my Georgy."

The Judge he looked over his left shoulder, saying "Lady, pray now be easy.
Georgy hath confessed and die he must. The Lord have mercy on Georgy."

Georgy shall be hanged in a chain of gold, such as you never saw many,
For Georgy's one of British blood, and he courted a virtuous lady,

Who for him hath wept both day and night, and could not drive her sorrow away,
But she hoped to see the happy day, to be blest once more with her Georgy.

Was I top of Proctor's Hill, where times I have been lately,
With my pistol cocked all in my hand I'd fight for the life of my Georgy.

The Bonny Lass of Anglesey

"The idea of a champion to do one's fighting is older than David and Goliath by far, only not many of them seem to be women. Peter Buchan said about **The Bonny Lass of Anglesey**: 'It is altogether a political piece and I do not wish to interfere much with it'. While echoing the 'much' in that statement, I have stretched the idea slightly, added a few verses, and she appears as a formidable sister-in-arms of **The Fair Maid on the Shore**, and all those others who are in despair of chauvinist males the world over. The melody is an Irish-American fiddle tune, one of several sharing the title of **Bonaparte's Retreat**, and I learned it from Tom Gilfellon."—Martin Carthy.

Source: Martin Carthy.

Recording: Martin Carthy, *Crown of Horn*, Topic 12TS300.

(Child 220)

There he sits and there he stands alone
And oh! What a frightened king is he.
Fifteen lords have all come down
To dance and gain the victory.

Our king he keeps a good treasure
And he keeps it locked with a silver key,
But fifteen lords who have all come down
Can dance his gold and his land away.

There he stands on the castle high
And oh! so loud, so loud I heard him cry,
"Go saddle your horse and bring to me
The bonny lass of Anglesey."

Some rode North and some rode South.
There was some to the East they rode straightway;
They spied her there on the mountain high,
The bonny lass of Anglesey.

Up she starts as white as the milk,
Between the king of all of his company,
Cries, "What is the prize I have to ask
If I do gain the victory?"

"Fifteen plows, a house and a mill!
I will give to thee till the day thou die
And the fairest knight in all my court
To take, your husband for to be."

"Fifteen plows, a house and a mill!
Come now, that's no prize for the victory
And there's no knight in all your court
That shall have me as a wife to be."

Up she starts as white as the milk.
She danced as light as the leaf on the broken sea,
Till fifteen lords all cried aloud
For the bonny lass of Anglesey.

She's taken fifteen one by one,
Saying, "Sweet, kind sir will you dance with me?"
But e'er it's ten o'clock of the night
They gave it o'er right shamefully.

But up and rose him the fifteenth knight
And oh! but an angry man was he.
He laid aside his buckle and sword
Before he's gone so manfully.

And he danced high and he's danced low
And he has danced the livelong day.
He says, "My feet shall be my death,
E'er she gains the victory."

"Oh my feet shall be my death,
E'er this lass shall gain the victory."
But e'er it's ten o'clock of the morn
He gave it o'er right shamefully.

She's taken the king all by the hand
Saying, "Sweet, kind sir will you walk with me?"
But e'er the king has gone one step
She danced his gold and his land away.

Says, "Fifteen plows, a house and a mill,
Come now, that's no prize for the victory."
And away she's gone with his treasure,
The bonny lass of Anglesey.

She's taken all their buckle and swords.
She's taken all their gold and their bright money
And back to the mountains she's away,
The bonny lass of Anglesey.

There's fifteen lords come a swaggering down
For to dance and gain the victory,
But fifteen lords and one high king
Go all ragged and bare today.

A Little Before Me Time

Child's generic title for this ballad was **Our Goodman**, from
a Scots version:

> *Hame cam oor goodman at een an' hame cam he*
> *An' he got a man intae the bed where nae man should*
> *be . . .*

Sounds like a serious situation! You can find this song all
over the USA and Canada and back to the Isles, usually en-
titled **Three (to Seven) Drunk Nights**. Many versions use
spoken parts for the husband and wife.

Source: Learned from Dave Surman.

Recording: Ewan MacColl, *Saturday Night at the Bull and
Mouth,* Blackthorne BR 1055. The Dubliners, *A Drop of
the Hard Stuff,* Epic BN26337.

(Child 274)

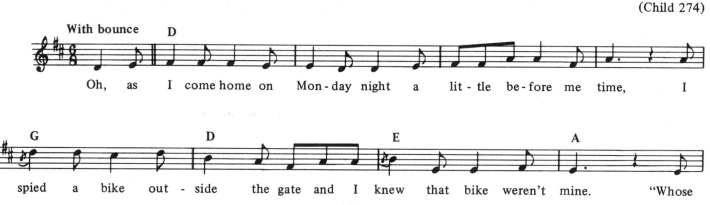

bike be this? Whose bike be that? Whose e-ver can __ it be?" Me

wife says, "That's a milk ma-chine me mam-my sent __ to me." I've

trav-elled this wide world o-ver, __ a hun-dred miles or more, But

han-dle-bars on a milk ma-chine I nev-er seen __ be-fore.

Oh, as I come home on Monday night a little before me time,
I spied a bike outside the gate and I knew that bike weren't mine.
"Whose bike be this? Whose bike be that? Whose ever can it be?"
Me wife says, "That's a milk machine me mammy sent to me."
I've traveled this wide world over, a hundred miles or more,
But handlebars on a milk machine I never seen before!

Oh, as I come home on Tuesday night a little before my time,
I spied a hat upon the rack and I knew that hat weren't mine.
"Whose hat be this? Whose hat be that? Whose ever can it be?"
Me wife says, "That's a chamber pot me mammy sent to me."
I've traveled this wide world over, a hundred miles or more,
But chamber pot with brim like that I never seen before!

Oh, as I come home on Wednesday night a little before me time,
I spied two boots upon the floor and I knew them boots weren't
    mine.
"Whose boots be this? Whose boots be that? Whose ever can they be?"
Me wife says, "Them's two flower pots me mammy sent to me."
I've traveled this wide world over, a hundred miles or more,
But flower pots with laces in I never seen before!

Oh, as I come home on Thursday night a little before me time,
I spied a coat upon the peg and I knew that coat weren't mine.
"Whose coat be this? Whose coat be that? Whose ever can it be?"
Me wife says, "That's a blanket that me mammy sent to me."
I've traveled this wide world over, a hundred miles or more,
But blanket there with buttons on I never seen before!

Oh, as I come home on Friday night a little before me time,
I spied a face upon the bed and I knew that face weren't mine.
"Whose face be this? Whose face be that? Whose ever can it be?
Me wife says, "That's a new-born babe me mammy sent to me."
I've traveled this wide world over, a hundred miles or more,
But whiskers on a new-born babe I never seen before!

The Jolly Beggar

Child rejects suggestions of royal composition in his introduction: "We are regularly informed by editors that tradition imputes the authorship of . . . **The Jolly Beggar** . . . to James V of Scotland. The tradition as to James V is, perhaps, not much older than the publication [of the Tea-Table Miscellany in 1724] . . . and has no more plausibility than it has authority."

Think what you like! The science of folklore is a different thing than folklore itself.

Source: Text and tune from J. Johnson, *The Scots Musical Museum*.

Recording: Planxty, *Planxty*, Polydor 2383 186.

(Child 279)

There was a jolly beggar, and a begging he was bound, And he took up his quarters into a land-'art town, And we'll gang nae mair a roving Sae late into the night, And we'll gang nae mair a roving, Let the moon shine ne'er sae bright, And we'll gang nae mair a roving.

There was a jolly beggar, and a-begging he was bound,
And he took up his quarters into a land'art town,
    And we'll gang nae mair a roving
    Sae late into the night,
    And we'll gang nae mair a roving,
    Let the moon shine ne'er sae bright,
    And we'll gang nae mair a roving.

He wad neither ly in barn, nor yet wad he in byre,
But in ahint the ha' door, or else afore the fire.
    And we'll gang nae mair a roving
    Sae late into the night,
    And we'll gang nae mair a roving,
    Let the moon shine ne'er sae bright,
    And we'll gang nae mair a roving.

The beggar's bed was made at e'en wi' good clean straw and hay,
And in ahint the ha' door, and there the beggar lay.

Up raise the goodman's dochter, and for to bar the door,
And there she saw the beggar standin' i' the floor.

He took the lassie in his arms, and to the bed he ran,
"O hooly, hooly wi' me, Sir, ye'll waken our goodman."

The beggar was a cunnin' loon, and ne'er a word he spake,
Until he got his turn done, syne he began to crack.

"Is there ony dogs into this town, Maiden, tell me true?"
"And what wad ye do wi' them, my hinny and my dow?"

"They'll rive a' my mealpocks, and do me meikle wrang."
"O dool for the doing o't, are ye the poor man?"

Then she took up the mealpocks and flang them o'er the wa',
"The deil gae wi' the mealpocks, my maidenhead and a'."

"I took ye for some gentleman, at least the Laird of Brodie;
O dool for the doing o't! are ye the poor bodie?"

He took the lassie in his arms, and gae her kisses three,
And four-and-twenty hunder mark to pay the nurice fee.

He took a horn frae his side, and blew both loud and shrill.
And four-and-twenty belted knights cam skipping o'er the hill.

And he took out his little knife, loot a' his duddies fa'.
And he was the brawest gentleman that was amang them a'.

The beggar was a cliver loon, and he lap shoulder height,
"O ay for sicken quarters as I gat yesternight."

The Golden Vanity

Londoner David Jones gave me this version of **The Golden Vanity** a few years back. A really fine singer, David is known in New York as "The Local Favorite," just as he was back on the Isle of Dogs in 1949 when he outclassed Smith of Lambeth in the South London School Boy Boxing Championship.

Source: David Jones

Recordings: David Jones, *Easy and Slow*, Minstrel JD-201. Ewan MacColl, *The English and Scottish Popular Ballads (Child Ballads)*, Folkways FG 3510.

(Child 286)

There once was a cap-tain, he was boast-ing by the quay, "I have a ship and a gal-lant ship is she, And of all the ships I know, well, she's the best for me And she's sail-ing in the

Low - lands low." In the Low - lands, — Low -

lands, she's sail - ing in the Low - lands — low. — "Well, — low. —

There once was a captain, he was boasting by the quay,
"I have a ship and a gallant ship is she,
And of all the ships I know, well, she's the best for me
And she's sailing in the Lowlands low."
In the Lowlands, Lowlands,
She's sailing in the Lowlands low.

"Well, I had her built in the North Country
And then I had her christened the *Golden Vanity.*
I armed her and I manned her and I sent her out to sea
And she's sailing in the Lowlands low."
In the Lowlands, Lowlands,
She's sailing in the Lowlands low.

Ah, then up stepped a sailor, just returned from sea,
"I was aboard of the *Golden Vanity,*
When we was given chase by the Spanish piratee,
As we sailed upon the Lowlands low."

"And we had on board of us a little cabin boy;
'What will you give me if the pirate I'll destroy'?
You can have my fairest daughter, she's my only pride and joy,
If you sink them in the Lowlands low."

So the boy bared his breast, plunged into the tide,
Swam until he came to the rascal pirate's side.
He climbed on board. He went below. By none was he espied
And he sank them in the Lowlands low.

Ah, some was playing cards, some was playing dice;
Some was in their hammocks, sporting with their wives,
But when he let the water in, he put out all their fires
And he sank them in the Lowlands low.

Then the boy swam back unto the starboard side.
"Captain take me up for I'm drifting with the tide!"
"I'll shoot you and I'll kill you if you claim my child as bride
And I'll leave you in the Lowlands low."

Then the boy swam around unto the larboard side.
"Messmates take me up for I'm drifting with the tide!"
They took him up so quickly, but on the deck he died.
They left him in the Lowlands low.

"Ah, they took him up so quickly but on the deck he died.
They laid him on his hammock which was so fine and wide.
They said a short prayer over him and dropped him in the tide
And they left him in the Lowlands low."

Here's a curse upon the Captain, where'er he may be,
For taking that poor cabin boy so far away to sea,
For taking that poor cabin boy so far away to sea
And to leave him in the Lowlands low.

David Jones Photo by Louise Sherman

Captain Ward and the Rainbow

In 1604 Kentishman John Ward led a mutiny aboard one of His Majesty's ships, turned pirate, and, together with a Dutchman named Dansekar, became the scourge of the seaways for the next five years. The **Rainbow** mentioned may have been one of four ships Sir Francis Drake used in his attack of Cadiz in 1587.

Source: Text from a broadside by Pitts; tune composed by Paul Kaplan and myself.

Recordings: Ewan MacColl, *The English and Scottish Popular Ballads (Child Ballads)*, Folkways FG 3510. Peter Bellamy, *Peter Bellamy*, Green Linnet SIF 1001.

Mixolydian of D

(Child 287)

Come all you lusty gallants and listen to me song,
For there is such a rover that over the seas is come.
His name is Captain Ward and full well it doth appear
There's not been such a robber found out these thousand years.

Well, he has sent unto the King, the sixth of January,
Asking that he might come in with all his company.
"And if the King will let me come till I my tale have told,
I will bestow for ransom full thirty ton of gold."

"Oh nay! Oh nay!" then said the King. "O nay! That must not be.
To yield to such a rover myself will not agree.
He has deceived the Frenchman, likewise the King of Spain.
Then how can he be true to me who has been false to twain?"

With that, the King's provided a ship of worthy fame;
Rainbow she is called, if you would know her name.
And when the gallant *Rainbow* did come where Ward did lie,
"Where is the captain of this ship?" *Rainbow* crew did cry.

"Oh, I am that," says Captain Ward. "There's no one bids me lie
And if you are the King's fair ship, you're welcome unto me."
"I'll tell you what," says *Rainbow*, "our King is in great grief
That you should lie upon the sea and play the errant thief."

"I never wronged an English ship, but Turk and King of Spain,
Likewise the blackguard Dutchman as I met on the main.
If I had known your own King but two or three years before,
I would have saved Lord Essex' life, whose death does grieve me sore.

"Go tell the King of England, go tell him thus for me,
He may reign the king on good dry land, I'll reign king over the sea!"

48

Johnny of Hazelgreen

Here's an Irish version of a well-enough-known Scots ballad.
It comes from Dáithí Sproule after the Donegal singer,
Packie Manus Byrne. Some texts have an additional verse
between our third and fourth:

"Now Hasilgreen is married, let all this talking be."
"If Hasilgreen be married, this day then woe to me;
For I may sigh and sob no more, but close my weeping
*   een,*
And hold my peace and cry no more, but dy for Hasil-
*   green."*

Dáithí uses a DADGAD guitar tuning and sings slowly, in
an unusually syncopated manner.

Source: Dáithí Sproule.

Recording: Dick Gaughan, *No More Forever*, Trailer LER
2072.

(Child 293)

ms 6, 7 and 8

shin - ing_____ clear,_____ I

ms 14-16, 30-32

for _____ her _____ dear._____ And

Ha - zel - green._____

One night as I rode o'er the vale, the moon was shining clear,
I overheard a fair young maid lamenting for her dear.
And she did cry as I passed by and painful to me it seemed,
For she was letting the tears roll down for Johnny of Hazelgreen.

"What troubles you, my darling girl, or what caused you to roam?
Are your mother and father dead, or have you got no home?"
"My parents they are both alive and plainly to be seen,
But I have lost my darling boy called Johnny of Hazelgreen."

"What kind of man is your Hazelgreen? He is one I do not know.
Well, he must be a fine young man for you to love him so."
"Well, his arms are long and his shoulders broad, he is comely to be seen
And his hair is rolled in chains of gold; he's my Johnny of Hazelgreen."

"Dry up your tears, my darling girl and come along with me.
I will have you wed to my own brave son. I never had one, but he.
And you could be a bride," I said, "to any lord or king."
"I would rather be a bride," said she, "to Johnny of Hazelgreen."

So she's got on her milk-white steed and I've got on my bay
And we've rode along through the moonlit night and part of the next day.
And when we got up to the gate, the bells began to ring
And who stepped out but that brave young lad called Johnny of Hazelgreen.

"You are welcome home, dear father," he said, "you are welcome home to me,
For you have brought my own dear girl that I thought I'd never more see."
And the smile upon her gentle face was as sweet as grass is green.
I hope she enjoys her married life with young Johnny of Hazelgreen.

The Maid and the Soldier

There's no end of good versions of this ballad (often known as **Seventeen Come Sunday** or **As I Roved Out**)—Scots, Irish, and English. Some I've seen have the maid and soldier wed at the end, but that seems a bit forced.

Source: Text from a broadside by E. Taylor of Birmingham; tune learned from Brian Brooks.

Recordings: Norman Kennedy, *Ballads and Songs of Scotland*, Folk-Legacy FSS-34. Harry Cox, *Traditional English Love Songs*, Folk-Legacy FSB-20.

(Child 299)

Pentatonic

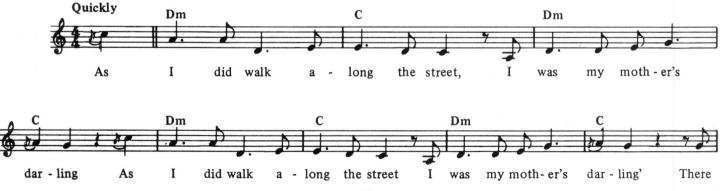

As I did walk a - long the street, I was my moth - er's

dar - ling As I did walk a - long the street I was my moth - er's dar - ling' There

I did meet a pret — ty fair maid, Just as the sun was ris - ing. With me

rue rum rah, fol de rid - dle dah, Di ree fol dee did- dle dair - ee o.

*As I did walk along the street,
I was my mother's darling,
As I did walk along the street,
I was my mother's darling,
There I did meet a pretty fair maid,
Just as the sun was rising.

*With me rue rum rah, fol de riddle dah,
Di ree fol dee diddle dairee o.*

*Her shoes were black, her stockings white,
The buckles were of silver.
Her shoes were black, her stockings white,
The buckles were of silver.
She had a black and a rolling eye
And her hair hung down her shoulders.

*With me rue rum rah, fol de riddle dah,
Di ree fol dee diddle dairee o.*

Where are you going my pretty fair maid?
Where are you going my honey?"
She answered me right cheerfully,
"On an errand for my mammy."

"How old are you my pretty fair maid?
How old are you my honey?"
She answered me right modestly,
"I'm seventeen come Sunday."

"Will you marry me my pretty fair maid?
Will you marry me my honey?
"With all my heart kind sir," says she,
"But I dare not for my mammy."

"But if you come to my mother's house
When the moon shines bright and clearly,
Then I'll come down and let you in
And my mammy shall not hear me."

I went up to her mammy's house
When the moon was shining clearly
And she came down and let me in
And I laid in her arms till morning.

"Oh, soldier, soldier will you marry me now?
Now is your time or never.
And if you will not marry me now,
I'm quite undone forever."

"I have a wife, she is my own,
How can I disdain her,
And every town that I go through
A girl if I can find her.

I'll go to bed quite late at night,
Rise early in the morning.
The bugle horn is my delight
And a pint of rum my darling.

*First two lines are repeated

Polly Vaughn

An old Celtic folk piece, **An Cailin Ban (The Fair Girl)** tells the story of a jealous maid who's afraid her love is going to see another when he goes out fowling. She changes herself into a swan, so as to follow him without his knowledge. He, or course, shoots her, and as she dies she changes back into her normal state.

The song is widely sung. In the USA it's known from Maine to Mississippi and from Florida to Michigan. In Ireland it's usually called **Molly Bawn**. John and Tony's version, used here, has a text collated from the singing of Harry Cox and A. L. Lloyd and an especially beautiful melody from Carrie Grover of Bethel, Maine.

Source: John Roberts and Tony Barrand.

Recordings: John Roberts and Tony Barrand, *Dark Ships in the Forest*, Folk-Legacy FSI-65. Packie Manus Byrne, *Singing Men of Ulster*, Green Linnet SIF 1005.

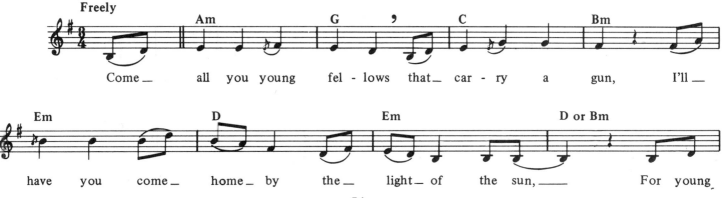

Come all you young fel - lows that car - ry a gun, I'll

have you come home by the light of the sun, For young

51

Jim - my was a fowl - er and a - fowl - ing a - lone, When he

shot his own __ true __ love in the room __ of a swan.

Come all you young fellows that carry a gun,
I'll have you come home by the light of the sun,
For young Jimmy was a fowler, and a-fowling alone,
When he shot his own true love in the room of a swan.

Come all you young fellows that carry a gun,
I'll have you come home by the light of the sun,
For young Jimmy was a fowler, and a-fowling alone,
When he shot his own true love in the room of a swan.

As Polly went walking, a rainstorm come on,
She hid under the bushes, the shower for to shun.
With her apron wrapped over her, he took her for a swan,
And his gun didn't miss, and it was Polly his own.

Then home rushed young Jimmy, with his dog and his gun,
Crying, "Uncle, dear Uncle, have you heard what I've done?
Oh, cursed be that gunsmith that made my old gun,
For I've shot my own true love, in the room of a swan."

Then out rushed bold uncle, with his locks hanging grey,
Crying, "Jimmy, dear Jimmy, don't you run away.
Don't you leave your own country till your trial come on,
For they never will hang you for the shooting of a swan."

Well, the funeral of Polly, it was a brave sight,
With four-and-twenty young men, and all dressed in white,
They took her to the graveyard and they laid her in the clay,
And they bid adieu to Polly, and all went away.

Now, the girls of this country, they're all glad, we know,
To see Polly Vaughn a-lying so low.
You could gather them into a mountain, you could plant them in
  a row,
And her beauty would shine amongst them like a fountain of snow.

Well, the trial wore on, and young Polly did appear,
Crying, "Uncle, dear Uncle, let Jimmy go clear,
For my apron was bound round me, and he took me for a swan,
And my poor heart lay a-bleeding all on the green ground."

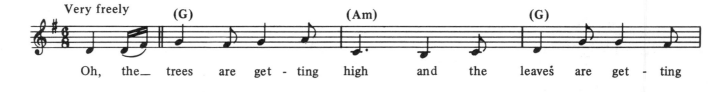

The Trees Are Getting High

An exceptional ballad well known in England, Ireland, and
Scotland. A song about an arranged marriage and mis-
matched lovers.

Source: Text collated from a number of sources; tune
learned from the singing of Dominic Behan.

Recordings: Dominic Behan, *Finnegan's Wake,* Folk-Legacy
FL113. Jean Redpath, *Song of the Seals,* Philo PH 1054.

Very freely (G) (Am) (G)

Oh, the __ trees are get - ting high and the leaves are get - ting

green. __ The times are gone and past that __ we __ have __ (D)

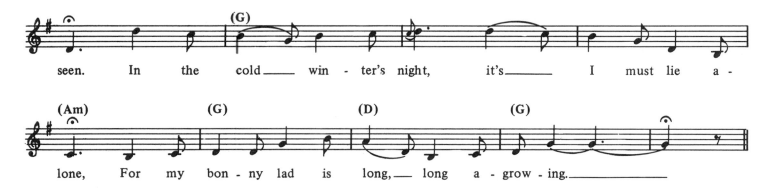

seen. In the cold winter's night, it's I must lie a-lone, For my bon-ny lad is long, long a-grow-ing.

Oh, the trees are getting high and the leaves are getting green.
The times are gone and past that we have seen.
In the cold winter's night, it's I must lie alone,
For my bonny lad is long, long a-growing.

"Oh, father, dear father, you've done me great wrong,
For you have wedded me to a lad who's far too young.
I am twice twelve and he is but thirteen.
He's a bonny boy but long, long a-growing."

"Oh, daughter, dear daughter, I've done you no wrong,
For I have wedded you to a noble lord's son
And he shall be the lord and you shall wait upon.
He's a bonny lad; he's young and he's growing."

"Oh, father, dear father, I'll tell you what we'll do.
We'll send him to the college for a year or two
And around about his college cap we'll tie those ribbons blue,
For to let the maidens know that he's married."

One day I was walking down by yonder churchyard wall.
'Twas there I spied the bonny boys and they all playing ball
And my own young love, he was the flower of them all.
He's a bonny boy; he's young and he's growing.

In his twelfth year he was a married man
And in his thirteenth he was the father of a son
And in his fourteenth year his grave it grew quite green.
Cruel death had put an end to his growing.

I will make my love a shroud of the ornamental brown
And while that I am weaving it the tears they will fall down
And while that I am weaving it the tears they will fall down
But I'll watch his bonny son while he's growing.

Come all your fair maidens and a warning take by me.
Don't ever place your love in the top of some growing tree,
For the leaves they will all wither and the roots they will decay
And the blushing of a young lad will soon fade away.

The Widow Woman's Daughter

Professor Child printed songs of incest, fratricide and the like, but shied away from this harmless song of a girl who, not only regained her maidenhead, but got her man in the end. Perhaps he thought it not sufficiently ancient, though it may have been too "indecent" without being morose.

This version is from Donal Maguire, a fine singer and mandolinist from Drogheda. He learned it from a recording by Eddie Butcher of Magilligan, Co. Derry.

Source: Donal Maguire.

Recordings: Eddie Butcher, *Ballads from Donegal and Derry*, Leader LEA 4055. Donal Maguire, *The Star of Sunday's Well*, Rossendal MUS 001. A. L. Lloyd, *The Bird in the Bush*, Topic 12T135

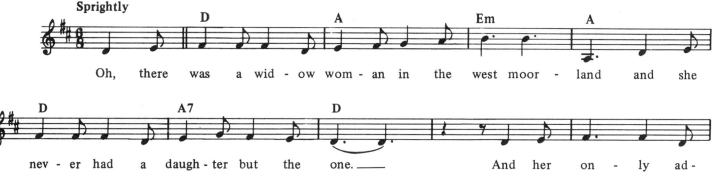

Oh, there was a wid-ow wom-an in the west moor-land and she nev-er had a daugh-ter but the one. And her on-ly ad-

vice ___ by ___ day   or   night   was   to   nev - er   give   her   maid - en-head   to

one. ___   "Oh,   hold   your   tongue,   dear ___   moth - er,"   she

says,   "and   there - fore   din - na   let   it   be, ___   For   there

was   a   jol - ly   sol - dier   in   the   Queen's   Life   Guards   last ___

night   stole   me   maid - en - head   from   me." ___

Oh, there was a widow woman in the west moorland and she never
  had a daughter but the one.
And her only advice by day or night was to never give her maidenhead to one.
"Oh, hold your tongue, dear mother," she says, "and therefore
  dinna let it be,
For there was a jolly soldier in the Queen's Life Guards last night
  stole me maidenhead from me."

"Oh go, oh go, you saucy jade and therefore dinna let it be
And bring me back the maidenhead you lost last night or another
  knight shall never lie with thee."
Now she is to the soldier gone with a heart both light and free,
Saying, "Give me back the maidenhead you stole last night, for me
  mammy, she's angry with me."

So he got her by the middle so small and he threw her into the bed
And he turned up her heels where her head ought to be and he gave
  her back her maidenhead.
Now she is to her mammy gone with a heart light and free,
Saying, "I'm as clear of all mankind as the very first night you had
  me."

Well, that fared well and so passed by, till the soldier's wedding, it
  came on.
And the widow woman dressed up her daughter so grand with a
  rose in every hand.
"Oh, who is that?" cries the bride's daddy," that stands so fine and
  braw?"
"It's the widow woman's daughter from the west moorlands and she
  tells her mammy all."

"Oh, how can she do it? Oh, how can she do it? Oh, how does she
  do it for shame?
For it's nine long nights I've lain with my love and I'm sure I never
  told anyone."
"If there's nine long nights you've lain with your love, another
  night you'll never lie with me
And he took the widow's daughter from the west moorland and he
  made her his braw lady.

Frog in a Cocked Hat

Old as it is, this is still a fairly modern version of a really ancient nursery rhyme and, as some say, originally a political parody. The song has been collected in Ireland, Wales, Scotland, and England. The brilliant Ozark singer Almeda Riddle has an especially fine version.

Source: Text from a broadside; tune from Mike Risinger of The Traditional Folk Music Club in New York.

Recordings: Packie Manus Byrne, *Singing Men of Ulster*, Green Linnet SIF 1005. Frankie Armstrong, *Lovely on the Water*, Topic 12TS216

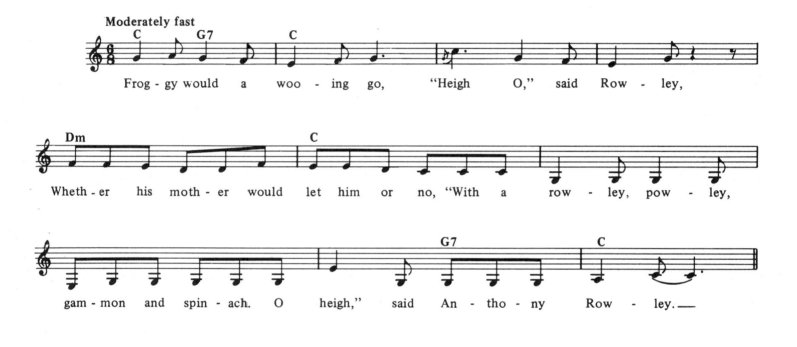

Froggy would a wooing go,
 "Heigh O, " said Rowley,
Whether his mother would let him or no,
 "With a rowley, powley, gammon and spinach.
 O heigh," said Anthony Rowley.

Off he went with his opera hat,
 "Heigh O,"...
On the road he met with a rat.
 "With a rowley ...

They soon arrived at mouse's hall,
They gave a loud rap and they gave a loud call.

"Pray, Mrs. Mouse, are you within?"
"Yes, kind sirs, I'm sitting to spin."

"Come, Mrs. Mouse, now give us some beer,
That Froggy and I may have some cheer."

"Pray, Mrs. Frog, will you give us a song?
Let the subject be something that's not very long."

"Indeed, Mrs. Mousey," replied the frog.
"A cold has made me as hoarse as a hog."

"Since you have caught a cold," she said,
"I'll sing you a song that I have just made."

As they were in glee and merrymaking,
A cat and her kittens came tumbling in.

The cat, she seized the rat by the crown;
The kittens, they pulled the little mouse down.

This put Mr. Frog in a terrible fright.
He took up his hat and wished them goodnight.

As Froggy was crossing over a brook,
A lily-white duck came and gobbled him up.

So here is the end of one, two and three;
The rat, the mouse and the little Froggy.

City
Streets
to the
t-Sugain
Road

The Rocky Road to Dublin

An emigrant on the road, perhaps on his way to Paddy West's house. **Rocky Road** is a slip jig favored both as a song and as a tune. Nonsmokers find it easier to master..

Source: Learned from Brian Brooks.
Recording: The Clancy Brothers and Tommy Makem, *The First Hurrah!* Columbia CS 8965.

Dorian of D

In the mer - ry month of June, from me home I start - ed, Left the girls of Tuam near - ly bro - ken heart-ed; Sa - lu - ted fa - ther dear, kissed me dar - ling moth - er, Drank a pint of beer, me grief and tears to smoth-er. Then, off to reap the corn and leave where I was born. I cut a stout black- thorn to ban - ish ghost and gob- lin. In a brand new pair of brogues, ratt - ling o'er the bogs And fright-en -ing all the dogs____ on the rock - y road to Dub - lin.

Chorus

One, two, three, four five: Hunt the hare and turn her down ____the rock - y road and all the way to Dub - lin. Wack - fol - lol - dee - ra! In ra.____

58

In the merry month of June, from me home I started,
Left the girls of Tuam nearly broken-hearted;
Saluted Father dear, kissed me darling mother,
Drank a pint of beer, me grief and tears to smother.
Then, off to reap the corn and leave where I was born,
I cut a stout blackthorn to banish ghost and goblin.
In a brand new pair of brogues, rattling o'er the bogs
And frightening all the dogs on the rocky road to Dublin.

One, two, three, four, five:
Hunt the hare and turn her down the rocky road
And all the way to Dublin. Wack-fol-lol-dee-ra!

In Mullingar that night I rested limbs so weary,
Started by daylight next morning bright and early.
I took a drop of the "pure" to keep me heart from sinking.
That's the Paddy's cure whenever he's up for drinking.
To see the lassies smile, laughing all the while
At me curious style, 'twould set your heart a-bubbling.
They asked if I was hired and the wages I required,
Till I was almost tired of the rocky road to Dublin.

One, two . . .

In Dublin next arrived, I thought it such a pity,
To be so soon deprived a view of that fine city,
So then I took a stroll all among the quality.
Me bundle it was stole all in a neat locality.
Something crossed me mind and when I looked behind,
No bundle could I find upon me stick a wobbling,
Enquiring for the rogue, they said me Connaught brogue
Wasn't much in vogue on the rocky road to Dublin.

From there I got away, me spirits never failing.
I landed on the quay just as the ship was sailing.
The Captain at me roared, said that no room had he.
When I jumped aboard, a cabin found for Paddy
Down among the pigs. I played some funny rigs
And danced some hearty jigs, the water round me bubbling.
When off Holyhead, I wished meself was dead
Or, better far instead, on the rocky road to Dublin.

The boys of Liverpool, when we safely landed,
Called meself a fool. I could no longer stand it.
Blood began to boil; temper I was losing.
Poor old Erin's isle they began abusing.
"Hurrah, me soul," says I. Me shillelagh I let fly.
Some Galway boys were by and saw I was a hobble in.
Then with a loud hurray, joining in the affray,
We quickly cleared the way for the rocky road to Dublin.

Feein' Time

A song from the open-air feeing markets or hiring fairs (as they were called in Ireland). Artie Trezise tells me that marriage was the best way out of the system. "The bothies were good for the crack, well enough, but if a fella wanted to get on he'd get married and the farmer would give him his own house. The same was true for the girl: she'd get out of the big house and into her own wee place."

In hiring for a certain term, the worker was essentially bound for that period, because he would receive no pay before the term was up. This, of course, caused a great reluctance to leave no matter how hard the conditions.

Source: Cilla Fisher.

Recording: Cilla Fisher, *For Foul Day and Fair*, Folk-Legacy FSS-69.

Me friend and I struck frae Mill-gye to Glas-ga toon we took our way, When all a-long the road was strung Wi' lads and bon-nie

las - ses gay. When draw - ing nigh, I one did spy, She was walk - ing slow - ly

by her - sel'; For fear the rain her claes would spoil,_ I did dis - play_ my um - ber - ell.

Me friend and I struck frae Millgye,
To Glasga toon we took our way,
When all along the road was strung
Wi' lads and bonnie lasses gay.
When drawing nigh, I one did spy,
She was walking slowly by hersel';
For fear the rain her claes would spoil,
I did display my umberell'.

"Where are you goin', my bonnie lass?
How far, then, are you gaun this way?"
"To Glasga toon, air, I am bound,
For this, you know, is feein' day.
Although the day seems wet to be,
Indeed the morning did look fine."
Smiling, she said, "I am afraid
I'll no be in by feein' time."

"Oh, cheer your heart, my bonnie lass,
For we'll hae guid weather bye and bye.
And don't be sad when wi' a lad,
A rovin' baker frae Millgye.
And if you will accept a gill
Of whisky, brandy, rum, or wine,
We'll hae a gill, and then we will
Be up to toon for feein' time."

She gave consent, and in we went
Tae an ale-house that was by the way;
Glass after glass around did pass,
Till we baith forgot it was feein' day.
The clock struck three, she smiled on me;
She said: "Young man, the fault is thine,
For nicht is on, and I'm frae home,
And, besides, I've lost ma feein' time."

"Oh, lass, don't grieve, for while I live
I ne'er intend tae harm you,
And marriage I will surely try,
For baker lads they aye prove true."
"But I'm too young to wed a man;
Besides, my mither has name but me,
But I'll comply and I'll ne'er deny,
And I'd wed before I tak' a fee."

Noo the nicht was spent in merriment,
And we got married the very next day,
And aye since syne my love has said,
"I'm glad ye lost the feein' day."
For my love and I we do agree,
I ne'er do think he will repine,
For every day he smiles and says,
"I'm glad ye lost the feein' time."

The Turfman from Ardee

For four months in 1974, I juggled a weekday career in
the airline business with a weekend job as Margaret Barry's
agent, chauffer, and singing companion. I've never laughed
so much in my life.

Margaret's repertoire became well known to me, and apart
from a couple of her slower ballads, this is my favorite of
her songs. Nothing much happens here, but **The Turfman's**
innocent repartee perfectly distills an Irish roadside scene.

Source: Margaret Barry.
Recording: Margaret Barry, *Her Mantle So Green*, Topic
12T123.

For the sake of health I took a walk one morn - ing in the dawn; I

met a jol - ly_ turf - man on _ the road _ as I went on.

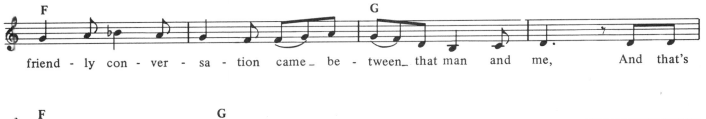

friend - ly con - ver - sa - tion came _ be - tween _ that man and me, And that's

how I came ac - quaint - ed ____ with the turf - man from Ar - dee.

For the sake of health I took a walk one morning in the dawn;
I met a jolly turfman on the road as I went on.
A friendly conversation came between that man and me,
And that's how I came acquainted with the turfman from Ardee.

O, we chatted very freely as we jogged along the road.
Said he, "Me ass I tired and I'd like to sell me load.
I've had no refreshment since I left my home you see,
And I'm tired out of traveling," says the turfman from Ardee.

Says I, "My friend your cart is worn your ass is very old.
It must be twenty summers since that animal was foaled."
"Yolked in a trap when he was born, September '43,
And he cantered for the midwife," says the turfman from Ardee.

"I know, me friend, me cart is worn but it's tough old Irish wood."
"It must be in use since the time of Noah's flood."
"The harness that was on his back was made by Sam McGee,
And he's dead these two and twenty years." says the turfman from Ardee.

"And many's the time I abused this beast with his rough hazel rod.
But I must own up I never did see poor old Jack unshod.
The axle never wanted grease in one year out of three;
It's the real old Carrick axle," says the turfman from Ardee.

It's then I heard a female voice that I knew very well,
Politely asking this poor man for his load of turf to sell.
I shook this steady hand of his and he bowed respectfully,
In hopes to meet some future day with the turfman from Ardee.

The Besom Maker

She walked through life, sweeping her past behind.

Source: Text from a broadside printed by Disley of St. Giles, London; tune learned from the singing of Lou Killen.

Recording: Johnny Handle, *The Lads of Northumbria,* Trailer LER 2007.

Lou Killen Photo by David Gahr

61

The Besom Maker

I am a besom maker, listen to my tale,
I am a besom maker, lives yonder in the vale.

Come buy my besoms, besoms fire and new,
Bonny green broom besoms, better never grew.

Sweet pleasures I enjoy both morning, night, and noon,
Going over hills so high a gathering of green broom.

Come buy my besoms . . .

One day as I was roving, over the hills so high,
I met with a rakish squire, all with a rolling eye.

He tipt to me the wink, I wrote to him the tune,
I eased him of his gink, a gathering of green broom.

One day as I was turning, to my native vale,
I met Jack Sprat, the miller, he asked if I'd turn tale.

His mill I rattled round, I ground the grits so clean,
I eased him of his gink, in gathering broom so green.

One day as I was turning to my native cot,
I met a buxom farmer, happy was his lot.

He ploughed his furrows deep, and laid his corn so low,
He left it there to keep, like green broom to grow.

When the corn grew up all in its native soil,
A sweet young baby soon on me did smile.
I bundled up my besoms and took them to the fair,
And sold them all by wholesale, nursing now's my care.

Come A' Ye Tramps an' Hawkers

A great song of the road! Kennedy prints another verse, from Davie Stewart, in *Folksongs of Britain and Ireland*:

> *I've seen the high Ben Nevis that gangs towerin' tae the moon*
> *I've been roun' by Crieff an' Callander and by Bonny Doon*
> *I've been by Nethy's silvery tide and places ill to ken*
> *Far up into the stormy north lies Urquart's fairy glen.*

Gretna Green is the last town in Scotland on the road from Glasgow to Carlisle. Braxie ham is meat from a sheep which has died naturally and partially putrified, prior to being butchered and cured.

Source: Text collated from various singers; tune is very common.

Recording: Ewan MacColl, *Street Songs of Scotland*, Washington 738.

Come a' ye tramps an' hawker lads an' gaitherers o' blaw,
That tramps the country roon' an' roon'. Come listen ane an' a'.
I'll tell tae ye a rovin' tale of sechts that I hae seen
Far intae the snowy north an' sooth by Gretna Green.

It's oft I've laughed untae mysel' when traivlin' on the road,
Two rags roon' my twisted feet; my face as broon's a toad.
Wi' lumps a cake an' tattie scones, wi' cheese an' braxie ham,
Ne'er gi'en a thoucht tae whaur I've been, nor less tae whaur I'm gaun.

I've done my share o' humpin' wi' the dockers on the Clyde.
I helped them Buckie trawlers haul the herrin' ower the side.
I helped tae build the mechty bridge that spans the busy Forth
An' wi' many an' Angus fairmers rig I've plood the bonny earth.

I'm happy in the Simmertime beneath the brecht blue sky,
No' thinkin' in the mornin' whaur at necht I'll hae tae lie,
In barn or byre or onywhaur oot aman the hay
An' if the weather treats me right, I'm happy every day.

I'm gaun back tae Paddy's Land; I'm making up my mind.
For Scotland's greatly altered noo, I canna' raise the wind,
But if I can trust in Providence an' Providence proves true,
I'll sing ye a' o'Erin's Isle when I come back tae you.

The Beggin'

A great song for busking. This version combines words I've learned over the years with others from Chappell's *Popular Music of the Olden Time*.

Source: Text is a collation; tune learned from the singing of John Cauldfield.

Recordings: Harry Broadman, *A Lancashire Mon*, Topic 12TS236. Ewan MacColl, *The Manchester Angel*, Tradition 2059.

Dorian of D

I am a jovial beggar. I have a wooden leg,
Lame from the cradle and forcèd for to beg.

And a-beggin' I will go, me lads,
A-beggin' I will go.

I've a little bag for me oatmeal, another one for me salt,
With me two wee bonny crutches you can see me swing and halt.

And a-beggin' . . .

I've a little bag for me wheat, sir, another one for me rye,
And a little bottle by me side to drink when I am dry.

Seven years I begged for my old master Wild.
He taught me how to beg, sir, when I was but a child.

I begged for me master and got him store of pelf.
But now, the Lord be praised, sir, I'm begging for meself.

In a hollow tree I live, sir, and there I pay no rent.
Providence provides for me and I am well content.

Oh, I've been blind a hundred times and deaf a score or more
And many's the right and willing lass I've bedded in the straw.

Of all the trades in England, beggin' is the best
For when a beggar's tired he can lay himself to rest.

Of all the trades in England, beggin' is the one
For we live a life of "going to do" and die with nothing done.

Bung Your Eye

"Bung Your Eye" was the common name for genever, a Dutch liquor of the vodka-gin-aguavit family and a popular drink of the 19th-century slum dweller. This song is from the England Jack the Ripper walked in; poor, cold, and hungry. The inhabitants of London's East End were futureless and attempted to ignore fate. While this ballad is humourous on one level, it is, of course, pitiful on another.

Variants of this "Derry Down" melody are often used in English folk song (see **The Dreadnaught**, p. 107, and **The Devil and Bonaparte**, p. 154).

Source: Text from a broadside by Wood of New Meeting Street, Birmingham; tune is very common.
Recording: The Dubliners, *The Dubliners*, Fiesta FLPS 1627.

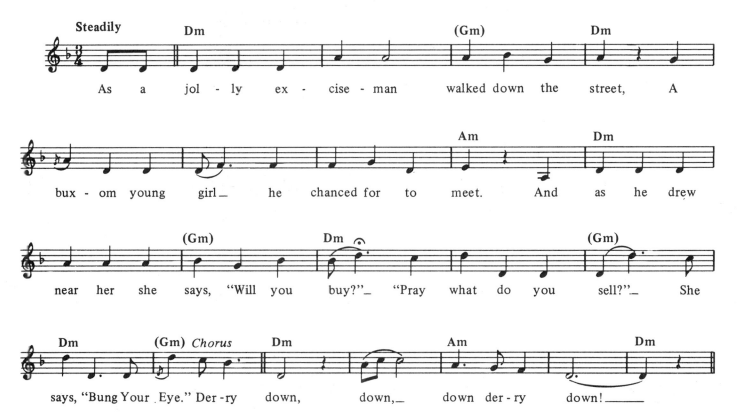

As a jolly exciseman walked down the street,
A buxom young girl he chanced to meet.
And as he drew near her she says, "Will you buy?"
"Pray what do you sell?" She says, "Bung Your Eye."

Derry down, down, down derry down!

"But now, to be serious, what have you got there?"
" 'Tis honest genever, I vow and declare,"
At the custom-house officers I look very shy,
"And to give it a nickname it's called Bung Your Eye."

Derry down . . .

"And if you're a gentleman as you appear,
To leave my genever I need not to fear
Till I speak to a customer that's just passed by,
I will leave you in charge of my sweet Bung Your Eye."

Now mark, my good friends, what I'm going to mention:
To look in her basket it was my intention,
But in two or three minutes a young child did cry,
Then up in my arms I took young Bung Your Eye.

Then I took the child home without more delay
And to have the child christened I hastened away.
Says the parson, "I'll christen the child by and by.
Pray what is its name?" I says, "Bung Your Eye."

"Bung Your Eye!" says the parson, "Why that's an odd name."
"Why yes, sir, it is and an odd why it came,
For I know all the people as I do pass by
They think me the father of young Bung Your Eye."

Now all you excisemen who walketh the street,
Beware of those girls if you chance them to meet.
With their honest genever they look very shy
But they'll soon make you father of young Bung Your Eye.

The Saucy Bold Robber

A David and Goliath story, this one, pitting a brave and unassuming Everyman against a giant whose only weakness, other than that he's a large target, is his greed.

The song is from Roy Harris, the fine Nottingham singer; He had it from Bert Lloyd.

Source: Roy Harris.
Recording: Roy Harris, *Champions of Folly*, Topic 12TS256.

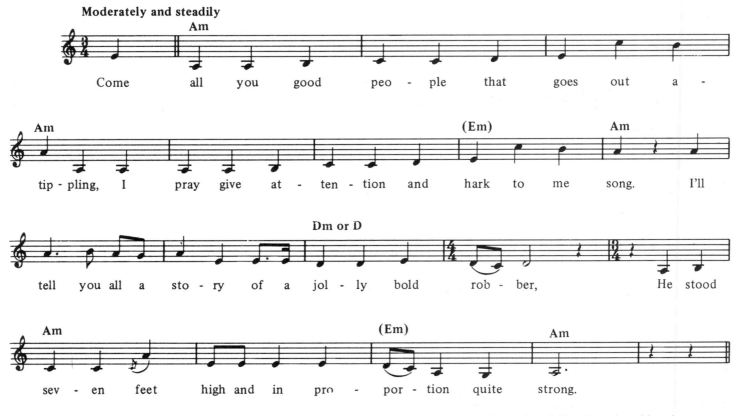

Come all you good people that goes out a-tipping, I pray give attention and hark to me song. I'll tell you all a story of a jolly bold robber, He stood seven feet high and in proportion quite strong.

Come all you good people that goes out a-tippling,
I pray give attention and hark to me song.
I'll tell you all a story of a jolly bold robber,
He stood seven feet high and in proportion quite strong.

He robbed lawyer Morgan and old Lady Dawkins;
Five hundred bright guineas from each one of them.
And as he was patrolling the sailor come strolling
And bold as a lion he slewèd up to him.

"Hand over your money, me gallant young sailor.
There's plenty of bulk in your pocket, I know."
"Oh aye," says the sailor, "I've got a bit of money,
But I'm damned if I see why I should give it to you.

"I've just left my ship, give the press-gang the slip,
And I'm bound down to London my sweetheart to see.
Seven shiny sovereigns will pay our sweet lodgings,
So I pray you, jolly robber, please leave it to me."

The robber caught hold of that gallant young sailor,
With a blow like a pick-axe knocked him to the ground.
"Oh aye," said the sailor, "You've hit me quite heavy,
But now I'll endeavour to repay you in kind."

It was then, boys, they stripped, like tigers they skipped,
And they fought blow for blow like two soldiers in the field.
At the ninety-seventh meeting it was the completing,
For this saucy bold robber by the sailor was killed.

Then the sailor looked down at that bloodstained old robber.
"I hope you'll forgive me, dear fellow," says he,
"But if I had just lifted a thousand bright gineas,
Well, I'm damned if I'd a-stopped a poor sailor like thee."

Roy Harris

Poor Murdered Woman

This is Martin Carthy's rendition of a local Surrey song. He replaced the tune (from the *Journal of the Folk Song Society,* Vol. 1) with the Scots **Blaeberry Courtship**, though nowadays, he says, he'd be just as happy with the original, collected by a parson, C. J. Shebbeare, at Milford in 1897.

Source: Martin Carthy.

Recording: Martin Carthy, *But Two Came By*, Topic 12TS343.

Dorian of D

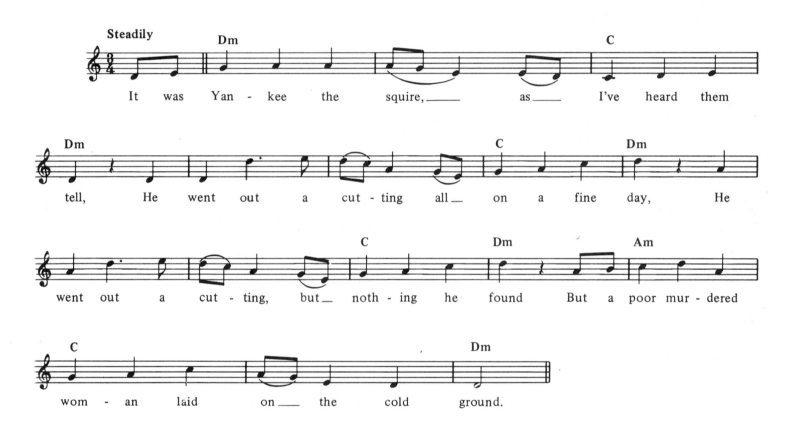

It was Yankee the squire, as I've heard them tell, He went out a-cutting all on a fine day, He went out a-cutting, but nothing he found But a poor murdered woman laid on the cold ground.

It was Yankee the squire, as I've heard them tell,
He went out a-cutting all on a fine day,
He went out a-cutting, but nothing he found
But a poor murdered woman laid on the cold ground.

About eight o'clock, boys, our dogs they throwed off
And off to the common, and that was the spot.
They tried all the bushes, but nothing they found
But a poor murdered woman laid on the cold ground.

They whipped their dogs off, and kept them away,
For I do think it's proper he should have fair play.
They tried all the bushes, but nothing they found
But a poor murdered woman laid on the cold ground.

They mounted their horses and rode off the ground.
They rode to the village, and alarmed it all round.
"It is late in the evening, I am sorry to say,
She can not be removed until the next day."

The next Sunday morning, about eight o'clock,
Some hundreds of people to the spot they did flock.
For to see that poor creature it would make your hears bleed.
Some cold-hearted violence had come to her head.

She was took off the common, and down to some inn.
And the man that has kept it, his name was John Sinn.
The coroner was sent for, the jury they joined,
And soon they concluded and settled their mind.

Her coffin was brought; in it she was laid,
And took to the churchyard in fair Leatherhead,
No father, no mother, nor no friend, at all
Come to see that poor creature put under the mould.

James McDonald

Here's a murder ballad with a story not unlike the American **Pretty Polly**. The victim's name in this case was Ann O'Brien and the locality Co. Longford in the Irish midlands. Though I haven't seen any research on the matter, I should think there's a good likelihood of there being a factual basis for the ballad.

The Scottish collector Gavin Greig contributed a weekly folksong column to his area newspaper, *The Buchan Observer*. (Ulsterman Sam Henry provided a similar column for the *Northern Constitution,* though Henry gave tunes and Greig did not.) **The Longford Murderer** is Greig's

title, and he has these comments about the gruesome recounting: "It must be allowed that the moral effect of these narrations tends in the right direction. For in them crime is ever followed by retribution, and even the criminal himself is represented as acquiescing to the justice of the sentence that condemns him to death."

Source: Text from a broadside, collated with Ord's *Bothy Songs and Ballads*; tune is my composition.

Recording: Cecilia Costello, *Cecilia Costello,* Leader LEE 4054.

Oh, young men and old, I must now make bold, pray lend to me an ear!
This is as cruel a murder as ever you shall hear.
All of a lovely female, her age was scarce sixteen;
And her beauty bright did me delight, I did her heart ensnare.

This fair maid being a servant girl and I a farmer's son,
All in the Co. Longford, convenient to Rathowen.
In private there we courted till I got her with child.
And then to take her precious life I planned all in my mind.

'Twas on a Sunday evening, as quickly you will hear,
I sent for her in private, and soon she came to me,
I said, "Dear Anne, if you comply, to Longford we will go.
It's there that we'll get married and no one here shall know."

'Twas late at night we both set out across the countryside.
While on the way I talked full gay, my secret plan to hide.
And tender words she spoke to me, would draw tears down from your eyes,
But I said, "We'll go no further, for it's here that you must die."

"Ah, James, think on your infant dear, and don't give me a fright,
And don't commit a murder this dark and dismal night,
I'll promise God all on my knees, if you will spare my life,
That I'll never come to trouble you, or ask to be your wife."

The words she said were all in vain. I struck her dreadful sore
And with a heavy loaded whip I left her in her gore
Her blood and brains flew like the rain, her moans would pierce your heart,
I was sure that I had murdered her before that I did part.

She was alive next morning just by the break of day,
There was a shepherd's daughter by chance came that way,
She saw her lying in her blood and came to her relief,
And Annie told her of my guilt and asked to see the priest.

The priest and doctor were sent for, and the policeman likewise,
They all got information and set out in disguise.
It's quickly they surrounded me, for she told my name,
They brought me back a prisoner and lodged me in Longford gaol.

And there I lay with troubled mind until my trial day.
The jury found me guilty, and the judge to me did say—
"For the murdering of an orphan girl, your countrymen shall see,
On the sixteenth of April you'll hang on the gallows tree."

Sam Hall

Jack (not Sam) Hall was a well-known burglar who was swung on Tyburn Hill during the heyday of public execution. Another famous criminal sang his last "goodnight" in that same year of 1701; Captain William Kidd was stretched in chains at Execution Dock, Wapping. Kidd, by the way, once resided at 56 Wall Street, New York City.

Both Kidd and Hall had songs using the same pattern and tune written about them; a third such is **Admiral Benbow**. Our version has a music hall influence.

Source: Text is a general collation; tune is commonly sung.

Recording: The Dubliners, *At Home with the Dubliners*, Tribune TRLP 1010.

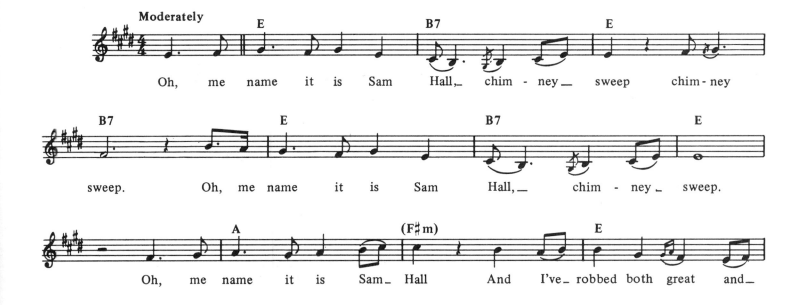

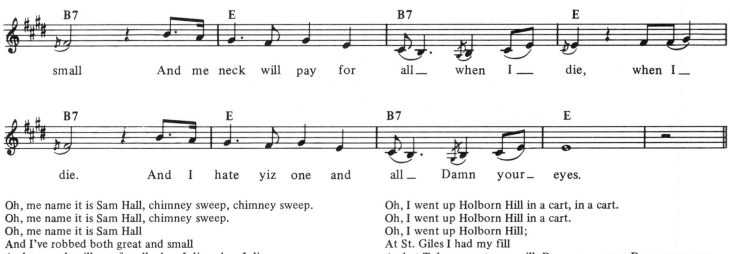

small And me neck will pay for all — when I — die, when I —

die. And I hate yiz one and all — Damn your — eyes.

Oh, me name it is Sam Hall, chimney sweep, chimney sweep.
Oh, me name it is Sam Hall, chimney sweep.
Oh, me name it is Sam Hall
And I've robbed both great and small
And me neck will pay for all when I die, when I die.
And I hate yiz one and all,
Damn your eyes.

Oh, I killed a man they said, so they said, so they said.
Oh, I killed a man they said, so they said.
Oh, I killed a man they said,
Yes, I bashed his bleeding head
With a great big lump a lead. Damn his eyes, Damn his eyes.
And I left him lying dead.
Damn his eyes.

Oh, they put me in the quod, in the quod, in the quod.
Oh, they put me in the quod, in the quod .
Oh, they put me in the quod
And they tied me to a log
Behind bars and iron rods. Damn their eyes. Damn their eyes.
And they left me there by God.
Damn their eyes.

Oh, the parson he did come, he did come, he did come.
Oh, the parson he did come, he did come.
Oh, the parson he did come
And he looked so very glum
And he talked of Kingdom Come. Damn his eyes. Damn his eye·
He can kiss my bleeding bum.
Damn his eyes.

Oh, I went up Holborn Hill in a cart, in a cart.
Oh, I went up Holborn Hill in a cart.
Oh, I went up Holborn Hill;
At St. Giles I had my fill
And at Tyburn wrote my will. Damn your eyes. Damn your eyes.
And at Tyburn wrote my will.
Damn your eyes.

Oh, the sheriff he came too, he came too, he came too.
Oh, the sheriff he came too, he came too.
Oh, the sheriff he came too,
With his little boys in blue
And all his bloody crew. Damn their eyes. Damn their eyes.
Saying, "Sam, we'll see you through."
Damn their eyes.

I saw Molly in the crowd, in the crowd, in the crowd.
I saw Molly in the crowd, in the crowd.
I saw Molly in the crowd
And I hollered right out loud,
"Now well, Molly, ain't you proud?" Damn your eyes. Damn your
  eyes.
Saying, "Molly, ain't you proud?"
Damn your eyes.

Up the ladder I did grope, that's no joke, that's no joke.
Up the ladder I did grope, that's no joke.
Up the ladder I did grope;
Then the hangman pulled the rope
And ne'er a word I spoke tumbling down, tumbling down.
And ne'er a word I spoke.
Damn your eyes.

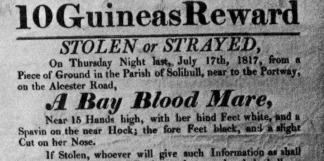

Broadside

Brennan on the Moor

Following Jack Hall by a hundred years or so came Willie Brennan, a highwayman who patrolled Munster but whose fame spread over seas and oceans. Alan Lomax collected a ten-verse version from Neil Morris in the Ozarks which has Willie getting a reprieve and joining the navy. This version is fuller than most.

Colm O Lochlainn writes that Brennan was hanged at Cork City in 1804 and Gordon McCulloch that he was shot during a holdup by a man named Jeremiah O'Connor in 1807.

Source: Broadside by Disley; tune is common, probably first heard from the Clancys.

Recordings: The Clancy Brothers and Tommy Makem, *The Clancy Brothers and Tommy Makem*, Columbia CS 8448. Enoch Kent, *Freedom, Come All Ye*, Topic 12T143.

It's of a fear-less high-way-man, a sto-ry I will tell, HIs name was Wil-lie Bren-nan, in Ire-land he did dwell, And on the Lim-er-ick Moun-tains he com-menced his wild ca-reer, Where man-y a wealth-y gen-tle-man be-fore him shook with fear, And it's Bren-nan on the moor, Bren-nan on the moor, Oh, bold and un-daunt-ed stood Bren-nan on the moor.

It's of a fearless highwayman, a story I will tell,
His name was Willie Brennan, in Ireland he did dwell,
And on the Limerick Mountains he commenced his wild career,
Where many a wealthy gentleman before him shook with fear,

And it's Brennan on the moor, Brennan on the moor,
Oh, bold and undaunted stood Brennan on the moor.

A brace of loaded pistols, he carried night and day,
He never robbed a poor man upon the King's Highway;
But when he'd taken from the rich like Turpin and Black Bess,
He always did divide it with the widow in distress.

And it's Brennan . . .

One night he robbed a packman; his name was Pedlar Bawn,
They traveled on together till day began to dawn.
The pedlar seeing his money gone, likewise his watch and chain,
He at once encountered Brennan and robbed him back again.

When Brennan seeing the pedlar was a good a man as he,
He took him on the highway his companion for to be.
The pedlar threw away his pack, without any more delay,
And proved a faithful comrade until his dying day.

One day upon the highway, as Willie he sat down,
He met the Mayor of Cashel, a mile outside the town.
The Mayor he knew his features, "I think, young man," said he,
"Your name is Willie Brennan. You must come along with me."

As Brennan's wife had gone to town, provisions for to buy,
When she saw her Willie, she began to weep and cry.
He says, "Give me that tenpence?" As soon as Willie spoke,
She handed him the blunderbuss from underneath her cloak.

Then with his loaded blunderbuss, the truth I will unfold,
He made the Mayor to tremble and robbed him of his gold;
One hundred pounds was offered for his apprehension there,
And with his horse and saddle to the mountains did repair.

Then Brennan being an outlaw, upon the mountain high,
Where cavalry and infantry to take him they did try;
He laughed at them with scorn, until, at length, it's said,
By a false-hearted young man he was basely betrayed.

In the country of Tipperary in a place they call Clonmore,
Willie Brennan and his comrade they did suffer sore,
He lay among the fern which was thick upon the field,
And nine wounds he did receive before that he did yield.

Then Brennan and his companion knowing they were betrayed
He with the mounted cavalry a noble battle made,
He lost his foremost finger, which was shot off by a ball,
So Brennan and his comrade, they were taken after all.

So they were taken prisoners, in irons they were bound
And conveyed to clonmel jail, strong walls did them surround.
They were tried and found guilty, the judge made this reply,
"For robbing on the King's Highway, you are both condemned to
 die."

"Farewell! Unto my wife, and to my children three,
Likewise my aged father, he may shed tears for me,
And to my loving mother, who tore her gray locks and cried,
Saying, 'I wish Willie Brennan, in your cradle you had died.' "

The Wild and Wicked Youth

A great fast song. The Johnstons popularized **The Newry Highwayman** version from O Lochlainn's *More Irish Street Ballads* in the early 1970s, and most renditions I hear would seem to stem from their performance. Mick Moloney recently told me he'd borrowed a 150-year-old mandolin for the recording session and that the instrument heaved a sigh and collapsed seconds after the last note was struck. The innate humor in such a situation usually surfaces only after a few years have passed. The "Fielding" referred to in the fifth verse was novelist Henry Fielding, a London judge in the latter eighteenth century, and his "gang" was London's first police force, the Bow Street Runners.

Source: Text from a broadside by Watts of Snow Hill, Birmingham; tune from the singing of the Johnstons.

Recordings: The Johnstons, *Ye Jacobites by Name*, Contour 2870 378. Clive Collins, *Here's a Health to the Man and the Maid*, Living Folk LFR 103.

Dorian of E

In New-ry town I was bred— and born. On Ste-phen's

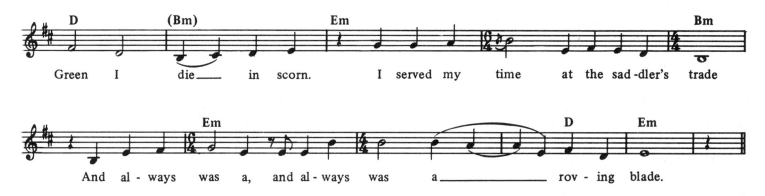

Green I die___ in scorn. I served my time at the sad-dler's trade

And al-ways was a, and al-ways was a _____ rov-ing blade.

In Newry town I was bred and born.
On Stephen's Green I die in scorn.
I served my time at the saddler's trade
And always was a, and always was a roving blade.

At seventeen I took a wife,
And I loved her dearly as I loved my life,
And to maintain her fine and gay
A-robbing went on the broad highway.

When my money did grow low
On the highway I was forced to go,
Where I robbed both lords and ladies high,
Brought home their gold to my heart's delight.

I robbed Lord Goldin, I do declare,
And Lady Mansfield in Grosvenor Square,
Closed up the shutters, bid them goodnight
And went away to my heart's delight.

To Covent Gardens I took my way,
All with my dear wife to see the play,
Till Fielding's gang did me persue.
Taken was I by that cursed crew.

My father cries, "I am undone!"
My mother sighs for her darling son.
My wife she tears her golden hair.
What shall I do; I'm in despair!

And when I'm dead and in my grave
A flashy funeral pray let me have,
Six highwaymen to carry me.
Give them good broadswords and liberty.

Six blooming girls to bear the pall;
Give them white gloves and ribbons all.
When I am dead they'll tell the truth,
He was a wild and a wicked youth.

Sylvie

Identical to **The Wild and Wicked Youth** in melody, **Sylvie**
is one of a host of good "transvestite" songs. Sometimes
the woman dresses in men's clothing to find a missing lover
(**I Am a Maid That Sleeps in Love**, p. 102) and sometimes
for adventure (**The Martinmas Time**) with the result being
misadventure (**The Handsome Cabin Boy**, p. 104). Sylvie
doubts her love's intentions and is reassured.

Source: Text is a general collation and adaptation.
Recording: Martin Carthy, *Martin Carthy*, Topic 12TS340.

Sylvie, Sylvie, when none could see,
Dressed in men's clothing and gear so free,
With a sword and pistol all by her side,
To meet her true love, to meet her true love,
Slyvie did ride.

As she was riding over the plain
She met her true love and bid him stand.
"Stand and deliver, kind sir," she said,
"Or else this moment,
"Or else this moment I'll shoot you dead."

Oh, when she'd robbed him of his store
She says, "Kind sir, there's one thing more;
A diamond ring which I know you wear.
Deliver it,
Deliver it and your life I'll spare."

"My diamond ring a token is.
The ring I'll save or my life I'll give."
Being tender-hearted just like a dove,
She rode away,
She rode away from her own true love.

Next morning in the garden green,
Just like two lovers they were seen.
He saw his watch hanging midst her robes
Which made him blush,
Which made him blush like a red, red, rose.

"What makes you blush, you silly thing?
I fain would have had your diamond ring,
'Twas I that robbed you on the plain.
So here's your watch, love,
So here's your watch, love, and gold again."

"I only did it for to know
Whether you was my true love or no,
But now I have a contented mind
My heart and all,
My heart and all, dear, they are thine."

The Farmers' Downfall

A song, presumably from about 1848 and a celebration of sorts after the repeal of the English Corn Laws. "Corn" by the way, is synonymous with "grain" rather than "maize" in England.

At the close of the Napoleonic Wars, legislation was brought about to prevent a sharp drop in corn prices. As population increased, so did demand and price. By 1839, the situation was critical; John Bright and Richard Cobden formed the Anti-Corn Law League. Seven years later, they were successful and the people got affordable food.

Source: Text from a broadside by Theophilus Bloomer of Birmingham; the melody is mostly mine.

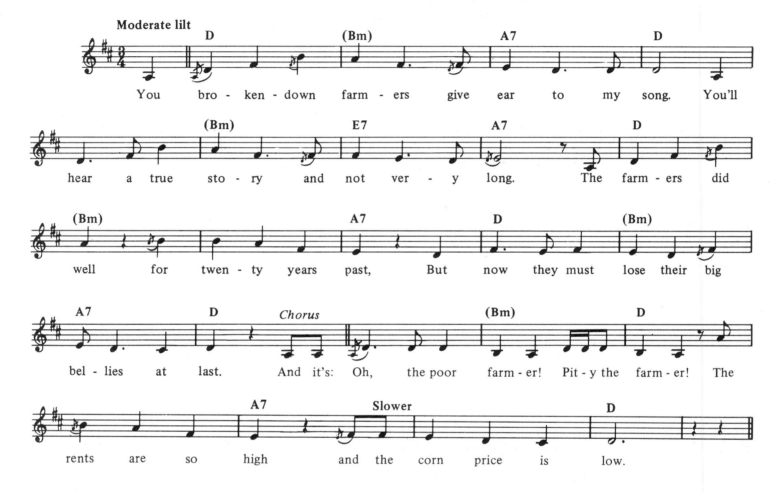

You broken-down farmers give ear to my song. You'll hear a true story and not very long. The farmers did well for twenty years past, But now they must lose their big bellies at last. And it's: Oh, the poor farmer! Pity the farmer! The rents are so high and the corn price is low.

M3, 22

ear ___ to my
corn price is

You broken-down farmers give ear to my song.
You'll hear a true story and not very long.
The farmers did well for twenty years past,
But now they must lose their big bellies at last.

And it's: Oh, the poor farmer!
Pity the farmer!
The rents are so high and the corn
price is low.

When the wheat for a guinea a bushel did sell,
It made all the farmers to laugh and to swell.
They said to themselves, "As the corn it sells now,
We can buy some fine horses and a fox hunting go."

And it's . . .

But the gentlemen said, as they joined in the chase,
"We will double the rents and alter the case.
We will double the rents or they shall quit the ground,
For they shall not be champions to follow the hounds."

But if they had gone on their old fashioned way,
They never would have had double rents for to pay,
But they got a new fashion of dressing so grand
And now they must work hard like another poor man.

A few years ago when the corn price did fall
They hoarded it up and would sell none at all,
But now they are glad to sell a bushel retail
For to keep their rents paid and themselves out of jail.

Now the rents are so high and the corn price so low,
The poor farmers cry out in sad grief and woe.
They grieve for the days that are over and past
And now they must lose their big bellies at last.

Remarks on the Times

Eighteen hundred-nine, the year mentioned in the song, came in the middle of twelve years of solid fighting with Napoleon. It was also a time of great unrest within Britain and Ireland, as new political, social, and economic systems of all makes were being superimposed on existing ones. There was turmoil everywhere.

Source: Text from a broadside by Edmunds; tune is an adaptation of a common traditional one.

Ye gentlemen of England, I pray you all draw near,
The distress of our country you quickly shall hear.
'Tis concerning the year eighteen hundred and nine,
The people complain of there being such hard times.

*The world's full of roguery as a poet's full of rhymes,
'Tis the lords and other great men make such hard times.*

They still keep continually to enclose the land,
So that the poor farmer cannot it withstand.
The wine drinking gentlemen have got all our rights
And the poor farmer he is ruined quite.

The world's full . . .

There's many a poor man that did keep a cow,
Two or three pigs and an old sow.
His rights are ta'en from him; he's nothing at all,
So now on the Parish his family must fall.

Poor tradesmen in Yorkshire, their case it is bad;
They're out of employment, no work to be had.
By the stoppage of trade, they're in poverty too.
Many hundreds and thousands for soldiers do go.

They say 'tis the war that makes things so dear,
Tea, sugar, soap, tobacco and beer.
I believe it is trade all the world o'er,
But the heaviest burden is laid on the poor.

We have nothing but roguery, I vow and protest.
Bakers, butchers and millers, as well as the rest,
They will cheat you with flour and blow up your meat
And if it stinks awfully they'll say it's quite sweet.

O, how the shop keepers palaver and cant,
Saying, "Ladies and gentlemen, what do you want?
We have fine congou tea, sugar white and brown."
They'll cheat you by weight and the scales bump down.

Another gang of villans ride up and down,
Corn factors and hucksters in every town,
Who buy up provisions and all kinds of grain
And they gain double fold when they sell them again.

By rogues such as these in our own country,
Our flourishing island's kept in poverty.
There's nothing but roguery; all cheat as they can
And the greatest of villans is thought the best man.

So now, brother thrasher, my song's at an end.
When all rogues are hanged, the times will mend.
A cartload of halters will scarce be enough.
There'll be no better doing till Jack Ketch does his stuff.

I Wish They'd Do It Now

The image of the "old bachelor" is no less humorous than that of the "old maid" and considerably less controversial nowadays.

I Wish They'd Do It Now was one of my father's favorites. The version he sang had double verses and came from his grandfather, Patrick McKay of Ennis, Co. Clare:

I was born in sweet Killarney one day when I was young
And that is just the reason why there's Blarney in my tongue.
Sure, the night was dark and stormy and the rain came pouring down

And the old nurse Judy Carney lived a long way out of town.
My father got the donkey out and off went with a crack
And with Judy stuck behind him, they very soon came back.
That I was a lovely baby, all the neighbours did allow.
They brought girls for to kiss me then. I wish they'd do it now.

Source: Text from a broadside with no imprint; tune learned from William Milner.
Recording: Bob Davenport, *Bob Davenport and the Marsden Rattlers*, Trailer LER 3008.

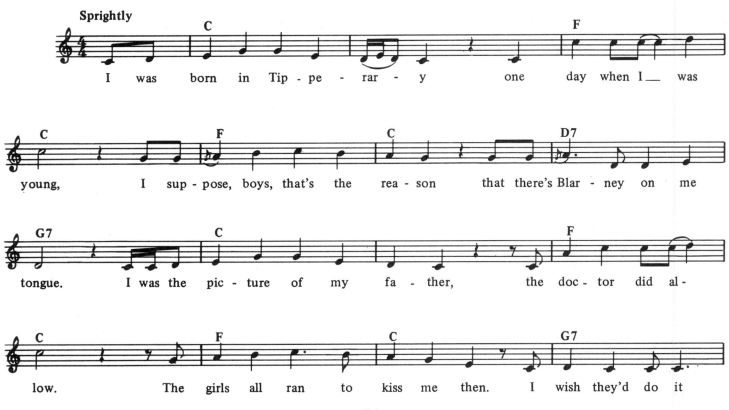

now.   Oh,   I   wish they'd   do   it   now!   Oh,   I   wish they'd   do   it

now!   The   girls   all   ran   to   kiss   me   then.   I   wish they'd do it— now.

I was born in Tipperary one day when I was young,
I suppose, boys, that's the reason that there's blarney on me tongue.
I was the picture of my father, the doctor did allow.
The girls all ran to kiss me then. I wish they'd do it now.

Oh, I wish they'd do it now! Oh, I wish they'd do it now!
The girls all ran to kiss me then. I wish they'd do it now. *

Then as that I grew older, how the girls would laugh with glee,
And they pressed me to their bosom, and nursed me on their knee.
They'd rock me in the cradle, but if I made a row,
They'd take me in to sleep with them; Oh, I wish they'd do it now.

Oh, I wish . . .

At twelve years old, a finer boy, I'm sure was never seen,
For the girls would coax me out to play, upon the meadows green.
They'd pick me all the butter-cups, to deck my boyish brow,
Then roll with me upon the grass; Oh, I wish they'd do it now.

Then the girls would take me out to bathe, when the weather it
   was mild,
And there we'd roll, and swim about, like little shrimps so wild.
They'd splash the water till it shone like pearls upon my brow,
Then they'd dry me nice all over; Oh, I wish they'd do it now.

Then my father sent me to the school, to learn my A B C,
But the little girls in my class, they would not let me be.
They'd pinch me in my breeches, it was not fair, you'll allow,
Then the master used to whack me; Oh, I wish they'd do it now.

It's very lonesome for a boy, to lead a single life
So, tonight, I've just made up my mind, to try and get a wife.
My fortune is six thumping pigs, likewise the big old sow,
There'll be lots of love and bacon, for the girl who'll have me now.

*Repeat last line of preceding verse.

Barney Leave the Girls Alone

As much as I like dance music for its own sake, I enjoy including a song in a medley of tunes occasionally, provided tempo and pitch can be accommodated. **Barney** would go well with a set of polkas in a band arrangement. The tune used here is **The Rakes of Mallow.**

Source: Text from a broadside by Wood of New Meeting Street, Birmingham; tune heard at innumerable sessions.

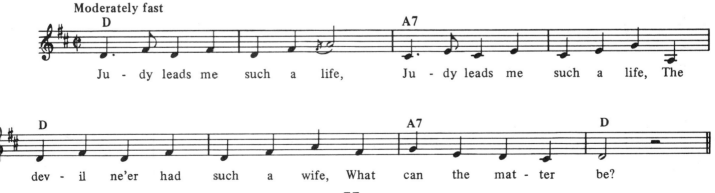

Ju - dy leads me   such   a   life,   Ju - dy leads me   such   a   life, The

dev - il ne'er   had   such   a   wife, What   can   the   mat - ter   be?

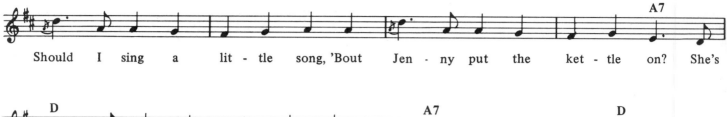

Should I sing a lit - tle song, 'Bout Jen - ny put the ket - tle on? She's

bark - ing at me day long. What can the mat - ter be?

Judy leads me such a life,
Judy leads me such a life,
The devil ne'er had such a wife,
What can the matter be?

Should I sing a little song,
'Bout Jenny put the kettle on?
She's barking at me all day long,
What can the matter be?

Put the muffins down to roast,
Put the muffins down to roast;
Blow the fire and make the toast,
And then we'll go to tea.

Barney leave the girls alone,
Barney leave the girls alone,
Barney leave the girls alone,
And let them quiet be.

Barney rock the cradle, oh!
Why don't you rock the cradle, oh!
Or else you'll get the ladle, oh!
When Judy comes to tea.

Barney leave the girls alone . . .

Barney you're a wicked boy,
Barney you're a wicked boy,
And what is more you'll kiss and toy
With all the girls you see.

Barney leave the girls alone . . .

Judy she loves whiskey, oh!
Judy she loves whiskey, oh!
And to my uncle's shop will go
Before she takes her tea.

Barney leave the girls alone . . .

Barney—what will Barney do!
Barney, what will Barney do!
Barney will get fuzzy too,
And drink and sing, God bless the King!
In a cup of whiskey tea.

Barney leave the girls alone . . .

Soldiers

Morrissey and the Russian Sailor

Bare-knuckle boxer Johnny Morrissey won the American championship on a foul from George Thompson in 1852. He was twenty-one. A native of Templemore, Co. Tipperary, he was raised in New York and went on the Gold Rush to California as a youth.

Morrissey beat the "Yankee Clipper," James Sullivan, on October 12, 1853 when Sullivan succumbed to taunts from Morrissey's supporters and launched out into the crowd after them — that was in the thirty-seventh round!

As far as is known, no fight took place between Morrissey and the Russian Sailor, at least not in Tierra-Del-Fuego.

Source: Text is a casual collation; tune learned from the singing of John Dillon, who learned it from Joe Heaney.

Recordings: Johnny McDonagh, *Irish Folk Songs*, Columbia AKL 4941. Joe Heaney, *Joe Heaney*, Philo 2004.

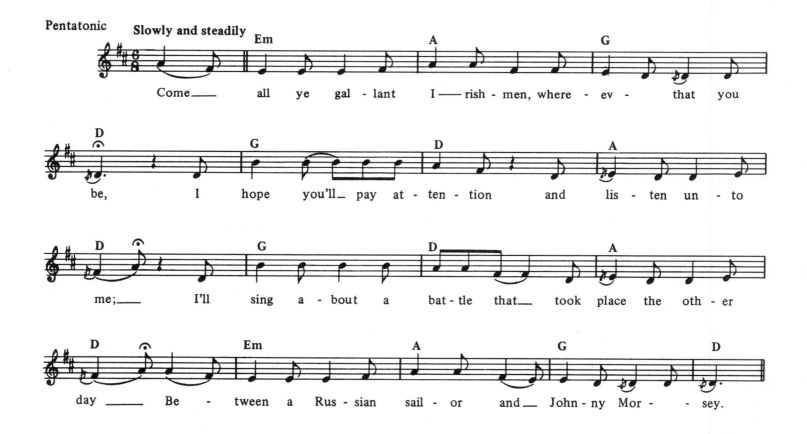

Come all ye gallant Irishmen, wherever that you be,
I hope you'll pay attention and listen unto me;
I'll sing about a battle that took place the other day
Between a Russian sailor and Johnny Morrissey.

'Twas in Terra-del-Fuego, in South America,
This Russian challenged Morrissey, these words to him did say,
"I hear you are a fighting man, and wear a belt I see,
Indeed, I wish you would consent to have a round with me."

Out spoke gallant Morrissey, with heart both brave and true,
"I am a valiant Irishman that never was subdued,
For I can whale the Yankee, the Saxon bull or bear;
In honour of old Paddy's land, I still the laurel wear."

Those words enraged the Russian boy upon the Yankee land,
To think, that he should be put down by any Irishman,
Says he, "You are too light a frame, and that without mistake,
I'll have you to resign the belt or else your life I'll take."

To fight upon the tenth of March those heroes did agree
And thousands came from every part the battle for to see.
The English and the Russians their hearts were filled with glee.
They swore this Russian sailor boy would kill brave Morrissey.

Those heroes stepped into the ring, most gallant to be seen,
And Morrissey put on the belt, bound round with shamrock green.
Full sixty thousand dollars then, as you may plainly see,
Was to be the champion's prize for him who'd gain the victory.

They shook hands and walked round the ring, commencing then to
  fight.
It filled each Irish heart with pride for to behold the sight.
The Russian, he floored Morrissey up to the eleventh round.
With Yankee, Russian and Saxon cheers the valley did resound.

A minute-and-a-half he lay before that he could rise;
The word went all about the field, "He's dead," were all their cries,
But Morrissey worked manfully and, rising from the ground,
From that unto the twentieth round the Russian he put down.

The Irish offered four to one that day upon the grass,
No sooner said than taken up and down they brought the cash.
They parried away without delay to the thirty-second round,
When Morrissey received a blow that brought him to the ground.

Up to the thirty-seventh round 'twas fall and fall about,
Which made the foreign tyrants then to keep a sharp look-out.
The Russian called his second for to have a glass of wine.
And our Irish hero smiled and said: "This battle will be mine."

The thirty-eighth decided all, the Russian felt the smart,
For Morrissey with a dreadful blow struck the sailor on the heart;
The doctor he was called for to open up a vein,
But he said it was quite useless, he'd never fight again.

Our hero conquered Thompson and the Yankee Clipper too,
The Benicia Boy and Sheppard he nobly did subdue;
So let us fill a flowing glass, and here is health galore
To noble Johnny Morrissey who came from Templemore.

Morrissey and the Buffalo Boy

Morrissey's opponent in this bout was John C. Heenan,
another star of both ring and ballad (e.g., **Heenan and
Sayers, Heenan and the Black**). Heenan was born in Troy,
New York, but was called the "Benicia Boy," after Benicia,
California, where he'd gone as a teenager. The two met at
Long Point, a peninsula on the Ontario side of Lake Erie,
in 1858. Heenan's hand was broken in the first round, but
he carried on until the eleventh.

Source: Text from a broadside printed by Henry Disley.

You gallant sons of Granuale, I pray attend awhile,
Unto these lines which I have penned, will cause you for to smile.
Concerning the great battle fought upon Columbia's shore,
By the Buffalo Boy and Morrissey, that came from Templemore.

He fought and conquered Thompson, in the year fifty-two,
The Yankee Clipper in fifty-three he nobly did subdue;
This conquest grieved the Yankees sore, and long disturbed the land
To think their champion was put down all by an Irishman.

The Buffalo Boy, a challenge sent our hero out of hand,
And said no man from Paddy's land before him e'er could stand.
Our hero smiled, and then replied, I'll meet you on the plain.
And let you know for Paddy's land, the laurel I'll maintain.

Thirty-five thousand dollars, the prize it was to be,
Long Island being appointed, in North America,
Both small and great from every state, in multitudes they ran,
The Yankees sure their champion would kill the Irishman.

These champions striped with courage bold, when they entered the
  ring,
For it was their full intention each other's blood to bring;
The American drew the first blood, and knocked our hero down,
The second round these heroes fought, they both came to the ground.

The third and fourth the American being floored it does appear,
The fifth, brave Morrissey came down—the Yankee they did cheer,
They boldly offered three to one, bright dollars on the ground,
The Irish independently, took up the bets all round.

Up to the tenth, by Morrissey, the Yankee down he went,
The know-nothings they shook their heads, being sadly discontent,
And called upon the Buffalo Boy, "exert your skills," they cried,
"Our country's credit and our cash, on you we have relied."

Then up spoke brave Morrissey, these words both brave and high.
"For Paddy's land I mean to stand, to conquer or to die;
Now abolish all the brags you've made, I mean to let you know;
The Irish cock is still true game wherever he does go."

With courage bold undaunted our hero stood his field,
The eleventh round decided all—the Yankee forced to yield;
Our Irish boys to crown their joys, they made the taverns roar,
They drank to gallant Morrissey, likewise the Shamrock shore.

Such a dreadful fight as this, 'tis said, has never been known,
The Americans in the future may let Granuale's sons alone;
The Buffalo Boy they bore away, being scarce fit to stand,
Brave Morrissey he cleared the ropes and cheered for Paddy's land.

Let the Americans no longer boast, nor Paddy's sons degrade,
For now they must surrender to our gallant Irish blade;
With honour now he wears the belt, the Yankees may deplore
The day they challenged Morrissey, that came from Templemore.

Morrissey Again in the Field

From a broadside probably printed in Belfast. The very journalistic heading reads: "A new song called JOHN MORRISSY [sic] AGAIN IN THE FIELD? Who is he to fight on the 1st of November, 1864."

After Morrissey whipped Heenan, he declined a rematch and retired to Saratoga Springs, a spa just below the Adirondack Mountains in New York. This ballad is a "one last go" from the scribes who'd serialized his exploits so well. John Morrissey was a classic Irish-American success story: A scrapper in his youth, a horse race promoter in middle age, a State Senator and Member of Congress later on. He died in 1878. I have to think he's probably doing as well in the afterlife.

Source: A broadside with no imprint.

Draw near you sons of Granuale, attend unto my song,
I'll sing for you a verse or two—I'll not detain you long;
'Tis of a valliant Irishman, his praises I will sing—
For ten thousand pounds on the first of June he has now challenged
 King.

" 'Tis true I am an Irishman from the town of Templemore,
And many a better man than King I left in all his gore,
'Tis not for money I'm going to fight, it's plainly to be seen,
But for old Ireland's credit and the dear old shamrock green.

"John Morrissey it is my name—my age is forty-three,
Some people say I am too old to gain the victory.
But on the first of November when I stand in the ring,
I'm sure I will play Patrick's Day upon the ribs of King.

"When I was joined in wedlock bans the truth I will relate,
A promise to my wedded wife I was obliged to make,
That fighting for the future I certainly would shun—
But I must have satisfaction for what John Heenan done.

"The first man that I ever fought it was the Buffalo Boy.
The Yankees all were sure that day my life he would destroy;
But John gained the victory and that without much noise,
I played for him that favorite tune the brave Tipperary Boys.

"Then Sam the Black he was the next I own I did subdue,
The Russian Sailor and Shepherd I have killed 'tis true.
I never feared an Englishman or Yankee in the ring,
But I tell you true, I will subdue the English bully, King.

"John Heenan to his country, oh, is now a disgrace—
And to America what's more he dare not show his face—
He has chosed the Orange for evermore as you may understand,
For a thousand pounds in ready gold he sold his native land.

" 'Tis not for the sake of money nor any other wealth,
Nor neither is it for the sake of the English Belt,
But for the honour of old Ireland as you may plainly see,
I'll fight or die all in the ring or gain the victory."

Now to conclude those verses, I have no more to say,
That courage may not fail him and may be gain the day,
Come fill the glasses to the top until they do flow o'er,
And feast to gallant Morrissey, the pride of Erin's shore.

General Wolfe

The Battle of Quebec in 1759 was the decisive engagement of the French and Indian War. It effectively removed France from the region, though to this day she controls St. Pierre and Miquelon, two small islands off the south coast of New-foundland.

James Wolfe, the battle's British commander, was mortally wounded in the fighting and, because of the personal trag-edy inherent in his victory, received a reputation as a "good bloke," though he probably wasn't.

Source: Text from a Disley broadside; tune learned from the singing of Ewan MacColl.

Recording: Bob Copper, *Sweet Rose in June,* Topic 12TS328.

Bold General Wolfe to his men did say,
"Come, come, my lads and follow me
To yonder mountains that are so high,
All for the honour, all for the honour of your King and country."

The French are on the mountains high,
While we poor lads in the valley lie;
I see them falling like moths in the sun,
Through smoke and fire,—through smoke and fire all from our
 British guns.

The first volley they gave to us,
Wounded our general in his left breast,
Yonder he sits for he cannot stand,
"Fight on so boldly, fight on so boldly, for whilst I've life I'll
 have command.

"Here is my treasure lies all in gold,
Take it and part it for my blood runs cold,
Take it and part it," General Wolfe did say,
"You lads of honour, you lads of honour, who made such gallant
 play.

"When to Old England you do return,
Pray tell my parents I'm dead and gone;
Pray tell my tender old mother dear,
Not to weep for me-o, not to weep for me-o, it is a death I wish
 to share.

"It's sixteen years since I first begun,
To fight for the honour of George our King;
Let our commanders do as I've done before;
Be a soldier's friend-o, be a soldier's friend-o, and boys they'll
 fight for evermore."

The Banks of the Nile

Although this Napoleonic song has an Irish tune, it's much more popular in England and Scotland. Many versions carry verses warning about lions and tigers, false notions of the ballad poet.

Source: Text from a broadside by Fortey of Bloomsbury, London; the tune is a slight adaptation of a very common one (see **The Flower of Sweet Strabane**, p. 176).

Recording: Ewan MacColl, *Classic Scots Ballads*, Tradition TLP 1015.

Pentatonic

Hark! The drums are beating low. I can no longer stay.
I hear the bugle sounding, that call I must obey.
We are sent out to Portsmouth and for many a long mile
To join the British Army on the banks of the Nile.

"Oh, Willie, dearest Willie don't leave me here to mourn.
You'll make me curse and rue the day that ever I was born,
For the parting of you, Willie, is the parting of my life,
So stay at home, dear Willie, and I will be your wife."

"Oh, Nancy, dearest Nancy, that's a thing that can't be so,
For our colonel has gave orders that no woman there can go.
We must forsake our own sweethearts, likewise our native soil,
To fight the blacks and heathens on the banks of the Nile."

"Then I'll cut off my yellow locks and go along with you.
I'll dress myself in velveteen and I'll go to Egypt too.
I will fight and bear your banner as fortune on us smiles
And we'll comfort one another on the banks of the Nile."

"Your waist it is too slender and your fingers are too small.
I fear you would not answer me when on you I would call.
Your delicate constitution would not bear that awful clime,
The hot and sandy deserts on the banks of the Nile."

My curse attend this cruel war and the hour that it began,
For it has robbed old Ireland of many a gallant man.
It took from my my own sweetheart and the protectors of our Isle.
With their blood streams the grass does weep on the banks of the Nile.

84

Jackie Munroe

A ballad combining two great broadside themes: A lover dispatched due to parental disapproval (**The Charming Beauty Bright, Young Edwin in the Lowlands Low**), and the warrior maiden (**The Lady Leroy, The Female Warrior**).

There's a twenty-nine-stanza Scots version in Greig's *Folk Songs of the North-East*.

Source: Learned from the singing of Bert Lloyd.

Recording: A. L. Lloyd, *Street Songs of England*, Washington VM 737.

Dorian of A

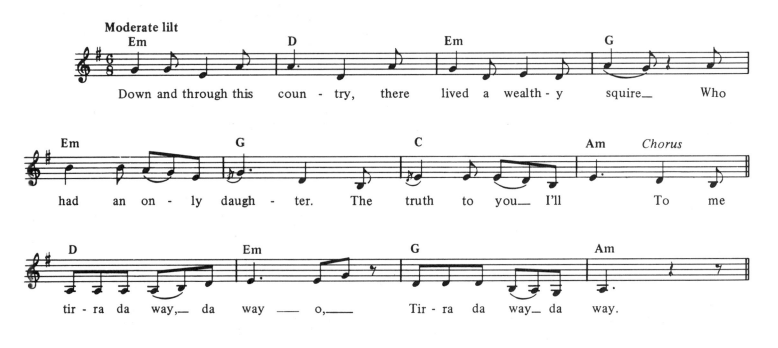

Down and through this country, there lived a wealthy squire
Who had an only daughter. The truth to you I'll tell.

To me tirra da way, da way-o,
Tirra da way da way.

She had sweethearts a-plenty, to marriage were inclined,
Though none but John the soldier could gain this lady's mind.

To me tirra . . .

When her father came to know, so angry then he swore.
"I'll give the gang ten guineas to press young John to the war-o."

But she robbed her father cleverly, got money at her command,
And went to enlist in the Army all dressed up like a man.

"Your waist is long and slender, your fingers fine and small
Your cheeks too red and rosy for to face the cannonball."

"It's true my waist is slender. My fingers are too small.
But it wouldn't change my countenance to see ten thousand fall."

"Before you join our regiment, your name I'd like to know?"
She smiled all over her face, she did, "They call me Jackie Munroe."

Well, she sailed all over the ocean, all over the deep, blue sea,
Till she was safely landed in the Wars of Germany.

Well, all across the battlefield, she fought it up and down,
Till among the dead and wounded, her darling boy she found.

"They have promoted me," she cries. "They have promoted me
Unto a Colonel's commission, so married we can be!"

Up then spoke the General, "Such things there never can be.
It's against the laws of our country, two men to married be."

And up then spoke the Chaplin, "Such things I can't allow."
She drew her broadsword from her side, "I'll make this do for you!"

Well, then these two were married, as you may plainly know,
And Johnny the wounded soldier got his little Jackie Munroe.

85

The Bonnie Lass O'Fyvie-O

A favorite of the 1960s folk boom. The Clancys, Ewan MacColl, Joan Baez, and Bob Dylan all recorded a version.

Source: Text adapted from Greig's *Folk Songs of the North-East*; tune is common.

Recording: Jean Redpath, *Skipping Barefoot Through the Heather*, Prestige International 13041.

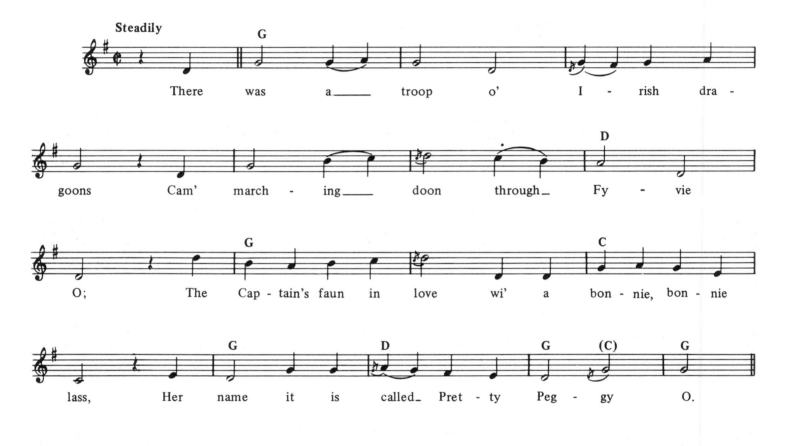

There was a troop o' Irish dragoons
Cam' marching doon through Fyvie O;
The Captain's faun in love wi' a bonnie, bonnie lass,
Her name it is called Pretty Peggy O.

"O come doon the stairs, pretty Peggy," my dear,
"O come doon the stairs, pretty Peggy O,
O come doon the stairs, comb aside your yellow hair,
Tak' the last farewell o' your daddie O."

"It's I'll gie ye ribbons, love, I'll gie ye rings,
And I'll gie ye necklaces o' lammer O.
And I'll gie ye silken gowns, flounced to your knees,
If ye would come doon to my chamber O."

"A soldier's wife I shall never be,
A soldier never shall enjoy me O,
For I never do intend to go to a foreign land,
So I never shall marry a soldier O."

"A soldier's wife ye shall never be,
For I'll make you the captain's lady O,
I'll make the regiment stand with their hats into their hands
When they come into the presence o' Peggy O.

"It's braw being a captain's lady, my dear,
It's braw being a captain's lady O,
To lie into your bed till your breakfast is made,
And dress till dinner be ready O."

The Colonel cries, "Mount, mount, Boys, mount,"
Cries, "Mount, boys, mount and get ready O,"
"O tarry for a while, for another day or twa,
Till we see if this bonnie lass will marry O."

"There is mony a bonnie lass in the toon of Auchterless
And mony a bonnie lass in the Garioch O,
There's mony a bonnie Jean into bonnie Aiberdeen,
But the flooer o' them a' is in Fyvie O."

Not lang on their way to Old Meldrum toon
Their captain grew sick and weary O,
Not lang on their way to bonnie Aiberdeen
They got their captain to bury O.

It was not the girl's beauty that I did admire,
But she was my only fancy O;
His name was Captain Ned, he died for a maid,
He died for the bonnie lass o' Fyvie O.

The Black Horse

Anti-recruiting songs were common in Ireland (three others follow), and this one and related versions called **Johnny Golicher** and **Pat Reilly** are among the most frequently seen.

There is a traditional tune in O Lochlainn's *Irish Street Ballads.*

Source: Text from a broadside probably in Ulster; the tune is mine.

Recording: Vin Garbutt, *The Young Tin Whistle Pest,* Leader LER 2081.

Pentatonic

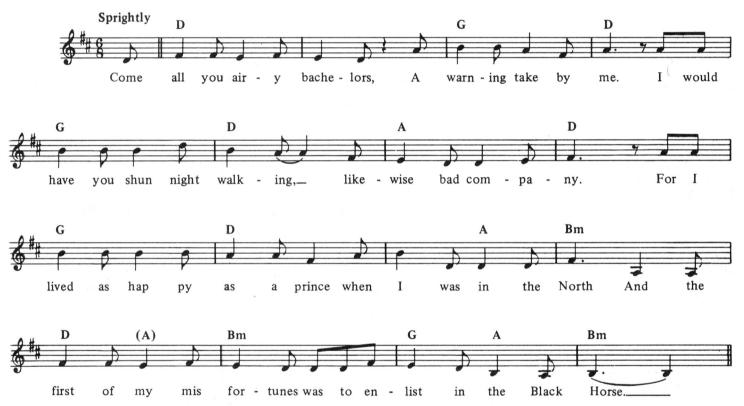

Come all you airy bachelors, a warning take by me.
I would have you shun night walking, likewise bad company.
For I lived as happy as a prince when I was in the North
And the first of my misfortunes was to enlist in the Black Horse.

It was on a certain Tuesday, to Galway I did go,
Meeting a small officer, which proved my overthrow.
I met with Sergeant Atkinson in the market as I went down.
And he says, "Young man, would you enlist and be a light dragoon?"

"Oh, no, kind sir, a soldier's life with me would not agree
Nor will I bind myself down from my liberty.
I live as happy as a prince, my mind does tell me so,
So fare you well; I'm just going down my shuttles for the throw."

"Are you in a hurry or are you going away,
Or won't you stand and listen to the words I'm going to say.
Or do you live far from this place? The town I wish to know.
And your name, kind sir, then, if you please before that you do go."

"Then I am in a hurry, my dwelling it is far.
My place of habitation lies six miles behind Armagh.
Charles Egan is my name, through Longford town I came.
And I never intend to do a crime that I should deny my name."

He says, "Now cousin Charles, perhaps you might do worse
Then to leave your native country and enlist in the Black Horse."
With all his kind persuasivness, with him I did agree,
And I left my native country, boys, to fight for liberty.

So fare you well, dear father, likewise my sisters three,
So fare you well, dear mother, your face I ne'er will see.
When I'm going down through Armagh town, you will all run
  through my mind,
So, farewell unto dear Ireland and the girl I left behind.

Arthur McBride

The classic anti-recruiting song, as two of the local lads treat the grand-talking sergeant and the rest of his train to a lesson in modesty. Recruiters were all swank, of course; they had to be. Those without hope would join all right, but what about anyone else? **Arthur McBride** represents the triumph of reality over jingoism.

Source: Text is a slight adaptation from Greig's *Folk Songs of the North-East*; tune is **The Bold Tennant Farmer**.

Recordings: Gordon McCulloch, *Freedom, Come All Ye*, Topic 12T143. Paul Brady, *Paul Brady – Andy Irvine*, Mulligan LUN 008.

Combined Major and Mixolydian of G

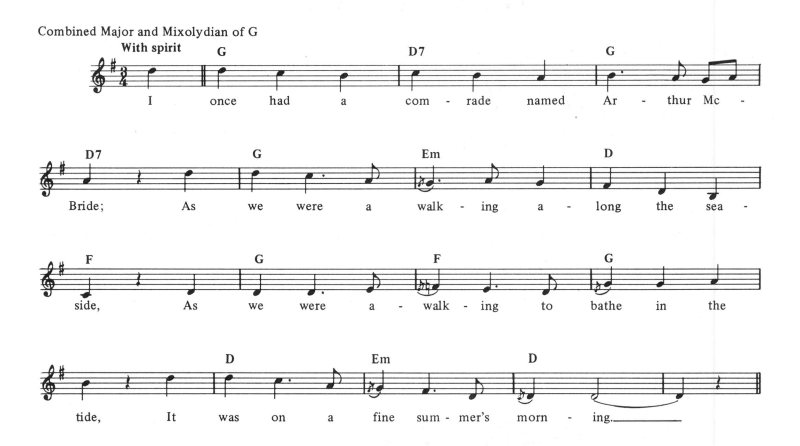

I once had a comrade named Arthur McBride;
As we were a-walking along the seaside,
As we were a-walking to bathe in the tide,
It was on a fine summer's morning.

As we were a-walking along the sea sand
we met Sergeant Napier and Corporal O'Hand,
And a little wee drummer called Patrick McDan,
They were going to the fair in the morning.

"O Arthur, my lad, if ye would but enlist,
Five guineas o' gold I will clap in your fist,
Besides five shillings to kick up the dust,
And drink the King's health in the morning."

"Na faith," says Arthur, "I ken it mysel',
I winna gae wi' ye to rin at your tail,
I winna gae wi' ye to rin at your tail,
And be at your command in the mornin'."

"Oh, if you go with us, I'm sure you'll go clean,
We're not like poor fellows goes dirty and mean,
We're not like poor fellows goes dirty and mean,
Get nothing but gruel in the morning."

"Ye needna be chattin' aboot your fine pay,
As you go a-marchin' and trampin' away,
For a' that ye hae is a shillin' a day,
To get you some food in the mornin'.

"Ye needna be chattin' aboot your fine clothes,
Ye've only the len' o' them as I do suppose,
Ye daurna sell them in spite o' your nose,
Or you will get flogged in the mornin'.

"I'm blessed," said the sergeant, "if I'll take more of that
From you or from any low cow feeding brat,
And if you tip me any more of your chat,
I will run you through in the morning."

88

But before they had time to draw out their blades,
Our whacking shillelahs came over their heads,
We soon let them see that we were the blades
That could temper their pows in the morning.

As for the wee drummer we labored his pow,
And made a fit ba' o' his row-didi-dow,
And kicket it to the ocean to rack and to row,
And take a bit bathe in the morning.

And as for the weapons that hung by their side,
We took them and pitched them far into the tide;
"May the deil gae wi' them," said Arthur McBride,
"If we ever see them returnin'."

The Kerry Recruit

Disley, the broadside printer of High Street, St. Giles, London, published a confused text which has our narrator simultaneously at the battle of Ballin-a-inch [*sic*] and away from Ireland. Ballynahinch, Co. Down, was the site of the defeat of General Henry Munro, a Protestant Irish leader of the 1798 uprising. **The Kerry Recruit** dates from the Crimean War (1853-1856). Disley called his ballad **The Irish Recruit**, but printed another, different one under this title; the song is a conversation between a recruiting sergeant and his prey:

"You'd better take a sword in hand, and fight for Queen Victoria,
And if you make a gallant stand, you'll surely be promoted;
If a wound you get you'll be pensioned off, with honour they'll discharge
And live at home for evermore from being a spalpeen fornach you [sic]."

He says, "Young man, come, have a drink, the day being very warm,

We'll drink enough to quench our thirst, with whiskey, beer and cordial";
When he slipped a shilling in my hand, saying, "Pay for what you've called for."

Tho' drunk I was, I knew right well the games of the old sergeant,
I threw him back his shilling again, saying "I can pay my own part";
He said, "Young man, be of good cheer, the trumpet sounds to call you,
Victoria's cash you took in hand, and you are bound for head quarters."

There is a great tradition of "playing- the-donkey" in Irish Satire. **The Kerry Recruit** is one of the best of such pieces.

Source: Text is a collation of the Disley broadside and a traditional one sung by Seamus Ennis; tune learned from the singing of the Dubliners, who had it from Ennis.
Recording: Seamus Ennis, *The Bonnie Bunch of Roses*, Tradition TLP 1013.

Pentatonic

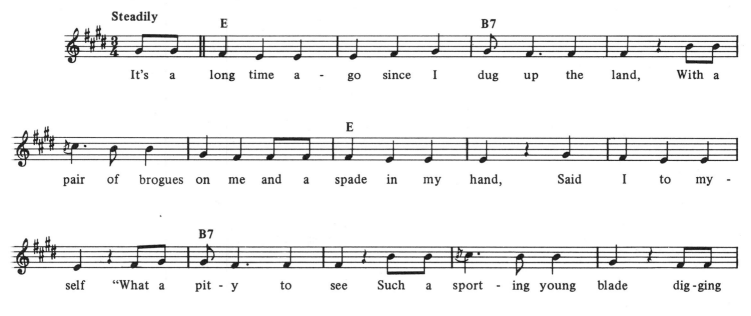

It's a long time a-go since I dug up the land, With a pair of brogues on me and a spade in my hand, Said I to my-self "What a pit-y to see Such a sport-ing young blade dig-ging

89

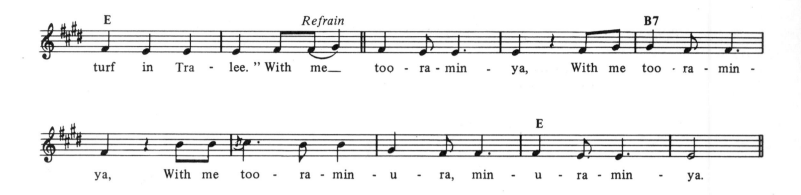

turf in Tra - lee." With me — too - ra - min - ya, With me too - ra - min -
ya, With me too - ra - min - u - ra, min - u - ra - min - ya.

It's a long time ago since I dug up the land,
With a pair of brogues on me and a spade in my hand,
Said I to myself, "What a pity to see
Such a sporting young blade digging turf in Tralee."

With me toora-min-ya,
With me toora-min-ya,
With me toora-min-u-ra, min-u-ra-min-ya.

I packed up my brogues, I shook hands with my spade,
And went off to the fair like a roving young blade,
When up came a sergeant and asked me to 'list,
"Och! sergeant," says I, "Can you tip me your fist?"

With me . . .

"There's five golden guineas, I have got no more,
When we go to headquarters you'll have half a score,"
"Oh! quarters, oh! quarters, oh! Sergeant," says I,
"Do you think I'll be quartered? No, sergeant, good-bye!"

The first thing they gave me it was a red coat,
With two stripes of leather they set me afloat;
They reached me a thing. I asked, "What was that?"
"It is a cockade that belongs to your hat."

The next thing they gave me 'twas a great gun,
And on the bold trigger I placed my left thumb;
Oh, my gun she spat fire, it made a great smoke,
She hit my own shoulder, the devil's own stroke.

The next place they sent me was down by the sea,
On board of a warship bound for the Crimea.
Three sticks in the middle all rowled round with sheets,
Faith, she walked through the water without any feet.

When at Balaklava we landed quite sound,
Both cold, wet and hungry we lay on the ground.
Next morning for action the bugle did call,
And we got a hot breakfast of powder and ball.

It's up came the sergeant a man of high rank,
To order my arms all into the rank;
"Sergeant," says I, "can't you let me alone,
Don't you see I've got arms and two legs of my own."

Then up came the captain a man of great fame,
To ask me my country and likewise my name;
I up wid my story, and told him again,
That my father and mother were two Irishmen.

Sure, it's often I thought of my name and my home
And the days that I spent cutting turf, ochahone.
When the bullets did fly, I let them to pass,
I dived down in a ditch to shelter my arse.

We fought at the Alma, likewise Inkerman,
But the Russians they whaled us at the Redan.
In scaling the walls there myself lost my eye,
And a big Russian bullet ran off with my thigh.

It was there I lay bleeding, stretched on the cold ground,
Heads, legs and arms were scattered all around.
Says I, "If my mam or my cleaveens were nigh,
They'd bury me decent and raise a loud cry."

They brought me the doctor, who soon staunched my blood
And he gave me an elegant leg made of wood,
They gave me a medal and tenpence a day,
Contented with Sheila, I'll live on half pay.

McCaffery

Easily one of the most widely distributed folk songs in Ireland and Britain, **McCaffery** comes straight from very real life.

Patrick McCaffery was born in Co. Kildare. An unwanted child, he was taken in by a family friend and brought to the squalid milltown streets of Lancashire. McCaffery eventually drifted into the army, where his troubled life continued. He had no interest in discipline, made no friends, and—worst of all—was increasingly singled out by his depot adjutant, Captain John Hanham, as a problem soldier.

The name-taking incident actually did take place; the children had previously broken windows in the officers' mess. McCaffery received a night's lockup and, shortly after his release, shot captain and colonel alike as they crossed the square at Fulwood Barracks, Preston. McCaffery's case received sympathetic treatment in the press, but to no avail; he was hanged in Liverpool on January 11th, 1862. Twenty-five thousand people are said to have watched in the pouring rain.

The version printed here comes from the singing of my father. He learned it in India about 1920.

Source: William Milner.

Recordings: Ewan MacColl, *British Army Songs*, Washington WLP 711. The Dubliners, *A Drop of the Hard Stuff*, Epic BN26337

William Milner

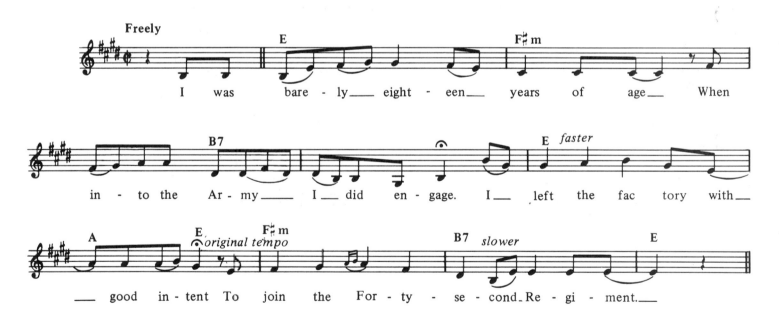

I was barely eighteen years of age
When into the Army I did engage.
I left the factory with good intent
To join the Forty-second Regiment.

To Preston barracks I had to go,
Some period to serve at that depot,
But out of trouble I couldn't be;
For Captain Hammon took a dislike to me.

While serving sentry out one day,
Some soldiers' children came out to play.
From out his quarters my Captain came
And ordered me to take their parents' names.

I went, but solemnly, against my will,
My Captain's orders to fulfill.
I took one name instead of three
And with neglect of duty they then charged me.

Next morn to the orderly room I had to go,
To tell my poor tale of woe.
My Captain says, "You're out of your mind!
Ten days to barracks you are now confined."

For seven nights and seven days,
My sentence turned upon my brain.
To shoot my Captain dead on sight
Was all that I resolved I'd do each night.

With loaded rifle I did prepare
To shoot my Captain on the barracks square.
It was my Captain I meant to kill,
But I shot my Colonel full against my will.

I did the deed, I shed the blood.
At Liverpool Assizes my trial was stood.
The judge said he, "McCaffery,
Prepare yourself for the gallows tree."

I have no father to take my part.
I have no mother to break her heart.
I have one friend and a girl is she,
Would give her life for McCaffery.

All you Irish boys take good warning by me.
Have nothing to do with the British Army,
For only lies and tyranny
Have made a murderer out of McCaffery.

Jerry Burns, an uncle from Castleblayney, Co. Monaghan,
served his time in the Gordon Highlanders. He got these
two extra verses from a Scots corporal in Germany in 1947.

In an English prison a young man died.
In an English churchyard his young body lies.
And every young soldier who passes that way
Says, "The Lord have mercy on John McCafferty."

Now all you young officers take a tip from me
And treat your men with some civility.
Although I'm gone, there's sure to be
Another man like John McCafferty.

Broadside

Sailors

The Royal Oak

I learned this song from Charles O'Hegarty, son of a Lon-gon-Irish stevedore, who was born and raised on the Isle of Dogs. Charlie is the wittiest and most genuinely endearing man I've ever met.

This version is very close to the one printed in *The Penguin Book of English Folk Songs*, collected by Clive Carey from Moses Mansfield at Haslemere, Surrey, in 1912.

Source: Charles O'Hegarty.

Recording: Charles O'Hegarty, *Songs of the Tall Ships*, Adelphi AD 1025.

As we were sailing all on the salt sea,
We hadn't been gone months but two or three
When we saw ten sail, ten sail of Turks;
All men-of-war, full as big as we.

"Haul down your colours, you English dogs.
Haul down your colours, do not refuse.
Haul down your colours, you English dogs,
Or your precious lives you will loose."

Our Captain being a valiant man
And a well-bespoken man was he—
"Let it never be said that we died like dogs,
So we shall fight most manfully.

"Go up aloft you cabin boys
And mount the mainmast at topsail high,
For to spread the news to King George's fleet
That we'll run the risk or else we'll die."

Now the fight began about six in the morn
And unto the setting of the sun.
And at the rise of the next dawn,
Out of ten ships, we couldn't see but one.

Now three we sank and three we burned
And three we caused to run away
And one we towed to Portsmouth harbour,
For to let them know we'd won the day.

If anyone, then, should enquire
As to our gallant Captain's name.
Captain Wellfounder was our commander
And the *Royal Oak* was our ship by name.

94

On Board a Ninety-Eight

A ship of the line carrying ninety-eight guns.

One often hears of the wayward youth who get coerced into the forces to be straightened out. What sheer delight to see that tale followed through to such an atmospheric conclusion. Who wrote this one? I'd love to know.

Source: Text from a broadside by Paul of Spitalfields, London; tune from Peter Bellamy.

Recording: Peter Bellamy, *Peter Bellamy*, Green Linnet SIF 1001. Roy Harris, *The Valiant Sailor*, Topic 12TS232.

When I was young and scarce eight-een, I drove a roaring trade, And ma-ny a sly trick I have played with ma-ny a pret-ty maid, My par-ents foond that would not do, I soon should spend their store, So they re-solved that I should go, on board a man-of-war.

Verse 2, m6

go to sea and

m7

ma-ny a pret-ty

95

When I was young and scarce eighteen, I drove a roaring trade,
And many a sly trick I have played with many a pretty maid,
My parents found that would not do, I soon should spend their store,
So they resolved that I should go, on board a man-of-war.

A bold press gang surrounded me, their warrant they did show,
And swore that I should go to sea and face the daring foe.
So off they lugged me to the boat; O, how I cursed my fate,
'Twas then I found that I must float on board a ninety-eight.

When I put my foot on board, how I began to stare,
Our Admiral, he gave the word; there is no time to spare.
They weighed their anchor, shook our sail, and off they bore me straight
To watch the foe in storm and gale on board a ninety-eight.

Before we reached America, they gave me many a drill,
They soon learnt me a nimble way to handle an iron pill,
In course of time a fight begun, when bold Jack Tars laid straight.
What I would give if I could run from on board the ninety-eight.

But as time flew I bolder grew and hardened was to war,
I'd run aloft with my ship's crew and valued not a scar,
So well I did my duty do, till I got Boatswain's mate
And damn me soon, got Boatswain too on board a ninety-eight.

So years rolled by at Trafalgar, brave Nelson fought and fell,
As they capsized that hardy tar I caught a rap as well,
To Greenwich College I came back because I saved my pate,
They only knocked one wing off Jack, on board a ninety-eight.

So now my cocoa I can take, my pouch with 'bacco stored,
With my blue cloths and three cocked hat, I am happy as a Lord,
I've done my duty, served my King, and now I bless my fate,
But damn me, I'm too old to sing; I'm nearly ninety-eight.

The Flying Cloud

One of the best of all the broadside ballads, this song is often sung at a fast clip, but never better than the slow, sweeping way Ewan MacColl recorded it over twenty years ago. This version is mine, after Ewan's, with a slightly more filled-out text.

In *Songs of the American Sailormen*, Joanna Colcord writes, "This song probably dates from somewhere between the years 1819 and 1825, when the West Indies were finally cleared of pirates by the joint efforts of the United States and several European naval powers." She also mentions

finding "reference to a raid on the Chesapeake region by a privateer squadron under Admiral Collier during the War of 1812 .... One of the British vessels was named the *Dunmore*," giving rise to the possibility the ballad story is factual.

Source: Text and tune from the singing of Ewan MacColl, with additional verses from other sources.

Recording: Ewan MacColl, *Haul on the Bowlin'*, Stinson SLP 80.

My name is Arthur Holleran, as you may understand. I was born ten miles from Dublin town, down by the salt sea-strand. When I was young and comely sure, then fortune on me shone. My parents loved me tenderly. I was their only son.

My name is Arthur Holleran as you may understand.
I was born ten miles from Dublin town, down by the salt sea strand.
When I was young and comely sure, then fortune on me shone.
My parents loved me tenderly. I was their only son.

My father he rose up one day and with him I did go.
He bound me as a butcher's boy to Pearson's of Wicklow.
I wore the bloody apron there for three long years or more.
Till I shipped on board of the *Ocean Queen*, belonging to Tramore.

It was on Bermuda's sunny isle I met with Captain Moore.
He was the skipper of the *Flying Cloud*, the pride of Baltimore.
I undertook with him on a slaving voyage to go
To the burning shores of Africa, where that sugar cane do grow.

It all went well until the day we come to Africa's shore.
Five hundred of them poor blacks, my boys, from their native lands
we tore.
We laid 'em down with links of chain as we made 'em walk below.
Juts eighteen inches space was all that each man had to show.

Well, the plague, it came and fever too and it killed 'em off like flies.
We dragged their bodies on the deck and we hove 'em in the sea.
For sure the dead were lucky for they'd have to weep no more
Nor drag the chain nor feel the lash in Cuba for evermore.

It was after stormy weather that we arrived off Cuba's shore.
We sold them to the planters there to be slaves for evermore,
For the rice and coffee seed to sow beneath the broiling sun,
And there to spend a wretched time until their lives were done.

It's now our money is all gone and we must go to sea once more.
Still, each man stayed to listen to the words of Captain Moore,
"There's gold and silver to be had if with me you remain.
We'll hoist that pirate flag aloft and sweep the Spanish Main!"

We all agreed but three young men who then asked us to land.
Two of them was Boston boys and one from Newfoundland.
I wish to God I'd joined those men and gone with them ashore,
Than to lead a wild and reckless life serving under Captain Moore.

We plundered many a gallant ship down on the Spanish Main,
Killed many a man and left his wife and children to remain.
To none we showed no kindness, but gave them a watery grave,
For the saying of our Captain was that dead men tell no tales.

We ran and fought with many a ship, both frigate and liner too,
Till, at last, a British man-o-war, the *Dunmore*, hove in view.
She fired a shot across our bow, as we sailed before the wind,
Then a chain shot cut our main mast off and we fell far behind.

They beat our crew to quarters as she drew up alongside
And soon across our quarter deck there flowed a crimson tide.
We fought until they killed our Captain and eighteen of our men,
Till a bombshell set our ship on fire and we had to surrender then.

It's now to Newgate we are sent bound down in iron chains,
For the sinking and the plundering of ships on the Spanish Main.
The judge he's found us guilty and we are condemned to die.
Young men, a warning by me take, and shun all piracy!

So, farewall Dublin city and the girl that I adore.
I'll never kiss your cheek again nor squeeze your hand no more,
For whiskey and bad company have made a wretch of me.
Young men, a warning by me take, and shun all piracy!

The Campañero

Collected and contributed by Ewan MacColl and Peggy Seeger. They had **The Campañero** from an old seaman, Ben Bright, in Edmonton, North London, in 1972.

Ewan says of Bright that "he was an extraordinary man, 76 years old, sprightly and youthful in appearance, had gone to sea when he was 12 years old and had been round the Horn twice by the time he was 16. He's in Australia now, bosunning for chartered yachts!"

Although **The Campañero** has been collected as a pumping shanty, Ben Bright's version is a forebitter or non-work-related sea song, with the shanty chorus incorporated into the second verse.

Source: Ben Bright.

Recording: Bernard Wrigley, *Rough & Wrigley*, Topic 12TS241,

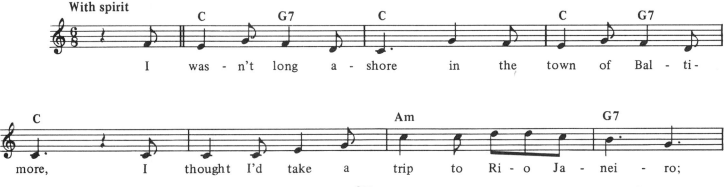

And a French - man gave me the chance, and like - wise a month's ad -

vance, And shipped me a - board of the barque, *The Cam - pa - ñe - ro.*

I wasn't long shore in the town of Baltimore,
I though I'd take a trip to Rio Janeiro;
And a Frenchman gave me the chance, and likewise a month's
   advance,
And shipped me aboard of the barque, the *Campañero.*

Next day I went aboard, me head it was whiskey-sore,
The crimp said, "In your bunk you'll find a square-O."
O, the square-O it was small and the Cockney drank it all,
Aboard o' the handy barque, the *Campañero.*

Next day she went away from the moorings where she lay,
Waiting for the wind unto blow fair, O.
On the following Saturday, O, we hauled her out to sea,
And we squared away in our yacht for Rio Janeiro.

Now, the wind blew down the bay all of our sails away,
And all of them we had unto repair, O;
For I lost me watch below, I was on the poop to sew,
Aboard o' the handy barque, the *Campañero.*

O, the mate he was a big bluff, and he tried to handle us rough,
Says I, "Is it me you're figuring for to scare, O?"
And a great big Russian Finn, O, we handed him over to him,
Aboard o' the handy barque, the *Campañero.*

In forty days or more, we sights Brazilian shore,
And the man in the top he said, "It's Rio Janeiro!"
O, the wind it was quite free and so straight ahead went we
And we dropped our hook that night in Rio Janeiro.

Now, the mate he went ashore, and we never saw no more,
The Skipper sent ashore his bag-shillero;
What with the mate, the skipper, the pump, I was nearly off me
   chump,
Aboard o' the handy barque, the *Campañero.*

And now the voyage is o'er and I'm back in Baltimore,
Of all the down-east ships that I'm aware, O,
If ever more I go to sea, no more Yankee ships for me!
They may be like the barque, the *Campañero.*

O.J. Abbott (L), Ewan MacColl (R) Photo by David Gahr

The Greenland Whale Fishery

A perennial favorite because of the great atmosphere it carries. **The Greenland Whale Fishery** was common to both British and American whalers. It's been dated to the tail end of the eighteenth century.

Source: Text from a broadside by Such; tune is very common.
Recording: The Dubliners, *At Home with the Dubliners*, Tribune TRLP 1010.

We can no longer stay on shore
Since we are so deep in debt,
So a voyage to Greenland we will go,
Some money for to get, brave boys,
Some money for to get.

In eighteen hundred and twenty-four,
On March the twenty third day,
We hoisted our colours up to our mast head,
And for Greenland bore away, brave boys.
And for Greenland bore away.

But when we came to Greenland,
Our good-like ship to moor,
O then we wished ourselves back again,
With the whores upon the shore, brave boys.
With the whores upon the shore.

The boatswain went to the mast-head,
With his spy glass in his hand,
"Here's a whale, a whale, a whalefish," he cried,
"And she blows on every span, brave boys.
And she blows on every span."

The Captain on the quarter deck
(A very good man was he),
"Overhaul, overhaul, your boat tackle fall,
And launch your boats to sea, brave boys.
And launch your boats to sea.

The boats being launched and the hands got in,
The whalefish appeared in view,
Resolved, resolved was each sailorman bold
To steer where the whalefish blew, brave boys.
To steer where the whalefish blew.

The whale being struck and the line paid on,
The fish gave a flurry with her tail.
She capsized the boat and we lost five men
Nor did we catch that whale, brave boys.
Nor did we catch that whale.

The losing of the fine 'prentice boys
Grieved our Captain sore,
But losing of that fine whalefish
Did grieve him ten times more, brave boys.
Did grieve him ten times more.

Come weight your anchor my brave boys,
For the winter star I see,
It is time we should leave this cold country,
And for England bear away, brave boys.
And for England bear away.

For Greenland is a barren place,
Neither light nor day to be seen,
Nought but ice and snow where the whalefish blow
And the daylight's seldom seen, brave boys.
And the daylight's seldom seen.

The Wings of a Gull

Although whaling voyages sometimes produced fantastic profits for all concerned, more often they ended this way— with the sailor's pay only slightly more than his indebtedness and years of his life wasted under the worst of conditions.

Source; David Jones.

Recording: David Jones, *Songs of the Tall Ships*, Adelphi AD1025.

Dorian of D

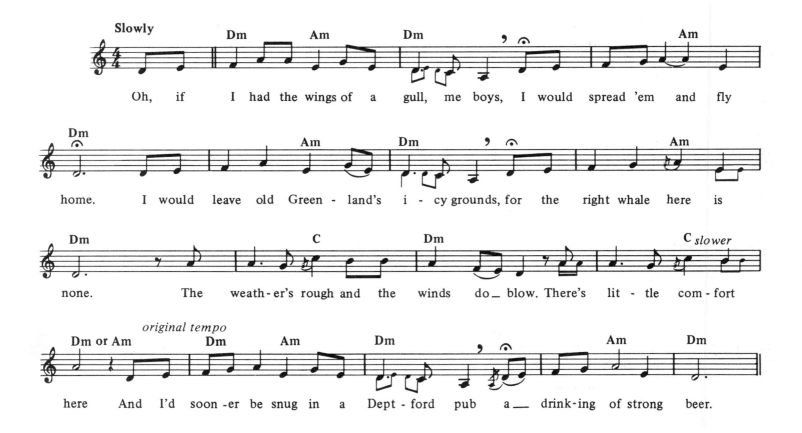

Oh, if I had the wings of a gull, me boys, I would spread 'em and fly home.
I would leave old Greenland's icy grounds, for the right whale here is none.
The weather's rough and the winds do blow. There's little comfort here
And I'd sooner be snug in a Deptford pub a-drinking of strong beer.

Oh, a man must be mad or he's wanting money bad to venture catching whales,
For he may be drown when the fish turns around or his head smashed in with its tail.
Though the work seems grand to a young green hand and his heart is high when he goes,
In a very short burst he'd as soon as hear a curse as the cry of: "There she blows!"

"All hand on deck now, for God's sake! Move briskly if you can."
And he stumbles on deck so dizzy and so sick, for his life he don't give a damn.
High overhead the great flukes spread and the mate gives the whale the iron
And soon the blood in a purple flood from his spout all comes a flyin'.

These trials we bear for nigh on four years till our flying jib points to home.
We're supposed for our toil to get a bonus on the oil and an equal share of the bone.
We go to the agent to settle for the trip and there we've cause to repent
For we've slaved away four years of our lives and we've earned about three pounds ten.

A Lady Fair

I came to "assemble" this broken token ballad while searching for new songs for The Flying Cloud. I recalled reading in
Colm O Lochlainn's *Irish Street Ballads* that **The Spanish
Lady** could be sung to his tune for **A Lady Fair** and reversed
the process, trimming the verses a bit. Necessity is the
father of invention.

Joe Heany has an excellent traditional version.

Source: Text adapted from C. O Lochlainn, *Irish Street
Ballads*; tune is *The Spanish Lady*.

Recordings: The Flying Cloud, *Traditional Music from Ireland, England and Scotland*, Adelphi AD 1029. Sarah Makem,
Ulster Ballad Singer, Topic 12T182.

101

A lady fair in her garden walking,
A gentleman came riding by.
He steps up to her, all to view her.
Says, "Fair lady, would you fancy I?"
"I am no lady, but a poor girl,
A poor young girl of low degree.
Therefore, kind sir, find another sweetheart.
I'm not fitting your servant maid to be."

Wack fol a laddie, toora laddie,
Wack fol a toor loora lay,
Wack fol a laddie, toora laddie,
Wack fol a toor loora lay,

"And oh, kind sir, I have a lover.
'Tis seven long years since I did him see.
If he stays away seven years longer
No man on earth shall marry me."
"What if your lover he is drownded,
Or maybe in some battle slain?
What if he is another's sweetheart
And you will never see him again?"

Wack fol a laddie . . .

"Well, if he's married, I hope he's happy
And, if he's dead, I wish him rest.
No other young man will 'ere enjoy me
For he's the one I love the best."
He put his hands into his waistcoat.
His fingers they were long and small.
Took out the ring was broke between them.
Down at his feet there she did fall.

He picked her up all in his arms
And he gave her kisses most tenderly
"You're my jewel; I'm your single sailor,
Returning home to wed with thee."
So all young maids who'd have a sailor,
Don't slight your love and he on the sea.
He'll come home and make you his own
And take you over to Amerikee.

I Am a Maid That Sleeps in Love

From the repertoire of Elizabeth Cronin, a sweet Cork lady from Macroom, and a favorite of the many collectors who visited her, including Jean Ritchie and George Pickow, from whom I have the ballad.

Mrs. Cronin was elderly in the early 1950s, when the recording was made, and sang in a hushed voice, but with great phrasing and rhythm.

Source: Elizabeth Cronin.

Dorian of D

I am a maid that sleeps in love and can-not tell my pain, For once I had a sweet-heart and John-ny was his name. And if I can-not find him I'll wan-der night and

day And it's for the sake of John - ny I'll cross the storm - y seas.

m3 and 4

can - not tell my pain For

m11

wan - der night and

I am a maid that sleeps in love and cannot tell my pain,
For once I had a sweetheart and Johnny was his name.
And if I cannot find him I'll wander night and day
And it's for the sake of Johnny I'll cross the stormy seas.

And I'll cut off my yellow locks, men's clothing I'll wear on
And, like a gallant soldier, this road I'll gang along,
Enquiring for a captain a passage to engage free
And to be his chief companion on the banks of Liberty.

The very first night the captain lay down on his bed to sleep.
These very words he said to me, "I wish you were a maid.
You're cherry cheeks and ruby lips they've often enticed me.
I wish to God, unto my heart, a maid you were to me."

"Oh, hold your tongue, dear Captain, and do not speak so strange
For, if the sailors heard of it, they'd laugh and make great game.
Now when we land on shore, brave boys, some pretty girls we'll find.
We'll roll and sport along with them for so we are inclined."

It was in three days after that we did land on shore.
"Adieu, adieu dear Captain, adieu forevermore.
A sailor I was on ship boy-o, but a maid I am on shore.
Adieu, adieu dear Captain, adieu forevermore."

"Come back, come back my blooming girl. Come back and marry me,
For I have a good fortune. I'll give it all to thee,
Five hundred guineas besides I will provide for thine
If you'll come back and marry me and say you will be mine."

"To marry you, dear Captain, is more than I can do
For once I had a sweetheart and he wore the jacket blue.
And if I cannot find him I'll wander night and day
And it's for the sake of Johnny I live and die a maid."

The Handsome Cabin Boy

I used to think ballads about female sailors/soldiers were just folklore and good singing until Charlie O'Hegarty, himself a Royal Marine Commando, told me the little he knows about Hannah Snell. Reputed to have once received as punishment a bareback lashing of five hundred strokes, Ms. Snell was a valiant marine for fifteen years during the middle part of the eighteenth century and was never discovered to be a Jane (rather than Jack) Tar. Of course, such a situation could only have been possible because of the grooming habits of the time; remember these same common folk have been referred to repeatedly as the Great Unwashed Masses.

Source: Text from a broadside; tune learned from Charles O'Hegarty.

Recording: Charles O'Hegarty, *Cruising Round Yarmouth*, Adelphi AD 1027.

Combined Mixolydian and Major of D

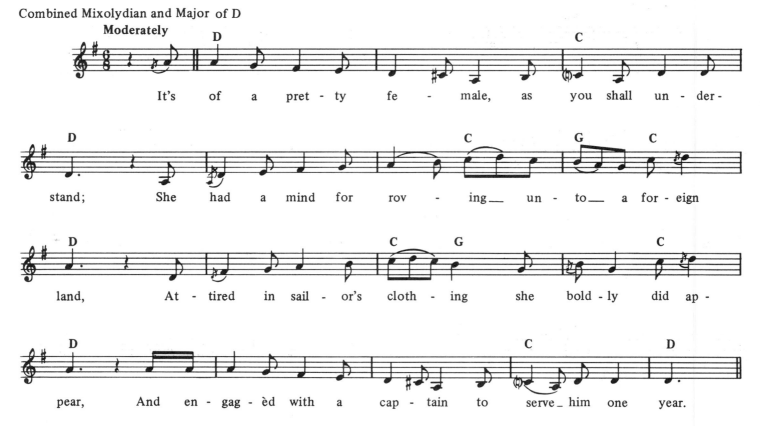

It's of a pretty female, as you shall understand;
She had a mind for roving unto a foreign land,
Attired in sailor's clothing she boldly did appear,
And engagèd with a captain to serve him one year.

She engaged with the captain as cabin boy to be;
The wind it was in favor, so they put out to sea.
The captain's lady being on board, she seemèd in great joy,
To think the captain had engaged the handsome cabin boy.

So nimble was that pretty maid, and done her duty well.
But mark what followed after, the song itself will tell;
The captain with that pretty maid did often kiss and toy
For he soon found out the secret of the female cabin boy.

Her cheeks appeared like roses, and with her side locks curled,
The sailors ofttimes smiled and said: "He looks just like a girl."
By eating captain's biscuits, her colour did destroy,
And the waist did swell of pretty Nell, the female cabin boy.

As thro' the Bay of Biscay their gallant ship did plough,
One night among the sailors there was a fearful row,
They bundled from their hammocks, it did their rest destroy,
And they swore about the groaning of the handsome cabin boy.

"O doctor! O doctor!" the cabin boy did cry,
The sailors swore by all was good, the cabin boy would die.
The doctor ran with all his might, and smiling at the fun,
For to think a sailor lad should have a daughter or a son.

The sailors, when they heard the joke, they all began to stare;
The child belonged to none of them they solemnly did swear.
The lady to the captain said, "My dear, I wish you joy,
It's either you or I betrayed the female cabin boy."

So they all took up a bumper and drank success to trade,
And likewise to the cabin boy, tho' neither man nor maid.
Here's hoping the wars don't rise again our sailors to destroy,
And here's hoping for a jolly lot more like the handsome cabin boy.

Spanish Ladies

A homeward-bound capstan shanty and forebitter which originated in the Royal Navy, according to Stan Hugill.

Ewan MacColl and Bert Lloyd recorded a South Sea whaler-man version:

Oh, it's I've been a sea cook and I've been a clipperman.
I can dance, I can sing, I can walk the jib boom.
I can handle a harpoon and cut a fine figure,
Whenever I get in a boat standing room.

Source: Text from a Henry Parker Such broadsheet; tune is common.
Recording: Lou Killen, *Fifty South to Fifty South*, South Street Seaport Museum SPT-102.

Farewell and adieu to you, Spanish ladies,
Farewell and adieu you ladies of Spain,
Since we've received orders to sail for old England,
In hopes in a short time to see you again.

We'll rant and we'll roar like true British heroes,
We'll rant and we'll roar like true hearts of oak,
And since we struck soundings in the channel of old England,
From Ushant to Scilly was thirty-five leagues.

O we hove the ship too, with the wind at the sou'west,
We hove the ship too, and soundings got we,
At thirty-five fathom. With a white sandy bottom,
We squared our main yards and up channel steered we.

O the first light we made it was called the Deadman,
The Ramhead, Plymouth, Star, Portland, and Wight,
We sailed past Beachy, by Farley and Dungeness,
Until we arrived off the South Foreland light.

O the signal was made for the grand fleet to anchor,
All in the downs that night for to lay,
It's stand by your stoppers, let go your shank painter,
Haul up your clue garnets, let fly tacks and sheets.

Let every man toss off a full bumper,
Let every man toss off a full bowl,
For we'll drink and be merry, and drown melancholy,
So here's a good health to all true hearty souls.

Boney

A short-haul shanty, **Boney** presents the Emperor's life in an historically straightforward manner. One point, though: the H.M.S. *Bellerophon* ("Billy Ruffian") took Napoleon to his final imprisonment on St. Helena off Africa's Atlantic coast.

Shantyman and sea-song scholar Stan Hugill has written that, to his knowledge, this is one of very few shanties which had no obscene version.

Source: Text is a collation; tune learned at South Street Seaport.

Recording: Brian Pearson, *Waterloo—Peterloo*, Argo ZDA 86.

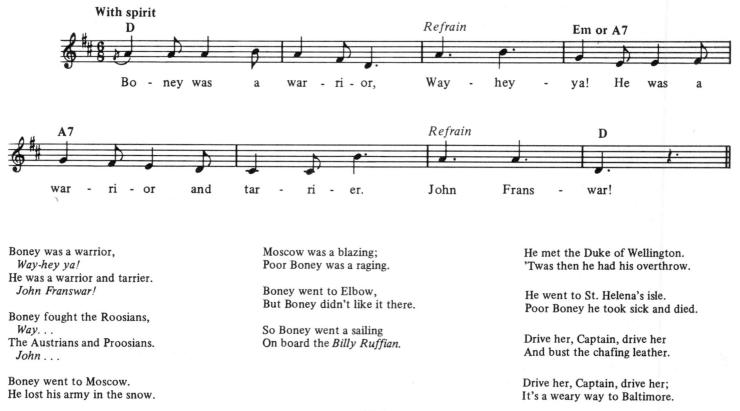

Boney was a warrior,
 Way-hey ya!
He was a warrior and tarrier.
 John Franswar!

Boney fought the Roosians,
 Way. . .
The Austrians and Proosians.
 John . . .

Boney went to Moscow.
He lost his army in the snow.

Moscow was a blazing;
Poor Boney was a raging.

Boney went to Elbow,
But Boney didn't like it there.

So Boney went a sailing
On board the *Billy Ruffian.*

He met the Duke of Wellington.
'Twas then he had his overthrow.

He went to St. Helena's isle.
Poor Boney he took sick and died.

Drive her, Captain, drive her
And bust the chafing leather.

Drive her, Captain, drive her;
It's a weary way to Baltimore.

The Dreadnaught

The Great Emigration saw a different seaman on deck. Packet ship sailors were likely to be from anywhere and to be any type of man. As the forebitter **Paddy West** indicates, they were as likely to have not seen a ship before. Handling such a diverse—and potentially wild—group of men required special skills, but no subtlety whatsoever.

The *Dreadnaught* was the called "the wild ship of the Atlantic," and her Captain, Samuel Samuels, was part lion-tamer. She was built to his specifications to be so strong that she could hold sails in nearly any weather. She was not the fastest, but could still fly, crossing westbound pilot to pilot in nineteen days once and regularly making the journey in twentyfour-and-one-half days.

Built in Newburyport, Massachusetts, in 1853, the *Dreadnaught* was large for her time, made of the best materials and hard-driven by Samuels. She was not *a* Liverpool packet, but *the* Liverpool packet, as Hugill points out, meaning that she traded to Liverpool rather than hailed from that city.

The *Dreadnaught* was shipwrecked in 1869 while rounding Cape Horn under the command of P. N. Mayhew.

Source: Text originally from S. Hugill, *Shanties from the Seven Seas*, altered with time; tune is common
Recording: Lou Killen, *Fifty South to Fifty South*, South Street Seaport SPT-102.

It's of a flash packet, a packet of fame,
She hails from New York and the *Dreadnaught*'s her name.
'Cross the wild Western Ocean, she's bound for to go.
She's a Liverpool packet. Oh Lord, let her go!

Derry down, down, down derry down.

Now the *Dreadnaught* is hauling out of Waterloo Dock
And the boys and the girls to the pierhead do flock.
They give us three cheers as their tears down do flow.
She's a Liverpool packet. Oh Lord, let her go!

Derry down . . .

Now the *Dreadnaught* is lying in the River Mersey,
'Waiting the *Independence* to tow her to sea
Out 'round the Rock Light where them salt tides do flow.
Bound away in the *Dreadnaught* to the westward we'll go!

Now the *Dreadnaught*'s a-howling down the wild Irish Sea,
Her passengers merry and they drinking so free.
Her sailors like lions walk the decks to and fro.
She's a Liverpool packet. Oh Lord, let her go!

Now the *Dreadnaught* is sailing the Atlantic so wide,
Where the high roaring seas roll along her black side.
With her sails taughtly set for the Red Cross to show,
She's a Liverpool packet. Oh Lord, let her go!

Now the *Dreadnaught* is crossing the Banks of Newfoundland,
Where the water's so green and the bottom's all sand.
The fishes of the ocean they swim to and fro.
She's a Liverpool packet. Oh Lord, let her go!

And now she is lying off the Long Island shore,
Where the pilot will board us as he's oft done before.
"Fill away your main topsail! Board your main tack also.
She's a Liverpool packet. Oh Lord, let her go!

And now we're arriving in old New York town.
We're bound for the Bowery and let sorrows drown.
With our gals and our beer boys, oh let the song flow.
And drink to the *Dreadnaught* where'er she may go!

Here's a health to the *Dreadnaught* and all her brave crew,
To bold Captain Samuels and his officers too.
You may talk of flash packets, *Swallowtail* and *Blackball*,
But the *Dreadnaught*'s the ship that can outsail them all!

Peter Street

One from Tony Barrand. He, in turn, had it from Enoch Kent of Glasgow and Toronto.

No one can deny that prostitutes and drink are a mixture flammable enough to burn any man. Because of the nature of their work, sailors came in for this more often than any class of landsmen, and songs like **Off to Sea Once More**, **New York Girls**, and **Peter Street** testify to it.

Source: Tony Barrand.

Recording: Tony Barrand, *Across the Western Ocean*, Swallowtail ST-4.

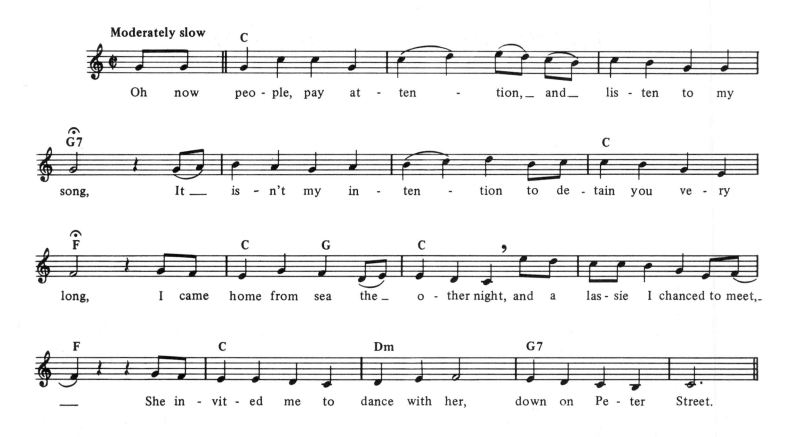

Oh now people, pay attention, and listen to my song,
It isn't my intention to detain you very long,
I came home from sea the other night, and a lassie I chanced to meet,
She invited me to dance with her, down on Peter Street.

Oh I said: My pretty fair maid, I do not dance too well,
And I am bound for Wigan town, where my parents they do dwell,
I have been at sea for seven long years, and I've saved up fifty pounds,
And my parents are expecting me tonight, in Wigan town.

Oh sir, if you were to go with me, you would surely have a treat,
We would have a glass of brandy, and something nice to eat,
And at six o'clock in the evening, I would convey you to the train,
And you'd be sure to call on me when you're in town again.

Well, this lassie was persuasive, and so nice to old Jack Tar,
So I agreed to go with her, and so we hired a car,
And the neighbors, they all stopped and stared, and I heard one of them say:
Bejasus! He'll need the jaunting car before he gets away.

Well now, when we got inside the house, oh then the whisky was brought in,
And when every man had had his fill, the dance it did begin,
And my love and I, we danced a reel to a good old-fashioned tune,
And I did a couple of double-shuffles all around the room.

When the dancing it was over, boys, then for bed we did prepare,
And when I awoke next morning, the truth I will declare,
My gold pocket-watch, and fifty pounds, and my lady-friend had fled,
And left me there Jack, all alone, stark naked on the bed.

When the daylight was departing, and night was drawing near,
I put on the shift and apron, and I walked down to the pier,
And as I crept on board the ship, I heard one sailor say:
Bejasus! Old Jack has got the ducks before he got away.

Well, I looked all around me, but nothing could I spy,
But a lady's shift and apron, a-hanging up to dry,
I tore my hair and I cursed the drink, Oh Lord! What will I do?
The Lord forgive me! Wigan town, will I ever again see you?

108

Oh, is that the new spring fashion, Jack, that you have brought
  from shore?
Where is the shop you bought it, boy, oh have they any more?
The last time that I spoke to you, you said you were homeward
  bound,
Christ, you might have got a better suit than that for fifty pounds.

Well, I might have got a better suit, if I had had a chance,
But I met a pretty fair maid who invited me to dance,
And I danced my own destruction with that lassie that was so neat,
So, no more will I go dancing, boys, down on Peter Street.

The Banks of Newfoundland

The packet rats were as poorly clothed as they were poorly trained. This sailor (and those from the next shanty) filled out his wardrobe with clothing from a steerage passenger's trunk.

The Banks of Newfoundland is a parody of the earlier poaching/transportation ballad **Van Dieman's Land**, p. 115.

Source: Learned from several singers at South Street Seaport in New York.

Recording: Ewan MacColl, *Blow Boys Blow*, Tradition TLP 1026.

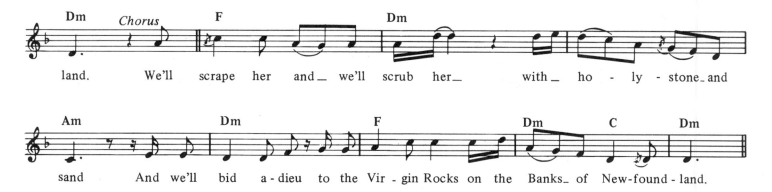

land. We'll scrape her and we'll scrub her with ho - ly - stone and

sand And we'll bid a - dieu to the Vir - gin Rocks on the Banks of New - found - land.

You rambling boys of Liverpool, I'll have Ye's to beware,
When you sail on a Yankee packet ship, no dungaree jackets wear,
But take a big monkey jacket, have it there at your command,
For there blows some cold Nor'westers on the Banks of Newfound-
land.

*We'll scrape her and we'll scrub her with holystone and sand
And we'll bid adieu to the Virgin Rocks and the Banks of Newfoundland.*

One night as I lay in my bed, a-dreaming all alone,
I dreamt I was in Liverpool, way up in Marrowbone,
With my true love beside me and a jug of ale in hand,
When I woke quite broken-hearted on the Banks of Newfoundland.

We'll scrape her . . .

We had Patrick Lynch from Ballinahinch, Jimmy Murphy and Mike
Moore.
It was the Winter of '73 and them sea boys suffered sore.
They pawned their gear in Liverpool, they sold it out of hand,
Not thinking on them cold North winds on the Banks of Newfound-
land,

The mate comes up on the foc'sle head and loudly he does roar,
"Just rattle he in, my lucky lads, we're bound for America's shore.
And wash the blood from that deadman's face and heave or you'll
be damned,
For there blows some cold Nor'westers on the Banks of Newfound-
land.

We had an Irish girl on board, Bridie Reilly was her name.
To me she promised marriage and on her I had a claim.
She tore up her flannel petticoats to make mittens for our hands,
For she wouldn't see them sea boys freeze on the Banks of New-
foundland.

Well it's now we're off the Sandy Hook and the ground's all covered
with snow.
We'll sight the tugboat, our hawser, and to New York we will go.
And when we get to the Black Ball docks, them boys and girls will
stand
And we'll bid adieu to sailing and the Banks of Newfoundland.

*We'll scrape her and we'll scrub her with holystone and sand,
For, while we're here, we can't be there on the Banks of Newfoundland.*

Tapscott (We're all Bound to Go)

This windlass shanty is one of a number I learned by osmo-
sis while singing with various groups at the South Street
Seaport Museum in New York. A. L. Lloyd recorded an
Indian Ocean whalers' version some years ago. He wrote
that the shanty would be sung "when the ship was being
warped out of harbor at the start of a trip. A long rope
would be made fast to a ring at the quayside and run round
a bollard at the pierhead and back to the ship's windlass.
The shantyman would sit on the windlass head and sing
while the spokesters strained to turn the windlass."

William Tapscott was an American packet ship broker who
kept offices on Regent's Road, Liverpool, and Eden Quay,
Dublin. He worked in conjunction with his brother, James,
who was New York-based and specialized in selling prepaid
passages to establish immigrants who now wished to bring
over loved ones. Together, they fleeced the unsuspecting in
the grand fashion of the laissez-faire businessman.

The Castle Garden still stands in lower Manhattan. It was
first an artillery position called Castle Clinton, then New
York City's civic and cultural center. The American Revolu-
tionary War hero, the Marquis de la Fayette, was received
there when he revisited the United States in 1824. The
"Swedish Nightingale," Jenny Lind, made her American
debut at the hall in a concert promoted by none other than
P. T. Barnum. From the middle of the nineteenth century
til 1892, the castle served as the U. S. Immigrant Station,
being the immediate forerunner of Ellis Island in that
regard. From 1896 to 1941 it housed the New York Aquari-
um. It's now empty, a national monument. Shame such an
active building wasn't kept in real use!

Source: Text from J. Colcord, *Songs of the American Sailormen*, somewhat changed in ten years of singing; tune learned
from my brother, Liam Milner.
Recording: John Roberts and Tony Barrand, *Across the
Western Ocean*, Swallowtail ST-4.

Tapscott (We're all Bound to Go)

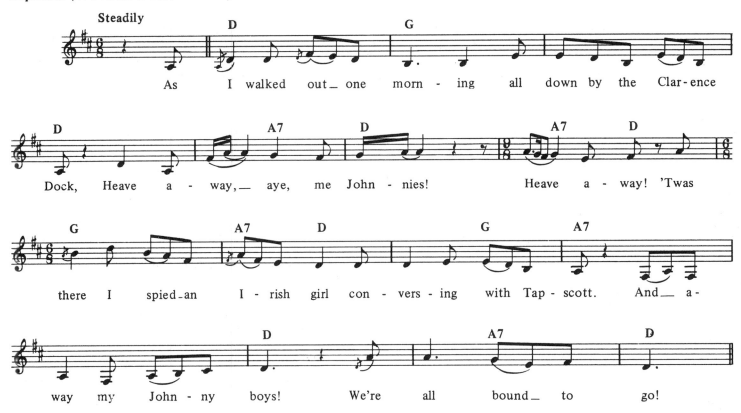

As I walked out one morning all down by the Clarence Dock, Heave a-way,— aye, me John-nies! Heave a-way! 'Twas there I spied an I-rish girl con-vers-ing with Tap-scott. And— a-way my John-ny boys! We're all bound— to go!

As I walked out one morning all down by the Clarence Dock,
Heave away, aye, me Johnnies! Heave away!
'Twas there I spied an Irish girl conversing with Tapscott.
And away my Johnny boys! We're all bound to go!

"Good morning, Mr. Tapscott." "Good morning, me dear," says he.
Heave away . . .
"Oh do you have a packet ship to bear me over the seas?"
And away my . . .

"Oh, yes, I have a packet ship. She's a packet of note and fame.
She's lying in the Waterloo Dock and the *Henry Clay*'s her name."

"Bad luck unto the *Henry Clay* and the day that she set sail,
For them sailors got drunk and broke into me bunk and they stole
  me clothes away.

"'Twas at the Castle Garden they landed me on the shore
And if I marry a Yankee boy I'll sail them seas no more."

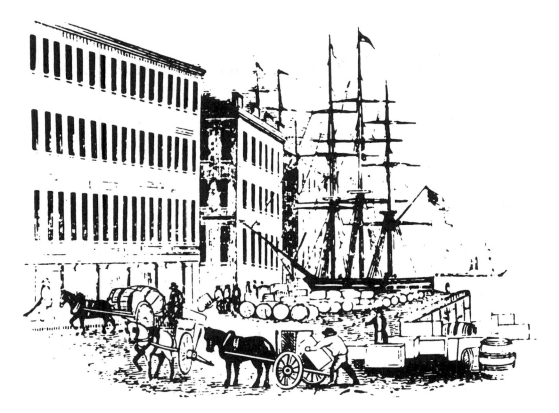

Transports and Immigrants

Henry the Poacher

Britain's lack of success in the War of American Independence caused her to look for another spot on which to "heap her garbage," as Peter Bellamy is fond of joking. In 1787, partially to rid the Thames of a number of convict ships full of condemned prisoners, the policy of transportation to Australia began. By 1816, transportation had come to be considered good government policy, if not downright good business, as the colony of New South Wales prospered and poaching was added to the list of crimes which could be punished in that way.

Source: Text from a broadside printed by William Fortey; tune learned from Christy Moore's recording.

Recording: Christy Moore, *Whatever Tickles Your Fancy*, Polydor 2383 344.

Come all you wild and wicked youths, wherever you may be,
I pray you give attention and listen unto me,
The fate of us poor transports as you shall understand,
The hardships that we undergo upon Van Dieman's Land.

Young men, all now beware,
Lest you are drawn into a snare.

My parents reared me tenderly, good learning gave to me,
Till bad company did me beguile which proved my destiny,
I was brought up in Warwickshire, near Southam town did dwell,
My name it is Young Henry in Harbourne known full well.

Young men, all . . .

Me and five more went out one night into Squire Dunhill's Park,
To see if we could get some game. The night it proved dark;
But to our great misfortune they trepanned us with speed,
And sent us off to Warwick gaol which made our hearts to bleed.

It was at the March Assizes to the bar we did repair,
Like Job we stood with patience to hear our sentence there;
There being some old offenders, which made our case go hard,
My sentence was for fourteen years, then I was sent on board.

The ship that bore us from the land, the *Speedwell* was her name
For full five months and upwards, boys, we ploughed the raging
  main;
Neither land nor harbor could we see; believe it is no lie.
All around us one black water, boys; above us one blue sky.

The fifteenth of September, 'twas then we made the land.
At four o'clock we went on shore all chained hand in hand.
To see our fellow sufferers we felt I can't tell how;
Some yolked unto a harrow, and others to a plough.

No shoes or stockings they had on, nor hat had they to wear,
But leathern frock and linsey drawers; their feet and heads were bare.
They chained them up by two and two like horses in a dray;
The driver he stood over them, with his Melackey cane.

Then I was marched to Sydney town, without no more delay,
Where a gentleman he bought me, his book-keeper to be.
I took this occupation, my master liked me well.
My joys were out of measure, and I'm sure no one can tell.

We had a female servant, Rosanna was her name,
For fourteen years a convict was, from Wolverhampton came.
We often told our tales of love when we were blest at home,
But now we're rattling of our chains in a foreign land to roam.

Van Dieman's Land

Van Dieman's Land is the state of Tasmania, Australia's
second oldest settlement. British colonization started in the
very early nineteenth century and was effected through the
irresistible joint means of land grants and convict labor.
Transportation was halted in 1853.

Source: Text from a broadside by Disley; tune very common.

Recording: Enoch Kent, *Freedom, Come All Ye*, Topic
12T143.

Come all you gallant poachers, that ramble free of care,
That walk out on moonlight nights with your dog, your gun, and
  snare,
The lofty hares and pheasants you have at your command,
Not thinking that your last career is to Van Dieman's Land.

Poor Tom Brown, from Nottingham, Jack Williams, and poor Joe,
We are three daring poachers, the country does well know,
At night we were trepanned, by the keepers hid in sand,
And fourteen years transported were unto Van Dieman's Land.

The first day that we landed upon this fatal shore,
The planters they came round us, full twenty score or more,
They ranked us up like horses, and sold us out of hand,
Then yoked us up to ploughs, my boys, to plough Van Dieman's
  Land.

It's often when in slumber I have a pleasant dream,
With my sweet girl sitting down by a pearly stream,
Through England I've been roaming with her at command,
Now I awaken broken-hearted upon Van Dieman's Land.

God bless our wives and families, likewise that happy shore,
That isle of great contentment, which we shall see no more,
As for our wretched females, see them we seldom can,
There's twenty to one woman upon Van Dieman's Land.

There was a girl from Birmingham, Susan Summers was her name,
For fourteen years transported, we all well know the same,
Our planter bought her freedom, and married her out of hand,
She gave to us good usage upon Van Dieman's Land.

So all young gallant poachers give ear unto my song,
It is a bit of good advice, although it is not long,
Throw by your dogs and snares, for to you I speak plain,
For if you knew our hardships you'd never poach again.

John Mitchel

Mitchel, the son of a Protestant minister, was a militant Irish writer during the days of the Great Famine, when millions of Irish either died or, if lucky enough, escaped to the New World. His nationalism and ardor for land reform were so strong and unbending as to cause his transportation in 1848 for treason.

Together with other Fenian prisoners, he escaped Van Dieman's Land in 1853 and went to America, where he fought in the Confederate Army. John Mitchel later returned to Ireland and was elected to Parliament shortly before his death in 1875.

Source: Text from P. Galvin, *Irish Songs of Resistance*; tune is *The Rocks of Bawn*.
Recordings: Joe Heaney, *Irish Traditional Songs in Gaelic and English*, Topic 12T91. Tommy Dempsey, *Irish Rebellion Album*, Folkways FH 5415.

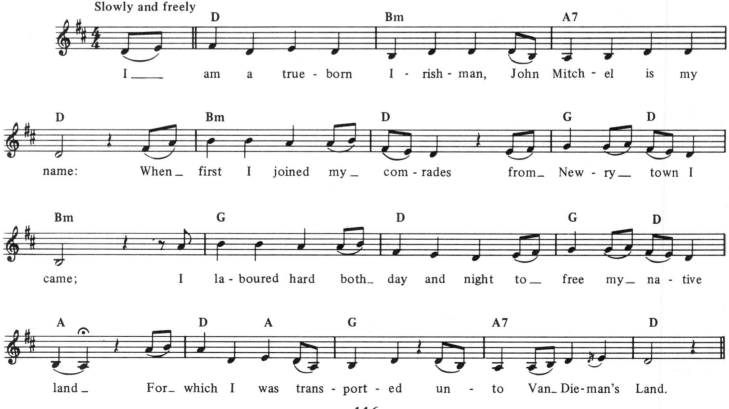

I ___ am a true-born Irish-man, John Mitch-el is my name: When ___ first I joined my ___ com-rades from ___ New-ry ___ town I came; I la-boured hard both ___ day and night to ___ free my ___ na-tive land ___ For ___ which I was trans-port-ed un-to Van ___ Die-man's Land.

I am a true-born Irishman, John Mitchel is my name:
When first I joined my comrades from Newry town I came;
I laboured hard both day and night to free my native land
For which I was transported unto Van Dieman's Land.

When first I joined my countrymen it was in forty-two;
And what did happen after that I'll quickly tell to you;
I raised the standard of Repeal, I gloried in the deed;
I vowed to heaven I ne'er would rest till Old Ireland would be freed.

Farewell my gallant comrades, it grieves my heart full sore
To think that I must part from you, perhaps for evermore;
The love I bear my native land, I know no other crime;
That is the reason I must go into a foreign clime.

As I lay in strong irons bound, before my trial day
My loving wife came to my cell, and thus to me did say:
'Oh, John, my dear, cheer up your heart, undaunted always be,
For it's better to die for Erin's rights than live in slavery.'

I was placed on board a convict ship without the least delay;
For Bermuda's Isle our course was steered: I'll ne'er forget the day,
As I stood upon the deck to take a farewell view
I shed a tear, but not for fear; my native land, for you.

Adieu! Adieu! to sweet Belfast, and likewise Dublin too,
And to my young and tender babes; alas, what will they do?
But there's one request I ask of you, when your liberty you gain
Remember John Mitchel far away, though a convict bound in chains.

Tattie Jock

"There's a farm called Craigie in north Fife, right enough, though I don't know if this is a true story.

The whole point of why we sing the song is that these men were only stealing potatoes—to *eat*. They were fed so very bad!"—Artie Trezise.

Source: Cilla Fisher and Artie Trezise

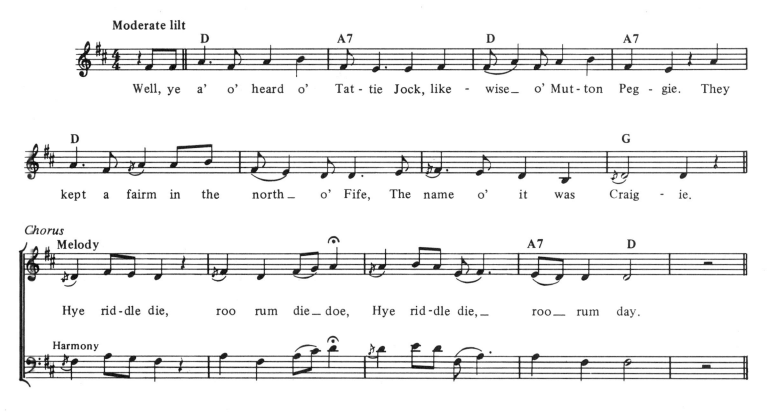

Moderate lilt

Well, ye a' o' heard o' Tat-tie Jock, like-wise_ o' Mut-ton Peg-gie. They kept a fairm in the north_ o' Fife, The name o' it was Craig-ie.

Chorus

Melody

Hye rid-dle die, roo rum die_ doe, Hye rid-dle die,_ roo_ rum day.

Harmony

Well, ye a' o' heard o' Tattie Jock,
Likewise o' Mutton Peggie.
They kept a fairm in the north o' Fife,
The name o' it was Craigie.

*Hye riddle die, roo rum die doe,
Hye riddle die, roo rum day.*

Three months we served with Tattie Jock
And weel we did agree.
Till we found oot that the tattie shed
Could be opened with the bothy key.

Hye riddle die . . .

Next morning in the tattie shed,
Our bags were hardly fu',
When Tattie Jock frae ahint the door
Cried, "Ah, my lads stand still."

117

Noo, the first he got was Willie Marr,
The next was Sandy Doo,
There was Jimmy Grey and Will Moncur
And Jimmy Pethrie flew.

Noo, he sent for ten big polismen
But nine there only cam',
And it dinged them for tae lift us that night,
Us bein' sic able men.

Noo, the youngest lad was the wisest lad,
The best lad o' us a'.
He joined a man o' war at Leith;
So he neednae stand the law.

As we were bein' marched up through Perth,
I heard a newsboy say,
"It's a shame tae see sic able men
Rade aff tae Botany Bay."

Noo, when we got oor sentence read
We all looked roon' and roon',
But when we heard o' the thirteen years
The tears cam' tricklin' doon.

When we get to Botany Bay
Some letters we will send,
Tae tell oor friends o' the harship we
Endure in a foreign.

The Donside Emigrant's Farewell

This parting song was sung by Charles Michie at a gathering
in his honor at Corriehoul, Corgarff, Aberdeenshire, in 1836,
just before he left for America. The assumption was he had
composed the song himself, though it now seems he merely
filled out an older text to suit his own circumstance. The
folk process.

Source: Text and tune learned from J. Ord, *Bothy Songs
and Ballads*, and G. Greig, *Folk Songs of the North-East*.

Dorian of D

Come all my old comrades, once more let us join,
And raise your sweet voices in chorus with mine;
Let us drink and be merry, from sorrow refrain,
For we may and may never meet all here again.

The time's fast approaching that I must away,
I bid you adieu for many's the long day;
With you, my dear comrades, so happy we've been here,
But away to Virginia my course I must steer.

May Heaven protect us with a prosperous gale,
And be our safeguard while we are under sail,
Lead us safe to the harbor across the proud wave,
We will trust to His mercy Who can sink or can save.

Ye hills and low valleys of Donside, farewell,
For if ever I return there is none here can tell;
Farewell to your lasses of every degree,
Long in vain will I wish for your sweet company.

Farewell to the jewel, to you I love best,
For you and your beauty excels all the rest;
But if you prove constant as constant can be,
Wherever I go, love, my heart is with thee.

Many hearts will be happy, but mine will be sad,
When I think on the joys that me and my love had;
When I mind on the time that you sat on my knee,
There was none in this world more happy than we.

Farewell to my joys, they are gone for a while,
Cold winter's away and the sweet summer smiles,
I have heard an old proverb, found it to be true—
That true love is better than gold from Peru.

Come all my dear comrades, let's drink up our glass,
Each lad drink a health to his darling sweet lass;
Drink a health to each lover whose sweetheart is true;
Here's a health, peace, and plenty; so farewell and adieu!

Lovely Ann

I've yet to meet anyone who knows a melody for this fine song. Greig includes a tuneless Scots version, **Sweet Charming Ann**, in *Folk Songs of the North-East* (No. CVIII). The words used here are from a broadside which bears no imprint, though it may have been published in Birmingham, and the tune is the same one which carries **Gleanntain Ghlas Gheoth Dobhair** and **The Shamrock Shore**. I use it because of its emigrant association and its great beauty.

Rathlin Island lies in the North Channel on the Antrim coast, not too far from the Giant's Causeway. Stan Hugill tells me the Union Line was a steamship company operating out of Belfast during the Great Emigration.

Source: Broadside with no imprint; tune is moderately common, first heard from Paul Brady.

Mixolydian of D

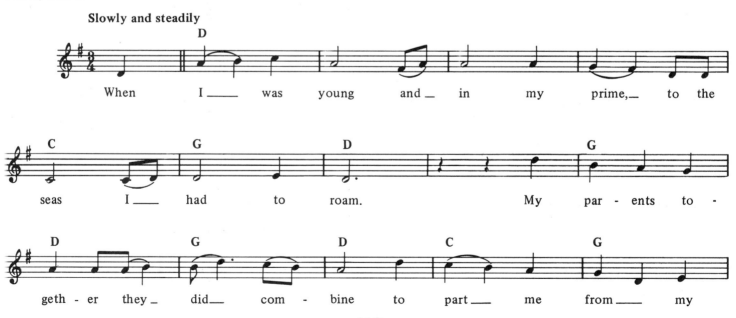

Slowly and steadily

When I was young and in my prime, to the seas I had to roam. My parents together they did combine to part me from my

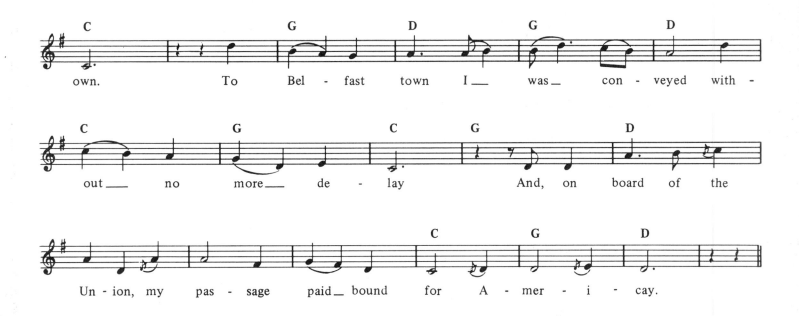

own.   To Bel-fast town I __ was __ con-veyed with-out __ no more __ de-lay   And, on board of the Un-ion, my pas-sage paid __ bound for A-mer-i-cay.

When I was young and in my prime, to the seas I had to roam.
My parents together they did combine to part me from my own.
To Belfast town I was conveyed without no more delay
And, on board of the Union, my passage paid bound for Americay.

'Twas on the fourteenth day of June from Belfast we set sail
And down the lough we bore straightway with a sweet and pleasant
    gale.
I bade farewell to the Shamrock Shore and the bonny banks of Bann
And to the girl I do adore, my charming lovely Ann.

Unto St. Andrews we were bound, our coast now for to clear.
Along the shores we bore away thinking no danger near.
At ten o'clock on the third night we received a dreadful shock —
Our ship she struck with all her might against some unknown rock.

It's of our hard fate to lament, just now I will begin.
In discontent, some hours we spent lying south-east off Rathlin,
Then overboard our stores we threw and our cargo to the waves
And numbers to the shrouds withdrew, their precious lives to save.

The raging sea ran mountains high and dismal were the skies.
Neither light nor land did we espy and fearful were our cries.
It's there we lay till break of day. Describe our state, who can?
And, to myself, these words did say, "Adieu, sweet lovely Ann."

When we received the first glimpse of light, our boats we did employ.
Towards the shore away we bore. Our hearts did leap with joy.
And Providence proved kind to us—His name I do adore!
There was not one soul left on board; we all got safe on shore.

I'll bid farewell to Americay and to the rocks of Rathlin.
No more I'll from my country stray to cross the raging main.
I'll go and see my bonny lass down by the River Bann
And all my days with her I'll pass. She's my charming lovely Ann.

The American Wakes

A conversation with Joe Heaney

Dan Milner: *Tell me about the American wakes, Joe.*

Joe Heaney: *Well, they weren't really wakes. The reason they called them that is that nine times out of ten the person never came back and saw his parents . . . he might come back and see the younger generation, but at that time it was so hard to come and, of course, they wanted to settle down and make a new life for themselves. But they didn't really wake someone; they had what you'd call 'a musical time'. That's the name they gave it.*
I was at four American wakes myself, as a boy. We were allowed to go till 10 o'clock and after that we had to skitter off home.
The night before the wake, the person that was going, whether it was a man or a woman, went around and kissed the old people and invited the young people to spend the night with them and there was plenty of music played until morning. It was to break the blow of that person going away.

DM: *How old is the custom?*

JH: *I don't know how far back it can go, but it continued to the early 1930s. Maybe it started when emigration started to America or maybe from the time of the Famine [in the late 1840s].*

DM: *So there'd be music, dancing, drink . . .*

JH: *Music, dancing, plenty of drink, and everybody was jolly until the crowd started going away from the house in the morning and they started shaking hands. That's when they started getting lonely and the mother would throw her arms around the neck of the person going away . . .*

> *Stór mo chrói* when you're far away from the home you'll
>   soon be leaving.
> And it's many a time by night and day your heart will be
>   sorely grieving.
> The stranger's land might be bright and fair and rich in
>   treasures golden,
> You'll pine, I know, for the long, long ago and the love that's
>   never olden.

Now she points out to him, even though he's going away to a strange land, that it's not all gold he'd find in the streets. "Even though you'll see a rich person, you'll see a poor person not far behind him and beware, no matter what you do, when you hear a voice behind you remember it could be me and it will be me. Always stand and think of where you were born. And that way you'll be okay."

Stór mo Chroí in the stranger's land there's plenty of wealth
   and wearing.
Whilst in gems adorned the rich and the grand there are faces
   with hunger tearing.
For the road is dreary and hard to tread and the lights of
   their city may blind you,
You'll think a store of long, long ago and the love you left
   behind you.

Stór mo Chroí when the evening sun over mountains and
   meadows falling,
Turn away from the throng and listen and maybe you'll hear
   me calling.
The voice that you'll hear will be surely mine for somebody's
   speedy returning.
Aroon, aroon will you come back soon to the one that will
   always love you?

*They took a chance. Some of them came to Boston, some came
to New York and a lot of immigrants, especially those that came
after the Famine, when they landed somewhere ∴ . . half of them
died on the sea anyway . . . they wouldn't be let on shore for
fear they carried a disease because of the hunger. Now a boat-
load, about five hundred, arrived in Boston one time . . . I think
it was 1852 . . . and they were turned away from Boston and
sent to New York and they were turned away from New York.
There were only about fifteen people of the five hundred left
living when they were finally allowed to land in Boston. Off
the St. Lawrence is fifteen hundred buried on three islands
because they wouldn't be allowed to land.*

DM: *And what could they expect if they arrived?*

JH: *Anybody who had anybody to meet them was alright, but
those that didn't was used by the Yankees and that's what
happened to* The Seven Irishmen.

DM: *It was sort of like the 'king's shilling' trick, wasn't it?*

JH: *A lot of people couldn't read. They weren't allowed to read at
one time anyway. It was against the law to teach a poor person
how to read in case he'd look in the paper and find out how
brainwashed he was, you know.
What they did was they met them and they offered them jobs.
They'd take them for a drink and "Sign this form." Now the
minute you signed the form you were signing yourself into the
army and that's how they got hundreds of people into the army.*

The Green Fields of America

Also the title of a very popular reel, this is an emigration song very positive in its view of the New World. The great Ulster singer Paddy Tunney sings it as **The Green Fields of Canada**, words used in our fourth verse.

Source: Text from a broadsheet of Henry Disley; tune learned from the singing of Paddy Tunney.

Recordings: Paddy Tunney, *Paddy Tunney*, Folk-Legacy FSE-1. Planxty, *Cold Blow and the Rainy Night*, Polydor 2383 301.

Combined Mixolydian and Aeolian of A

bond - age   I____ ne'er   can   be   hap -   py,   The green
fields   of   A - mer - i - ca   is____ sweet - ter   by ____   far.

Farewell to the land of shillelagh and shamrock,
Where many a long day in pleasure I spent,
Farewell to my frields I leave here behind me,
To live in old Ireland if they are content.
Now, sorry am I for to leave this green island,
Whose cause I supported in both peace or war,
To live here in bondage I ne'er can be happy,
The green fields of America is sweeter by far.

I remember the time when our country it flourished
When tradesmen of all kinds had plenty of money
But our manufactory has crossed the Atlantic,
And we, boys, must follow to America.
No longer I'll stay in the land of oppression,
No cruel task masters shall rule over me,
To the country of liberty I'll bid 'good morrow',
In the green fields of America we will be free.

Oh, who could stay here among want and starvation
To hear the poor children crying for bread?
And many poor creatures without habitations,
Or without a roof to cover their head.
Come, pack up your store, and consider no longer,
Six dollars a week, it's not very bad pay,
No taxes or tithes to devour up your labour,
When you are in the green fields of America.

My father is old and my mother she is feeble,
To leave their cottage their hearts feel sore,
The tears down their cheeks in large drops are falling
To think they must die on a foreign shore.
But little I care where my bones are buried,
If in peace and comfort I spend my life,
The green fields of Canada daily are blooming,
And then we will end all misery or strife.

Farewell to the groves of the sweet County Wicklow
Likewise to the girls of Erin all round,
May their hearts be as merry as ever I wish them,
'Tho now far away on the ocean I'm bound.
If ever it happens in a foreign climate,
A poor friendless Irishman comes in my way,
To the best I will make him right welcome,
At my home in the green fields of America.

The ship is now waiting, the anchor is weighing,
Farewell to the land I am going to leave,
My Mary she left both her father and mother,
With me to cross the western wave.
I'll fill a bumper when we're on our passage,
And this is the toast from my heart I will say,
Here's health and long life to those that have courage,
To go to the free land of America.

Towards Irish Independence

The Seven Irishmen

The musical pipeline between Ireland and North America certainly has always been two-way. One immediately thinks of the use of the banjo in Irish music, the great popularity in Ireland of the recordings of Michael Coleman (made in the USA), Sam Henry's collecting from traditional sources such Canadian and American songs as **Shanty Boy** and **The Lakes of Pontchartrain** and the frequency of American-experience ballads like the Morrissey series and **The Seven Irishmen**.

Numerous Irish fought for the Union or Confederacy during the American Civil War, many in separate ethnic units.

'Twas the night before battle and, gathered in groups, the soldiers lay close at their quarters,
A-thinking, no doubt, of their loved ones at home, of mothers, wives, sisters and daughters.
With a pipe in his mouth sat a handsome young blade and a song he was singing so gaily,
His name was Pat Murphy of Meagher's Brigade and he sang of the land of shillelagh.

Says Pat to his comrades, "It's a shame for to see brothers fighting in such a queer manner,

But I'll fight till I die, if I shouldn't get killed, for America's bright starry banner."
Far away in the East there's a dashing young blade and a song he is singing so gaily;
It's honest Pat Murphy of the Irish Brigade and he sings of the splintered shillelagh.

Well, the morning came soon and poor Paddy awoke on the Rebels to have satisfaction.
The drummers were beating The Devil's Tatoo, a-calling the boys into action.
Then the Irish Brigade in the battle was seen, their blood for the cause shedding freely.
With their bayonet charges, they rushed on the foe with a shout for the land of shillelagh.

These seven were anxious to see America, but not in blue suits; they could have stayed at home and had the King's shilling.

Source: Joe Heany, a favorite song of his father.

Recording: Joe Heany, *Joe Heany*, Philo 2004

Joe Heaney (L), Liam Clancey (R) Photo by David Gahr

The Seven Irishmen

All— you that love the Sham-rock green, at - tend— both young and old.—

— I feel it is— my du - ty those lines for to— un-

fold. Con - cern - ing sev - en pas - sen - gers who— late - ly sailed— a-

way, To seek a - bet - ter live - li -hood all— in— A-mer - i - cay.

ms 1, 2

you that love—the Sham-rock green at —

m11

late - ly— sailed a-

m13

seek a bet - ter—

All you that love the Shamrock green, attend both young and old.
I feel it is my duty those lines for to unfold,
Concerning seven passengers who lately sailed away,
To seek a better livelihood all in Americay.

On the fourteenth day of April our gallant ship did sail,
With fifty-five young Irishmen, true sons of Granuale.
They landed safely in New York on the nineteenth day of May,
To see their friends and relatives all in Americay.

Some of them had their friends to meet as soon as they did land,
With flowing bumber drank a health to poor old Paddy's land.
These who had no friends to meet their hearts were stout and bold,
And by the cursed Yankees they would not be controlled.

Seven of those young Irishmen were walking down George's Street
When a Yankee officer they happened for to meet;
He promised them employment in a brickyard near the town,
There he did conduct them, their names were taken down.

He brought them to an alehouse and called for drink galore.
I'm sure such entertainment they never had before.
While he thought he had them drunk, those words to them did say,
"You are listed now as soldiers to defend Americay."

They looked at one another, those words they then did say,
"It's not to 'list that we did come into Americay
But labor for our livelihood, as we often did it before,
That we lately emmigrated from the lovely Shamrock shore."

Twelve Yankees dressed as soldiers came in without delay,
They said, "My lads you must prepare with us to come away.
This is one of our officers, you cannot now refuse.
So you need not strive or yet resist, you can no longer wait."

The Irish blood began to rise, one of those heroes said,
"We have an only life to lose, therefore we're not afraid.
Although we are from Ireland, this day we'll let you see,
We'll die like sons of Granuale and keep our liberty."

The Irish boys got to their feet, it made the Yankees frown,
As fast as they could strike a blow, they knocked the soldiers down.
With bloody heads and broken bones, they left them in crimson gore
And proved themselves St. Patrick's Day throughout Columbus shore.

You swear it was a slaughterhouse in where those Yankees lay;
The officer with all his men on cars were dragged away;
With bloody heads and broken bones, they'll mind it evermore,
With a drop of sweet shillelagh that came from Erin's shore.

A gentleman from Ohio had seen what they did do.
He said, "I will protect you from this criminal Yankee crew.
I'll take you to Ohio while I have authority,
And you shall be in my service while you are in this country."

So Irishmen both great and small, listen and draw nigh,
Offer up a fervent prayer both morning, noon and night,
In hopes that God will save them all men that's far away,
And keep them from all danger while they're in Americay.

The Woods of Trugh

Apart from its beautiful melody, I particularly like this ballad for the evenhanded way it deals with the dual themes of love and patriotism. Both are often overdrawn with the pen.

The Battle of Benburb (The Proud Peak) was a catastrophic defeat for the Anglo-Scots army which faced O'Neill's gathered clans. Over three thousand were either killed in battle or mercilessly slain in their flight to the sea.

Trugh is in Co. Monaghan and the goings-on described from the seventeenth century, though the song is newer.

Source: Learned from Cathal McConnell.

Recording: Frank Harte, *And Listen to My Song*, Ram RMLP 1013.

Mixolydian of D

128

Out from the shady woods of Trugh, McKenna rides at noon.
The sun shines brightly, not a cloud darkens the skies of June.
No eye has he for nature's charms; they don't distract his brain,
As through flowery vales he makes his way and never draws a rein.

Before him stands the tall gray towers of Glaslough castle old.
It holds a treasure in its walls more dear to him than gold,
For in it waits his own true love, the dark eyed young Maureen,
Who he hopes will bless his home one day in the woods of Trugh
   so green.

"I have come to look upon you love for tomorrow I must go
With my brave Trugh men to Benburb, there to meet Owen Roe,
I have come to look upon you love and hear your answer sweet,
For I might in the battle fall we never more might meet."

"Go forth my love, my blessings take, and smite the Saxon hoarde.
I'll be your bride when you return without one other word.
With a warm embrace they bid adieu as the evening sun went down
Behind those western wooded hills that o'erlook Glaslough town.

McKenna lightly mounts his steed at the twilight of the eve.
It leads him over Dava Hills through Trugh's green shady leaves.
Tonight he meets with his brave men on the dark hills of Tyronne
And then the army of the North, likewise the fearless Owen.

Right well O'Neill was pleased to see those gallant mountaineers
Who kept the Saxon wolves at bay 'round ancient Trugh for years.
Full well they fought on Benburb's plain as the English flag went
   down.
And few that night escaped them toward Carrickfergus town.

When Autumn's gold lay in the woods and the berries ripe and red.
McKenna and his young bride to Glaslough church were led
And never in her father's hall a fairer maid was seen
Than McMahon's only daughter, the dark eyed young Maureen.

Erin's Green Shore

The representation of Ireland or Irish Liberty in a feminine
form is common—nearly expected—in folk song, and it
would be safe to claim close relationship between our
heroine and the "fine old woman" of Tommy Makem's
Four Green Fields.

Surprisingly, this particular song has been frequently collected in North America and is now all but unknown in the
Isles.

Source: Text adapted from a broadside printed by A. Jackson of Moor Street, Birmingham; tune learned from the
singing of Hedy West.

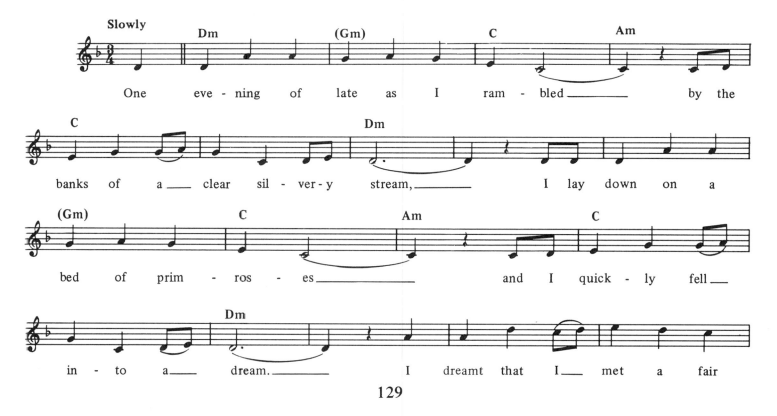

One eve-ning of late as I ram-bled _____ by the
banks of a ___ clear sil-ver-y stream, _____ I lay down on a
bed of prim-ros - es _____ and I quick-ly fell ___
in - to a ___ dream. _____ I dreamt that I ___ met a fair

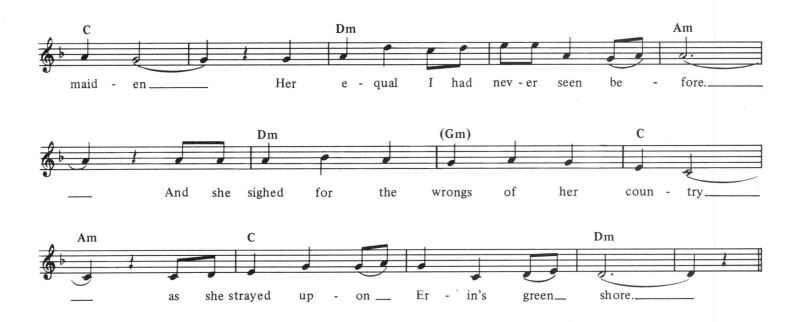

maid - en _____ Her e - qual I had nev - er seen be - fore.

_____ And she sighed for the wrongs of her coun - try _____

_____ as she strayed up - on ____ Er - 'in's green ____ shore. _____

One evening of late as I rambled by the banks of a clear silvery stream,
I lay down on a bed of primroses and I quickly fell into a dream.
I dreamt that I met a fair maiden. Her equal I had never seen before.
And she sighed for the wrongs of her country as she strayed upon Erin's green shore.

Her eyes were like two sparkling diamonds or the stars on a cold, frosty night.
Her cheeks were like two blooming roses and her skin like the ivory so white.
She dressed in the richest of clothing and green was the mantle she wore.
It was trimmed with a rose and the shamrock that grows along Erin's green shore.

I quickly addressed this fair maiden, "Oh, my jewel, come tell me your name,
For really to me you're a stranger, or I shouldn't have asked you the same."
"I'm the daughter of Daniel O'Connell and from London I've lately sailed o'er.
I've come to awaken my brothers who slumber on Erin's green shore.

"Well I think you're a true son of Ireland and my mind unto you I'll disclose.
Now go to the meeting at Belfast and truly your enemies expose.
For when you bind your hands round in Union, no landlords can stay by your door
And the blessings of freedom will beam on the poor sons of Erin's green shore."

From transports of joy I awakened, but I found this was only a dream.
This beautiful fair one had vanished. How I long for to meet her again!
May the angels of God be our guardians, for I fear I shall see her no more.
May the shining bright warm rays of freedom beam down upon Erin's green shore.

Broadside

Dunlavin Green

Nine years after the Bastille was stormed, the 1798 rebellion broke out in Ireland. It had a number of causes—the inability of the new Irish Parliament to bring about full religious emancipation; the Parliament's own undemocratic and corrupt makeup; and the systems of field enclosures, tithes, and high taxes prevalent throughout the countryside.

The town of Dunlavin lies near where the Wicklow Mountains fold below the Curragh of Kildare. On May 26, 1798, thirty-six suspected United Irishmen were tricked into assembling by the military, then taken off to the village green and shot.

Michael Dwyer, mentioned in the fifth verse, was a rebel leader who held out in the Wicklow Mountains for several years after the rebellion. After his surrender, he was transported to New South Wales, where he later became the chief constable of Parramatta, a few miles from Sydney.

Patrick Galvin prints a very close version of this song both textually and melodically; O Lochlainn a different tune.

Source: Learned from the singing of Frank Harte.
Recordings: Frank Harte, *Through Dublin City*, Topic 12T218. Dan Milner, *Traditional Music from Ireland, England and Scotland*, Adelphi AD 1029.

In the year of one thousand, seven hundred and ninety-eight,
A sorrowful tale unto you I'll now relate,
Of thirty-six heroes who are gone from the world, can't be seen,
Through false information they were shot on Dunlavin Green.

Bad luck to you Saunders, for you did their lives betray.
You said a parade would be held on that very day.
Our drums they did rattle and our fifes they did sweetly play,
Surrounded we were and quite privately marched away.

Quite easily they led us as prisoners through the town.
To be shot on that plain we were first made to kneel down.
Such grief and such sorrow were never before there seen,
When the blood ran in streams down the dikes of Dunlavin Green.

There's young Matty Farrell has plenty of cause to complain
Likewise the two Duffys who were shot down on that plain
And young Andy Ryan, his mother distracted will run
For the loss of her darling, her own beloved eldest son.

Some of the boys to the hills they are going away,
Some of them are shot and more of them going to sea.
Mickey Dwyer in the mountains to Saunders he owes a spleen,
For the loss of his brothers who were shot on Dunlavin Green.

Bad luck to you, Saunders, bad luck may you never shun!
May the widow's curse melt you like now melts in the sun!
The cries of the orphans their murmurs you cannot screen,
For the loss of their fathers, who were shot on Dunlavin Green.

131

Nell Flaherty's Drake

Not the easiest song to remember, but a great one to sing. Sam Henry published a similar song, **The Bonny Brown Hen**, in "Songs of the People," number 88, July 18, 1925. It's from the famed Magilligan district of Co. Derry (home of the Butcher family) and uses the same devices and glowing terms to praise the hen and its lineage in a most literal sense. This song, of course, is allegorical and has little to do with the family *Anatidae*, or Flaherty either!

Source: Text from a broadside with no imprint; tune is common.

Recording: Tommy Makem, *Irish Songs of Rebellion*, Tradition 2070.

Oh, my name it is Nell, quite can-did I tell, And I lived in Clon-mel, which I'll nev-er de-ny, I had a large drake, and the truth for to speak, My grand-moth-er left me, and she go-ing to die; He was whole-some and sound; he weighed twen-ty pound, And the u-ni-verse, 'round I would rove for his sake. Bad luck to the rob-ber, be he drunk or so-ber, That mur-dered Nell Fla-her-ty's beau-ti-ful drake.

Oh, my name it is Nell, quite candid I tell,
And I lived in Clonmell, which I'll never deny,
I had a large drake, and the truth for to speak,
My grandmother left me, and she going to die;
He was wholesome and sound; he weighed twenty pound,
And the universe 'round I would rove for his sake.
Bad luck to the robber, be he drunk or sober,
That murdered Nell Flaherty's beautiful drake.

His neck it was green—he was rare to be seen,
He was fit for a Queen of the highest degree,
His body so white, it would give you delight,
He was fat, plump and heavy, and brisk as a bee;
My dear little fellow, his legs, they were yellow,
He would fly like a swallow, and swim like a heak.
Until some wicked savage, to grease his white cabbage,
He murdered Nell Flaherty's beautiful drake.

May his pig never grunt, may his cat never hunt,
May a ghost always haunt him in the dead of the night,
May his hen never lay, may his ass never bray,
May his coat fly away like an old paper kite;
May the lice and the fleas the wretch ever tease,
May the pinching north breeze make him tremble and shake,
May a four-year-old bug build a nest in the lug,
Of the monster that murdered Nell Flaherty's Drake.

May his cock never crow, may her bellows ne'er blow,
And a—pot or po, may he never have one,
May his cradle not rock, may his box have no lock,
May his wife have no smock to shield her back bone,
May his duck never quack, and his goose turn quite black
And pull down the turf with his long yellow beak.
May scurvy and itch, not depart from the breech,
Of the monster that murdered Nell Flaherty's Drake.

May his pipe never smoke, may his teapot be broke,
And to add to the joke may his kettle not boil,
May he—the bed 'till the moment he's dead
May he always be fed on lob-scouse and fish oil,
May he swell with the gout, may his grinders fall out,
May he roar, bawl and shout, with the horrid toothache.
May his temples wear horns, and all his toes corns,
The monster that murdered Nell Flaherty's Drake.

May his spade never dig, may his sow never pig,
Every nit on his head be as large as a snail,
May his house have no thatch and his door have no latch,
May his turkey not hatch, may the rats eat his meal,
May every old fairy from Cork to Dunleary,
Dip him in snug and easy in some pond or lake,
Where the eel and the trout may slime in the snout,
Of the monster that murdered Nell Flaherty's Drake.

May his dog yelp and growl with hunger and cold,
May his wife always scold 'till his brain goes astray,
May the curse of each hag, that e'er carried a bag,
Alight on his nag till his beard it turns grey,
May monkeys still bite him, and man-apes affright him,
And everyone slight him asleep or awake,
May weasels still gnaw him, and jackdaws still claw him,
The monster that murdered Nell Flaherty's Drake.

Then all the good news I have to diffuse,
'Tis for Peter Hughes, and blind Peter M'Free,
There's big nosed Bob Manson, and buck-toothed Ned Hanson,
Each man has a grandson of my darling Drake,
My bird he had dozens of nephews and cousins,
And one I must get or my heart it will break,
To keep my mind easy or else I'll run crazy,
So this ends the song of Nell Flaherty's Drake.

The Yorkshire Pigs

A local song from the north Kerry-west Limerick border. I
learned it from a Galwayman who was "not too sure" of
the town name, "Gloshen," in the third verse.

Irish butter, by the way, is regularly less expensive in London than in Dublin.

Source: Wishes to remain anonymous.

Steadily

G   Em   G   D7

A - roon and a - roon! What shall we do?— Our name, it is fast go - ing

G   Am   G   Am   C

down.   The hu-mour is gone from ev - 'ry man in coun - try and in

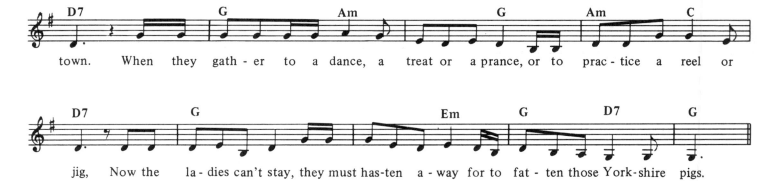

town. When they gath - er to a dance, a treat or a prance, or to prac - tice a reel or

jig, Now the la - dies can't stay, they must has - ten a - way for to fat - ten those York - shire pigs.

Aroon and aroon! What shall we do? Our name, it is fast going down.
The humour is gone from ev'ry man in country and in town.
When they gather to a dance, a treat or a prance, or to practice a reel or jig,
Now the ladies can't stay, they must hasten away for to fatten those Yorkshire pigs.

When I was a boy there was credit and joy and butter and milk galore.
We had it to share, we didn't spare for the bonham or the boar
While craythurs keep small we'll give tay to them all, aye, and bread made with raisins and figs,
But I hear them say, "There's the devil to pay!" when it comes to the Yorkshire pigs.

Up and down and aroon' through Gloshen in June and from Brosna to Rathkeale
There's slips and stores and well bred boars to supply the whole country
But they'll regret their conduct yet with their high-heeled shoes and sprigs
For the creamery soon will give cheques in the moon for to fatten those Yorkshire pigs.

Oh, my sweet garsún, who toils neath the moon, take the sleep from your weary eyes
For the men of the mill in Abbeyfeale are building their factories high.
And here's to the man who lives while he can and success to the man who digs!
May we all live to see old Ireland free and to hell with the Yorkshire pigs.

The Blackbird of Avondale

The "Blackbird" was Charles Stuart Parnell, born at Avondale in Co. Wicklow in 1846. He was the son of an American woman and a member of the Anglo-Irish landowning class, an M. P. for Meath, and an ardent Irish nationalist who worked to bring about land reform and home rule. Like many of the greatest patriots, Parnell was not a Roman Catholic.

In 1889, after impeding Parliament in order to draw attention to the Irish Question, Parnell was named as a correspondent in a divorce proceeding and effectively ruined by a Church-Government alliance.

Source: Fr. Charles Coen.
Recording: Geordie Hanna, *On the Shores of Lough Neagh*, Topic 12TS372.

Slowly and freely

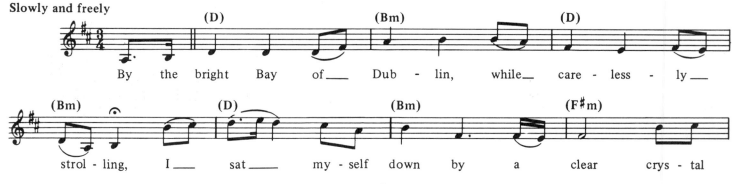

By the bright Bay of___ Dub - lin, while___ care - less - ly___

strol - ling, I___ sat___ my - self down by a clear crys - tal

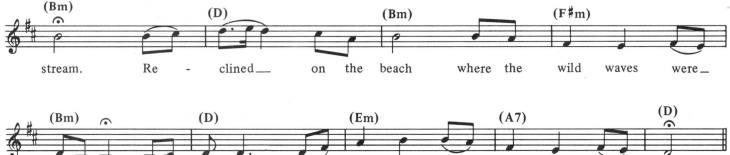

stream. Re - clined___ on the beach where the wild waves were___

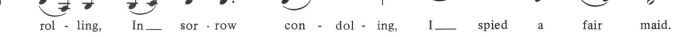

rol - ling, In sor - row con - dol - ing, I___ spied a fair maid.

ms 2 and 3, 14 and 15

Dub - lin, while___ care - less - ly___
dol - ing, I___ spied a fair___

ms 5, 9

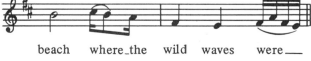

sat___ my - self
clined___ on___ the

ms 10, 11

beach where___the wild waves were___

By the bright Bay of Dublin, while carelessly strolling,
I sat myself down by a clear crystal stream.
Reclined on the beach where the wild waves were rolling,
In sorrow condoling, I spied a fair maid.

Her robes changed to mourning, that once were so glorious,
I stood in amazement to hear her sad tale.
Her heartstrings brought forth in wild accents deploring,
Saying, "Where is my blackbirds of sweet Avondale?"

To the fair Counties Meath, Kerry, Cork and Tipperary,
The notes of his country, my blackbird will sing,
But, woe to the hour we'll part light and airy,
He flew from my arms in Dublin to Queens.

Oh Erin, my country, awake from your slumber
And bring back my blackbird so true unto me.
Let everyone know by the strength of his murmur
That Ireland, a nation, would long to be free.

Now the birds in the forest, for me, have no charm.
Not even the voice of the sweet nightingale.
Her notes are so charming, fills my heart with alarm,
Since I lost my poor blackbird of sweet Avondale.

Skibbereen

Some of my earliest memories are of immigrant parties my family attended in Toronto, Boston, and Brooklyn. There was music and dancing and drink; I scavaged the dregs from a case of beer bottles in Toronto and fell down the cellar steps, so I *know* there was drink! My father, brother, and I were the singers at these affairs and were always called upon for a few favorites.

Skibbereen was always the request of My Aunt Mary Mahoney, because she came from close by the place, and my father was the singer.

Source: Text from P. Galvin, *Irish Songs of Resistance*: tune is common.

Recording: Joe Heaney, *Joe and the Gabe*, Green Linnet SIF 1018.

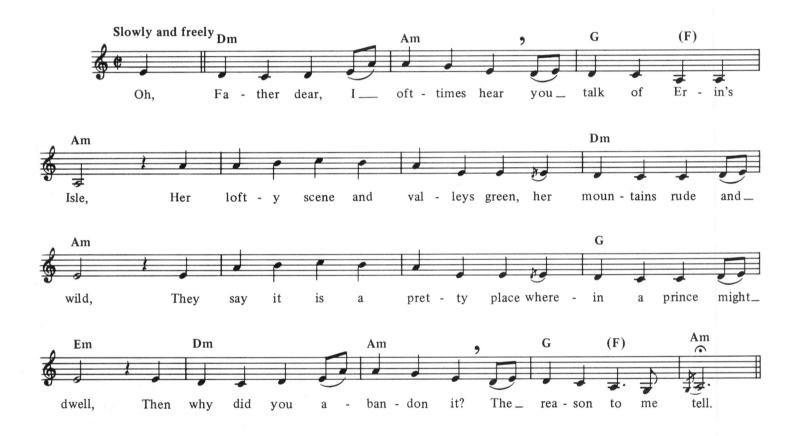

Oh, Father dear, I oft-times hear you talk of Erin's Isle, Her lofty scene and valleys green, her mountains rude and wild, They say it is a pretty place wherein a prince might dwell, Then why did you abandon it? The reason to me tell.

Oh, Father dear, I oft-times hear you talk of Erin's Isle,
Her lofty scene and valleys green, her mountains rude and wild,
They say it is a pretty place wherein a prince might dwell,
Then why did you abandon it? The reason to me tell.

My son, I loved our native land with energy and pride
Until a blight came on the land, and sheep and cattle died,
The rent and taxes were to pay, I could not them redeem,
And that's the cruel reason why I left old Skibbereen.

It's well I do remember that bleak December day;
The landlord and the sheriff came to drive us all away,
They set my roof on fire with their demon yellow spleen,
And that's another reason why I left old Skibbereen.

It's well I do remember the year of forty-eight,
When I arose with Erin's boys to fight against the fact,
I was hunted through the mountains for a traitor to the Queen,
And that's another reason why I left old Skibbereen.

Oh, Father dear, the day will come when vengeance loud will call,
And we will rise with Erin's boys and rally one and all,
I'll be the man to lead the van beneath our flag of green,
And loud and high we'll raise the cry: 'Revenge for Skibbereen!'

Country Life

Johnnie Sangster

A harvesting song, said to be the composition of William Scott of Fetterangus, Aberdeenshire, **Johnnie Sangster** dates from the first part of the nineteenth century.

Source: Learned from J. Ord, *Bothy Songs and Ballads.*

Recording: Ray Fisher, *The Bonny Birdy*, Trailer LER 2038.

O a' the seasons o' the year when we maun work the sairest,
The hairvest is the foremost time and yet it is the rarest.
We rise as seen as mornin' licht. Nae craters can be blyther.
We buckle on oor finger-steels and followed oot the scyther.

For you, Johnnie, you, Johnnie, you, Johnnie Sangster!
I'll trim the gavel o' my sheaf for ye're the gallant bandster.

A mornin' piece to line oor cheek afore that we gae further.
Wi' clouds o' blue tabacco reek, we then set oot in order.
The sheaves are risin' fast and thick and Johnnie he maun bind them.
The busy crew, for fear they stick, can scarcely look behind them.

For you, Johnnie . . .

I'll gie ye bands that winna slip; I'll pleat them weel and thraw them.
I'm sure they winna tine the grip hooever weel ye draw them.
I'll lay my leg oot ower the sheaf and draw the band sae handy
Wi' ilka strae as straucht's a rash and that will be the dandy.

If e'er it chance to be my lot to get a gallant bandster,
I'll gar him wear a gentle coat and bring him gowd in handfu's.
But Johnnie he can please himsel', I wadna wish him blinket;
Sae aifter he has brewed his ale, he can sit doon and drink it.

A dainty cowie in the byre for butter and for cheeses,
A grumphie feedin' in the sty wad keep the hoose in greasies,
A bonnie ewie in the bucht wad help to creesh the ladle
And we'll get ruffs o' cannie woo' wad help to theek the cradle.

Tally Ho! Hark Away

A ballad of a fox chase which stretched over a few hundred miles of the poet's mind.

The type of fox hunting dealt with in this song is a sport of the Anglo-Irish gentry and comes, of course, originally from England. The Irish peasant classes the fox as vermin, for it competes with him for the wild hare and his own chickens. Fox hunting is work to him, and he goes about it with a spade and a terrier, first to dig out the burrow and then to drive the fox to his gun.

Source: Text from a broadside with no imprint, probably printed in Ulster; tune learned from Tony Callanan.

Recording: Sweeney's Men, *1968*, Transatlantic TRA SAM 37.

Combined Mixolydian and Major of D

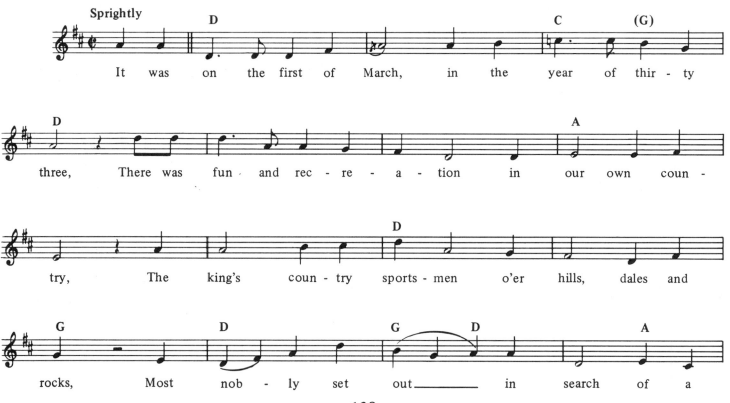

It was on the first of March, in the year of thir-ty three, There was fun and rec-re-a-tion in our own coun-try, The king's coun-try sports-men o'er hills, dales and rocks, Most nob-ly set out_____ in search of a

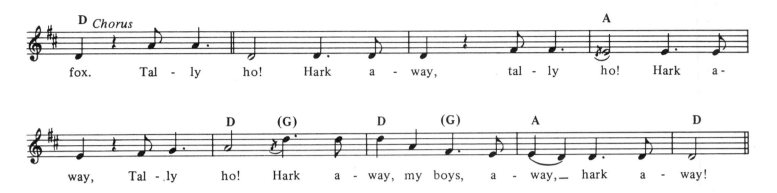

fox. Tal - ly ho! Hark a - way, tal - ly ho! Hark a -

way, Tal - ly ho! Hark a - way, my boys, a - way,— hark a - way!

It was on the first of March, in the year of thirty three,
There was fun and recreation in our own country,
The King's country sportsmen o'er hills, dales and rocks,
Most nobly set out in search of a fox.

Tally ho! Hark away, tally ho! Hark away,
Tally ho! Hark away, my boys, away, hark away!

When they started poor Reynard, he faced to Tullamore,
Through Wicklow and Arklow, along the seashore.
They kept him in view the whole length of the way,
And closely pursued him through the streets of Roscrea.

Tally ho! Hark away . . .

When Reynard was started he faced down the hollow,
Where none but the huntsmen and hounds they could follow,
The gentlemen cried, "Watch him!" Saying, "what shall we do here?
If the hills and dales don't stop them, he will cross to Kildare."

There were one hundred twenty sportmen went down to Ballyland.
From that to Ballyboyne and Ballycuminsland,
But Reynard, sly Reynard arrived on that night,
And said they would watch him until the daylight.

It was early next morning the hills they did resound
With the echoes of the horn and the cry of the hounds,
But in spite of his action, his craft, and his skill,
He was taken by young Donohoe going down Cootehill.

When Reynard was taken his losses to fulfill,
He called for pen, ink, and paper to write his last will,
And what he made mention of you'll find it is no blank,
For he gave them a check on the National Bank.

Here's to you, Mr. Jackson of Curraghmore estate,
And to you, Mr. Gambler, my money and my plate,
And to you, Sir John Power, my whip, spurs and cap,
For you crossed the walls and ditches and never looked for a gap.

Féach A Phadraig (Look, Patrick)

Fr. Charlie Coen learned this hymn at home in Woodford,
Co. Galway, from a schoolteacher, Paddy Felle. "He had a
large repertoire of traditional songs and a rare gift for
music. He could spin off the notes of any song in 'tonic-sol-
fa.'

"Very freely, it's a hymn in praise of St. Patrick for bringing the True Faith to Ireland. Ireland is compared to a garden in which the foremost flower is Jesus Christ and the
garden is cared for by his mother, Mary."

Source: Fr. Charles Coen.

Recording: Fr. Charles Coen, *Father Charlie*, Green Linnet
SIF 1021.

Combined Mixolydian and Major of A

Slowly and freely

Féach_ a Phad - raig As - pal Éire - ann Thug gan Stao - nadh grá - dar

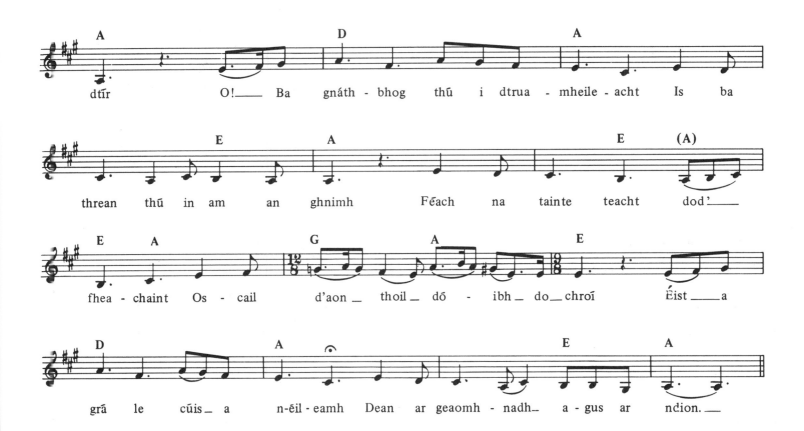

dtír O!___ Ba gnáth - bhog thú i dtrua - mheile - acht Is ba

threan thú in am an ghnimh Féach na tainte teacht dod'___

fhea - chaint Os - cail d'aon ___ thoil ___ dó — ibh ___ do ___ chroí Éist ____ a

grá le cúis ___ a n-éil - eamh Dean ar geaomh - nadh ___ a - gus ar ndion. ___

(text)	Is dearg bhláatha ag sceith 'nar dtír	De le fás an creidhimh fhir
(phonetic)	*Iss jar-igg vlah-ha egg shkay nawr jeer*	*Jay lay fawse on krediv ear*

Féach a Phadraig Aspal Eireann
Fay-ach ah Faw-rick Oss-pill Ayr-en

Is Éire naomhtha bhi ba bhláth-gort
Iss Eire nave-ha vee bah vlaw-gurt

Cuiris feirscrios er na táinte
Keer-iss fair-skreese er nah thawn-cha

Thug gan Staonadh grá dar dtír
Thug gone Stay-noo graw dawr jeer

Oscail d'aon thoil dóibh do chroí
Us-keil dain hell doh-eeve doh hkree

Diabhal le gnas an tsolais ghil
yowl lay nawse on thol-ess yeel

O! Ba gnáth-bhog thú i dtruamheileacht
Oh Baw gnaw-vug thu ee drew-vale-acht

Éist a grá le cúis a n-éileamh
Aye-shh ah graw lay coo-ish ah nail-evv

D' fhág siud eire ag mhuire mathair
Dawg shood eire egg muee-ra wah-hair

Is ba threan thú in am an ghnimh
Iss bah hhrain who in om on gneeve

Dean ar geaomhnadh agus ar ndion.
Jane awr gave-noo ogus awr neen.

Is ag Árd-Mac Dé fá snaidhmh.
Iss egg Awrd Mock Jay faw sneeve.

Féach na tainte teacht dod' fheachaint
Fay-nch nah tawn-cha chockt dode aye-kent

Cuir do bhreithre bláatha bána
Keer doh vray-rah blaw-ha bawna

The Holly and the Ivy

A bouncy English hymn simultaneously celebrating the Christian Nativity with the pagan rite of the magical evergreens, holly and ivy.

Source: John Roberts and Tony Barrand.

Recording: John Roberts and Tony Barrand with Fred Breunig and Steve Woodruff, *Nowell Sing We Clear*, Front Hall FHR-013.

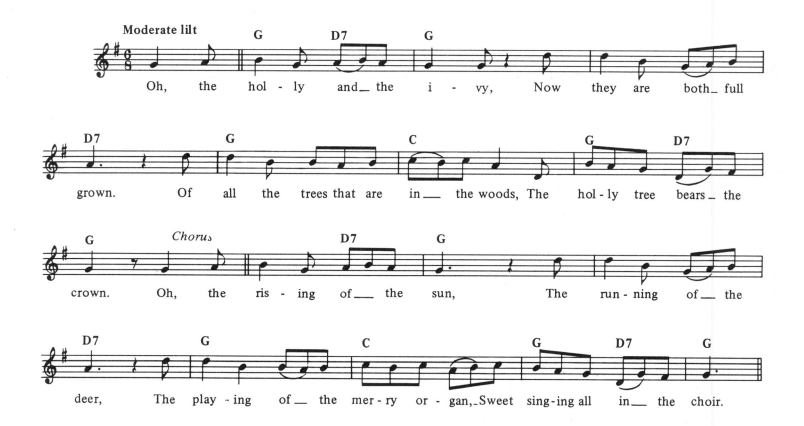

Oh, the holly and the ivy,
Now they are both full grown,
Of all the trees that are in the woods,
The holly tree bears the crown.

Oh, the rising of the sun,
The running of the deer,
The playing of the merry organ,
Sweet singing all in the choir.

The holly tree bears a blossom
As white as any milk
And Mary bore sweet Jesus Christ
All wrapped up in silk.

Oh, the rising . . .

The holly tree bears a berry
As red as any blood
And Mary bore sweet Jesus Christ
To do poor sinners good.

And the holly bears a bark
As bitter as any gall
And Mary bore sweet Jesus Christ
To do redeem us all.

The holly tree bears a prickly leaf
As sharp as any thorn
And Mary bore sweet Jesus Christ
On Christmas Day in the morn.

All the Little Chickens in the Garden

One of the Watersons' most popular songs. Collected from
Joe Udall, a Cumbrian shepherd, in 1974 by Norma Waterson and Martin Carthy.

Source: The Watersons.
Recording: The Watersons, *For Pence and Spicy Ale*,
Topic 12TS265.

When first I come down York-shire, not man-y years a-
go, Why, I met with a lit-tle York-shire girl and I'll have yez all to
know That she was so blithe, so bux-om, so beau-ti-ful and
gay. Now lis-ten whilst I tell you what her dad-dy used to
say: "Treat me daugh-ter de-cent. Don't do her an-y
harm And when I die I'll leave you both me ti-dy lit-tle
farm, Me cow, me pigs me sheep and goat, me stock, me fields and
barn And all the lit-tle chick-ens in the gar-den."

143

When first I come down Yorkshire, not many years ago,
Why, I met with a little Yorkshire girl and I'll have yez all to know
That she was so blithe, so buxom, so beautiful and gay.
Now listen whilst I tell you what her daddy used to say:

"Treat me daughter decent. Don't do her any harm
And when I die I'll leave you both me tidy little farm,
Me cow, me pigs, me sheep and goat,
Me stock, me fields and barn
And all the little chickens in the garden."

When first I went to court the girl, she was so awful shy.
Why she never said a blummin' word while other folks stood by.
But as soon as we were on our own she made me name the day,
Now listen while I tell you what her daddy used to say.

"Treat me daughter decent . . .

And so I'll wed me Yorkshire girl so pleasing to me mind,
I always been proved true to her and she's proved true in kind.
We've had three bairns, they've growed up now with a grandun' on
   the way
And when I look into her eyes I can hear her father say.

Martin Carthy (L), Norma Waterson (R)

The Nice Little Window

Here's an Irish version of the Scots **Bonny Wee Window**.
Fr. Charlie Coen learned it from his own father, Mike Coen.
Vance Randolph found it in Missouri.

The ballad speaks for itself.

Source: Fr. Charles Coen.

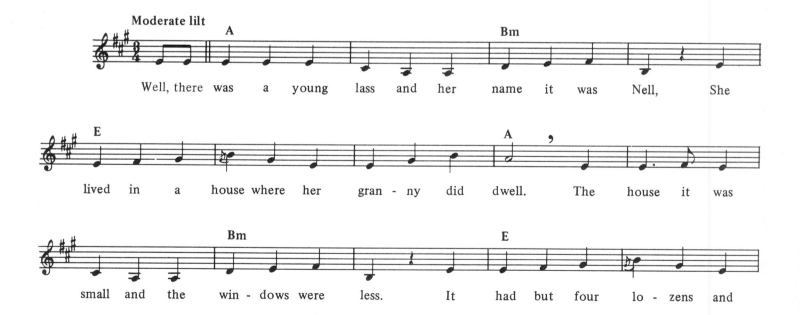

Moderate lilt

Well, there was a young lass and her name it was Nell, She lived in a house where her gran-ny did dwell. The house it was small and the win-dows were less. It had but four lo-zens and

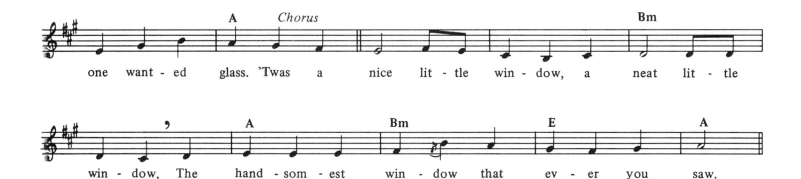

one want-ed glass. 'Twas a nice lit-tle win-dow, a neat lit-tle win-dow, The hand-som-est win-dow that ev-er you saw.

Well, there was a young lass and her name it was Nell,
She lived in a house where her Granny did dwell.
The house it was small and the windows were less.
It had but four lozens and one wanted glass.

'Twas a nice little window, a neat little window,
The handsomest window that ever you saw,

Well, it happened one night, Granny went to her bed
And Johnny the blithest young lad that Nell had
Came over the hills his fond lover to see
And under the window right planted got he.

'Twas a nice little window . . .

Well, they weren't long there and they hadn't much said
Till Granny cries out, "Nellie come to your bed."
"I will then, dear Granny," now Nellie did say,
So "Goodbye, dear Johnny, but come back next day."

To this nice little window . . .

"Oh lassie, dear lassie, don't take it amiss
Before I go away won't you give me one kiss?"
And to get this dear kiss Johnny rammed his head through
For what wouldn't love make a fond lover do.

To a nice little window . . .

Well, a kiss all got Johnny and sweet was the smack,
But for all his life could he get his head back.
He wrugged, he tugged, he bawled and he cursed
While Nell's sides with laughter were now fit to burst.

With his nice little window . . .

Now, Johnny was shouting and roaring with pain,
With his head in the window he had to remain
Till the lintels gave way and the sash width it broke
And off went poor Johnny with the wool 'round his throat.

Of that nice little window . . .

O'er mountain and glen, sure, he sped like the wind.
He went like a march hare and n'er looked behind.
The women all shouted, the children all squealed
And dogs, sticks and stones all went band at his heels.

With his nice little window . . .

When Johnny got home, sure, the hatchet he got
And ridded himself of that wooden cravat
And he vowed that the devil might have him for his ain
If he e'er kissed a lass through a window again.

'Twas a nice little lassie, a bonnie wee lassie,
The handsomest wee lassie that ever you saw.

Dame Durden

A harvest home piece well known from the singing of the Coppers of Rottingdean, Sussex. This version is from Dave Surman, melodeon player, world traveler, schoolteacher, judo expert, and all-around good bloke from Kiddlington, Oxfordshire.

Source: Dave Surman.

Recording: Bob and Ron Copper, *English Shepherd and Farming Songs*, Folk-Legacy FSB-19.

Dame Durden

Dame Durden kept five servant maids to carry the milking pail.
She also kept five laboring men to use the spade and flail.

'Twas Moll and Bet and Doll and Kit and Dorothy Draggletail,
John and Dick and Joe and Jack and Humphrey with his flail.
And John kissed Molly
And Dick kissed Betty
And Joe kissed Dolly
And Jack kissed Kitty
And Humphrey with his flail
Kissed Dorothy Draggletail
And Kitty she was a pretty maid to carry the milking pail.

Dame Durden in the morn so soon, she did begin to call.
To rouse the servant maids and men she then began to bawl.

'Twas Moll and Bet . . .

'Twas on the morn of Valentine the birds began to prate.
Dame Durden's serving maids and men they all began to mate.

The Crabfish

A song common in west Clare, popularized by Willie Clancy. I've often heard David O'Docherty sing **The Crabfish**, though it was always so insanely late at night I never thought of asking him for the words. These came from Donal Maguire, who had them from Kevin Burke, plus one extra verse from Mick Moloney.

Kevin lived in New York in the early '70s and had a good deal to do with popularizing Irish music among folk enthusiasts. Mick, of course, is a brilliant instrumentalist, a fine singer, a crystalline lecturer, a tireless organizer, and a general uplift to all who meet him.

Source: Donal Maguire and Mick Moloney.

Recordings: John Roberts and Tony Barrand, *Across the Western Ocean*, Swallowtail ST-4. Arthur Argo, *A Wee Thread o' Blue*, Prestige International 13048.

Oh, there was a lit-tle man and he had a lit-tle horse And he sad-dled it and bri-dled it and threw his leg a-cross. Mis-ter rad-dle-dum, a-fad-dle-dum, Oh,___ Mis-ter rad-dle-dum, a-fad-dle-dum a-day.___

Oh, there was a little man and he had a little horse
And he saddled it and bridled it and threw his leg across.

Mister raddle-dum, a-faddle-dum
Oh, Mister raddle-dum, a-faddle-dum a-day.

Well, he rode and he rode, till he came to a brook
And there he saw a fisherman fishing with his hook.

Mister raddle-dum . . .

"Oh fisherman, fisherman, fisherman," says he,
"Have you got a little lobster fish you would see to me?"

"Oh no, sir. Oh no, sir. Oh no, sir," said he.
"But I've got this little crabfish I will sell to thee."

Well, he grabs this crabfish by the backbone,
Put it o'er his shoulder and galloped off for home.

Well, when he got indoors he couldn't get a dish,
So he put it in the pot where his missus used to piss.

In the middle of the night she got up for to squat
And the crabfish it caught her by the glory-be-to-God!

"Oh husband, Oh husband, Oh husband come hither!
The devil's in the piss pot and he's got me on his tether."

Well, she grabbed the brush and he grabbed the broom
And they bate this little crabfish all around the room.

They bate him in the head and they bate him in the side
And they bate him in the bollix till the poor old bugger died.

Now the moral of this story is very plain to see:
Have a deco [good look] in the piss pot before you have a pee.

The Suckling Pig

Rents, tithes, and taxes didn't leave much but resentment.

Source. Text from a broadsheet; tune learned from the singing of Mike Herring.

Recording: Mike Herring, *The Painful Plough*, Impact IMP-A 103.

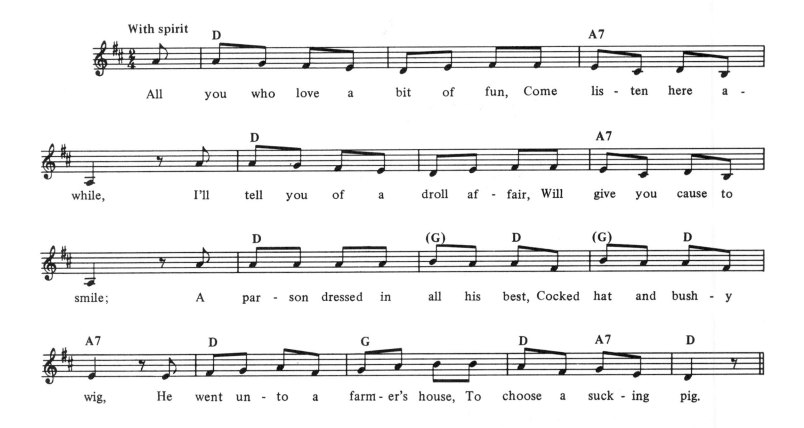

All you who love a bit of fun, Come lis-ten here a-while, I'll tell you of a droll af-fair, Will give you cause to smile; A par-son dressed in all his best, Cocked hat and bush-y wig, He went un-to a farm-er's house, To choose a suck-ing pig.

All you who love a bit of fun,
Come, listen here awhile,
I'll tell you of a droll affair,
Will give you cause to smile;
A Parson dressed in all his best,
Cocked hat and bushy wig,
He went unto a farmer's house,
To choose a sucking pig.

"Good morning," says the Parson,
"O! good morning sir, to you,
I'm come to claim a sucking pig,
You know it is my due;
Therefore I pray go fetch me one,
That is both plump and fine,
Since I have asked a friend or two
Along with me to dine."

Then in the stye the farmer goes,
Amongst the pigs so small,
And chooses for the Parson,
The least amongst them all;
But when the Parson saw the same,
How he did ramp and roar,
He stamped his foot, and shook his wig,
And almost cursed and swore.

"O," then replied the farmer,
Since my offer you refuse,
I pray, sir, walk into the stye,
There you may pick and choose."
Then in the stye he ventured,
Without any more ado,
The old sow ran with open mouth,
And at the Parson flew.

O, then she caught him by the coat,
And took off both his skirts,
Then ran her head between her legs,
And threw him in the dirt;
The Parson cursed the very hour,
He ventured for the pig,
You'd laugh to see the young ones,
How they shook his hat and wig.

Then next she caught him by the breech
While he so loud did cry,
"O, hold me from this cursed sow,
Or I shall surely die."
The little pigs his waistcoat tore,
His stockings, and his shoes,
The farmer cries; "Your welcome, sir,
I hope you'll pick and choose."

At length he let the Parson out,
All in a handsome trim,
The sow and pigs so neatly
In the dirt had rolled him;
His coat was to a spencer turned,
His brogues was ripped, we find,
Besides his backside was all bare,
And his shirt hung out behind.

He lost his stockings and his shoes,
Which grieved him full sore,
Besides his waistcot, hat and wig,
Were all to pieces tore;
Away the Parson scampered home,
As fast as he could run,
The farmer almost split his sides,
With laughing at the fun.

The Parson's wife stood at the door
All waiting his return,
And when she saw his dirty plight
She into the house did turn;
"My dear what is the matter,
And where have you been?" she said.
"Get out, you Bitch," the Parson cryed,
For I am almost dead.

"Go fetch me down a suit of clothes,
Go fetch them down, I say,
And bring me my old greasy wig,
Without any more delay;
And for the usage I've received,
All in the cursed stye,
I ne'er shall relish sucking pig
Until the day I die."

The Gallant Poacher

The Agricultural Revolution which started in 1701 allowed foodstuff for the cities to grow, but, through the enclosure of lands, brought hardship to the countryside. Common folk who had hunted game freely over open fields now risked imprisonment, death, or transportation for following the same custom. Times were hard, as more crops were being produced by fewer men. There was hardship in the midst of plenty . . . and there was trouble.

Source: Text from a broadside by W. S. Fortey, General Steam Printer and Publisher, 2 & 3, Monmouth Ct., Seven Dials; tune from Dave Surman.

Recording: The Watersons, *A Yorkshire Garland*, Topic 12T167.

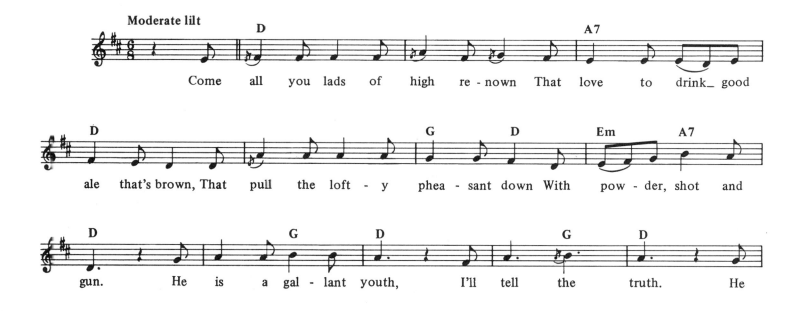

Moderate lilt

Come all you lads of high re-nown That love to drink_ good ale that's brown, That pull the loft-y phea-sant down With pow-der, shot and gun. He is a gal-lant youth, I'll tell the truth. He

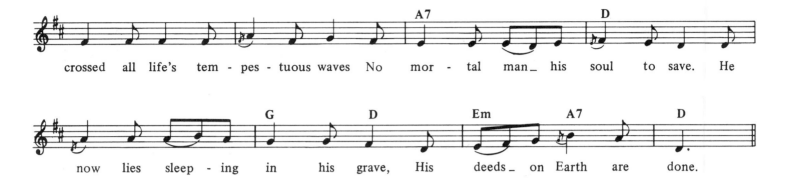

crossed all life's tem-pes-tuous waves No mor-tal man_ his soul to save. He

now lies sleep-ing in his grave, His deeds_ on Earth are done.

Come all you lads of high renown
That love to drink good ale that's brown,
That pull the lofty pheasant down
  With powder, shot and gun.
    He is a gallant youth,
    I'll tell the truth.
He crossed all life's tempestuous waves
No mortal man his soul to save.
He now lies sleeping in his grave,
  His deeds on Earth are done.

Me and five more a poaching went,
To kill some game was our intent.
Our money being gone and was all spent,
  We had nothing else to try.
    The moon shone bright,
    Not a cloud in sight.
The keeper heard us fire the gun;
To the spot he quickly run
And swore before the rising sun
  That one of us should die.

The bravest lad among the lot,
'Twas his misfortune to be shot.
His deeds shall never be forgot
  By all his friends below.
    For help he cried,
    But was denied.
His memory ever shall be blest;
He rose again to stand the test,
Whilst down upon his gallant breast
  The crimson blood did flow.

This youth, he fell upon the ground,
And in his breast a mortal wound.
While through the woods the gun did sound
  That took his life away.
    In the midst of life he fell,
    His sufferings are known full well.
Deep was the wound the keeper gave;
No mortal man his life could save.
He now lies sleeping in his grave
  Until the judgement day.

His case, it makes our heart's lament.
We comrades to the gaol were sent;
Our enemies seemed quite fully bent
  That there we should remain.
    But Fortune changed her mind
    And unto us proved kind!
Two more locked up in their midnight cells,
To hear the turnkeys boast their bells.
Those crackling doors we bid farewell
  And the rattling of those chains.

The murderous hand that did him kill
And on the ground his blood did spill
Must wander sore against his will
  And find no resting place.

Tatties an Herrin'

From the singing of Tom Spiers of Aberdeen; I believe he
had it from his father. A slightly satirical piece with a justi-
fiable pride in the fine staple food of the North-East coastal
towns and villages. This was when fish was very cheap! An
unusual song for the times, but with a fine chorus and dry
Scots tongue-in-cheek humor. The "roast beef devourers"
are, of course, the effete English!

Source: Allan Carr.
Recording: Ewan MacColl, *The Best of Ewan MacColl*,
Prestige International 13004.

Oh, your Scots work-in' man, he's gone cra-zy I fear. Ev-ery

day he mun' hae his bit beef an' his beer. Nae mair does he turn tae the

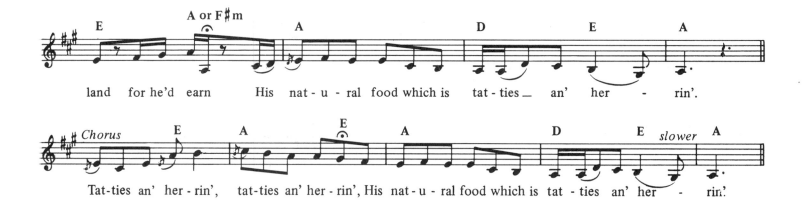

land   for he'd earn   His nat - u - ral food which is   tat - ties ___ an'   her - rin'.

Tat-ties an' her - rin',   tat-ties an' her - rin', His nat - u - ral food which is tat - ties an' her - rin'.

Tat - ties   an' her - rin',

Oh, your Scots working man he's gone crazy I fear
Every day he mun' hae his bit beef an' his beer
Nae mire dis he look tae the land far he'd earn
His natural food which is Tatties and Herrin'.

Tatties and Herrin', Tatties and Herrin'.
His natural food which is Tatties and Herrin'.

When the Queen's wantin' sodgers tae fecht wi' her foes,
It's no tae the roast beef devourers she goes.
But she looks tae the land o' the brave and the darin',
Tae the lads that were brocht up on Tatties and Herrin'.

Tatties and Herrin', Tatties and Herrin',
Tae the lads that were brocht up on Tatties and Herrin'.

Wi' ten bob in the week, ye can aye pay yer fee,
Wi' a tanner for baccy, two shillings fer ye.
Aye tho' it's nae much it'll aye pay yer fairin',
Wi' seven and sixpence for Tatties and Herrin'.

Tatties and Herrin', Tatties and Herrin',
Wi' seven and sixpence for Tatties and Herrin'.

When the Harbour O' Refuge wis first spoke aboot.
Aiberdeen and Stanehive they were fair pitten oot.
For the Queen kent her convicts wid get their best fairin',
Upon guid Buchan tatties and Peterheed herrin'.

Tatties and Herrin', Tatties and Herrin,'
Upon guid Buchan tatties and Peterheed herrin'.

Tony Barrand

The May Morning Dew

This song comes from Séamus Walker, one of a group of riotous Dublin singers who live in and around Boston. He remembers it from the Clare institution at the Tradition Club in Dublin—Siney Crotty. Shay sings this one as a true folk lyric. The song is short, the images concisely defined, the ornaments tight, and the presentation sweeping.

Source: Séamus Walker

Recording: John Lyons, *The May Morning Dew*, Topic 12TS248.

Dorian of A

How sweet it's in sum - mer to sit by the hob,

List - en - ing to the growls and the bark of a _____ dog _____

As you wan - der through the green _ fields where the wild _ dai - sies grew

Or to pluck the wild flow - ers in the May morn - ing dew.

m 13

wild _____ dai - sies

How sweet it's in summer to sit by the hob,
List'ning to the growls and the bark of a dog
As you wander through the green fields where the wild daisies grew
Or to pluck the wild flowers in the May morning dew.

Oh, summer is coming. Oh, summer is near,
With the trees all so green and the sky bright and clear.
And the birds they are singing. Their loved ones are winging
And the wild flowers are springing in the May morning dew.

God be with the old folks who are now dead and gone;
Likewise my two brothers, young Dennis and John,
As they trip through the heather, the wild heron persue
And the wild hare they hunted in the May morning dew.

The house I was raised in is a stone on a stone
And all 'round the garden wild thistles have grown
And to all the fine neighbors I once ever knew
Like the red rose have vanished in the May morning dew.

152

Napoleon!

The Devil and Bonaparte

Of the many songs about Napoleon, few are hostile.

Source: Text from a broadside by Wood of Birmingham;
tune is common.

"Good morrow, kind friend, it's for you I look.
Your name is recorded, the first in the book—
Bonaparte the great, what a wonder to tell!
A saint upon earth but a devil in hell."

Derry down, down, down derry down.

"Nay, hold Mr. Devil and do not torment.
I'm wicked it's true, yet there's time to repent."
"But sir, you're so hardened, I know it full well,
Your heart is quite callous, your portion is hell."

Derry down . . .

"Indeed Mr. Devil, I feel a great pain
But while I'm on Earth I'm determined to reign.
All laws I'll destroy, religion as well,
But pray Mr. Devil, what news comes from hell?"

"All hell is resounded to hear of your name,
Great Cromwell himself can't boast of such fame.
Tormented in fire, his crying does tell,
He was sovereign on Earth, but now subject in hell.

"Alexander and Caesar and Pompey and more,
When they was on Earth I did them adore,
But still their great projects and schemes you excell.
And so, my boy, you shall serve me in hell.

'Great Corsican despot, look back at deed,
You caused many thousand brave fellows to bleed.
You served me it's true and wonderful well,
You beat men on Earth that will beat you in hell.

'The clerk of my kingdom has penned every trick.
In Jaffa I read that you poisoned the sick
And turned to Mohammed, the Turks know it well.
But Mohammed will pay you when you go to hell.

"You talk of invading a kingdom it's ture,
But Britannia's brave sons will make you to rue.
The white cliffs of Albion you do not suit well,
In your flat bottom boats they'll send you to hell."

"Indeed, Mr. Devil, myself I'll not go,
Many thousands of French I'll send you know,
For if they're destroyed by Britons quite well,
You ought to reward me—not send me to hell.

"I've strove all my life your laws to obey
And acknowledge that over me you have the sway.
So now, Mr. Devil, pray leave me quite well,
I'm a torment on Earth, don't torment me in hell.

"Adieu," said the devil, "now from you I go
Down, down to my regions of darkness below."
He vanished in fire. Poor Boney, he fell
And cried out aloud, "Who will save me in hell?"

The Plains of Waterloo

The annual *Fleadh Cheoil na h-Eirann* is an orgy of music which serves as the competition platform to select "champions" in various age/instrument categories. Fr. Charlie Coen has represented New York well in years he's competed, wining gold medals for concertina, tinwhistle, flute, and singing. He suspects, incidentally, that being a cleric has had both a positive and adverse affect on his fortune.

Fr. Charlie learned this song at the 1977 *Fleadh* from a west Clare flute player, John Flanagan. Many songs have this title, but this one is alone in that the soldier fought *with* Bonaparte. Such, the London broadside printer, had a different version, which closed with

So unto George our gracious King, my voice I mean to raise,
And to all gallant commanders I wish to sing their praise,
The Duke of York and family, and Wellington also,
And all the soldiers brave that fought that day, on the plains of Waterloo.

Source: Fr. Charles Coen.

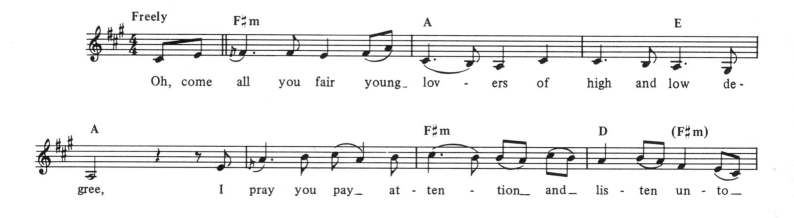

me.   It's all a - bout_ a young_ man_ and his tale I'll_ tell to_

you,   How he fought in Spain and _ Por - tu - gal and was slain at Wa - ter - loo. __

ms 2,14

lov - ers of
Por - tu - gal and was

ms 6 and 7,10 and 11

ten - tion and___ lis - ten ___ un - to ___
young___ man and ___ his tale I'll ___ tell to ___

Oh, come all you fair young lovers of high and low degree,
I pray you pay attention and listen unto me.
It's all about a young man and his tale I'll tell to you,
How he fought in Spain and Portugal and all slain at Waterloo.

This young man that I speak about, he was proper tall and thin.
He's mild in his behavior, he's complete in every limb.
His cheeks they were a rosy red and his eyes a sparkling blue.
Ah, there's no one here that I would compare with my love at
  Waterloo.

My love, he was a soldier with his knapsack and his gun;
When Ireland fell and traitors roved, his rambles first begun.
To Bonaparte he was faithful and he wore the soldiers' blue,
How little he thought that would be his lot, to be slain at Waterloo.

When bonny stars were in the sky, my love he want away.
He told me that he loved me and would marry me someday.
He stood upright with his sword so bright, like the timeless one so
  true.
Ah, but now he lies with sightless eyes on the plains of Waterloo.

When Bathurst was taken and our leaders all were dead,
The plains around with carnage lay to show how much we'd bled.
Ten thousand men lay in their gore and those that ran were few,
Ah, but we marched on to fight once more on the plains of Waterloo.

And it's many the river I have crossed, through water and through
  mud,
And many the battle I have fought though ankle deep in blood
Though heart and home were calling me, I left them all for you,
To see you fight for our land once more, on the plains of Waterloo.

And if I can't have the man I love, no man on earth I'll take.
Down lonely roads and shady groves, I'll wander for his sake;
Down lonely roads and shady groves, o'er hills and valleys too,
I'll wander far for my love was slain on the plains of Waterloo.

The Mantle So Green

The hill on our front was fringed by the enemy's cannon, and we advanced to our new position amid a shower of shot and shells . . . . We halted and formed square in the middle of the plain. As we were performing this movement, a bugler of the fifty-first, who had been out with skirmishers, and had mistaken our square for his own, exclaimed, 'Here I am again, safe enough.' The words were scarcely out of his mouth, when a round shot took off his head and spattered the whole battalion with his brains, the colours and the ensigns in charge of them coming in for an extra share. One of them, Charles Fraser, a fine gentleman in speech and manner, raised a laugh by drawling out, "How extremely disgusting!" A second shot carried off six of the men's bayonets, a third broke the breastbone of Lance-Sergeant Robinson. These casualties were the affair of a second."—Ensign Keppel, the fourteenth Regiment of Foot Guards.

Source: Text from a broadside; tune learned from Margaret Barry.
Recording: Margaret Barry, *Her Mantle So Green*, Topic 12T123.

157

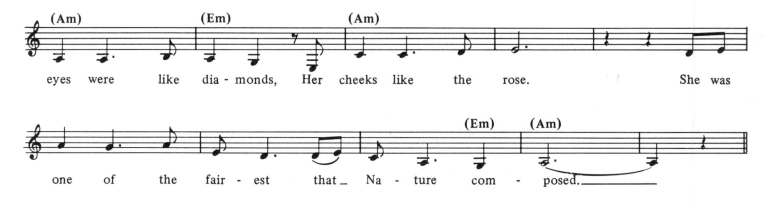

eyes were like dia - monds, Her cheeks like the rose. She was

one of the fair - est that __ Na - ture com - posed. _____

As I went a-walking one morning in June
To view the fields and the meadows in bloom,
I espied a young damsel, she appeared like a queen,
With her costly fine robes and her mantle so green.
I stood with amazement and was struck with surprise.
I thought her an angel that fell from the skies.
Her eyes were like diamonds, her cheeks like the rose.
She was one of the fairiest that Nature composed.

I said, "My pretty fair maid, if you'll come with me,
We'll both join in wedlock and married we'll be.
I'll dress in rich attire, you'll appear like a queen
With your costly fine robes and your mantle so green."
She answered me, "Young man, you must me excuse,
For I'll wed with no man. You must be refused.
To the woods I will wander and shun all men's views,
For the lad that I love lies in famed Waterloo."

"Well, if you won't marry, tell me your lover's name,
For I, being in battle, just might know the same."
"Draw near to my garment and there will be seen
His name all embroidered on my mantle so green."
In raising her mantle I did there behold
His first name and surname in letters of gold.
William O'Reilly appeared to my view—
"He was my chief comrade in famed Waterloo!

"We fought so victorious where wild bullets did fly.
In the field of high honour your true love does lie.
We fought for three days till the fourth afternoon,
He received his death summons on the eighteenth of June.
When he was dying, I heard his last cry,
'If you were here, Nancy, contented I'd die!'
Peace is proclaimed. The truth I declare.
Here is the love token, the gold ring I wear."

She stood in amazement and paler she grew.
She flew to my arms with a heart full of woe.
"To the woods I will wander for the lad I adore."
"Rise up, lovely Nancy, your faith I'll restore.
Oh, Nancy, dearest Nancy, 'tis I won your heart
In your father's garden that day we did part."

The Green Linnet

Maria Louisa's lamentation, a song both Dick Gaughan and
Joe Heaney sing very well. Joe has his version from the late
Willie Claney of Miltown Malbay. Co. Clare, one of the
finest uillean pipers and most loved musicians of his time.

Source: Text from a broadside by Disley; tune learned from
the singing of Dick Gaughan.

Recordings: Dick Gaughan, *No More Forever*, Trailer LER
2072. Joe Heaney, *Joe Heaney*, Philo 2004

Mixolydian of D

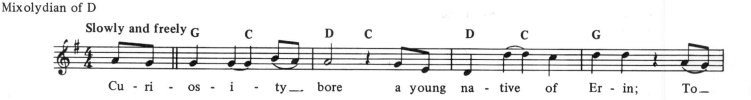

Cu - ri - os - i - ty __ bore a young na - tive of Er - in; To __

view the gay banks of the Rhine, When an em-press he saw and the robe she was wear-ing All o-ver with dia-monds did shine. A god-dess in splen-dor was nev-er yet seen, To e-qual this fair one so mild and se-rene, In soft mur-mur she says, "My sweet lin-net so green, Are you gone, will I nev-er see you more?"

Curiosity bore a young native of Erin
To view the gay banks of the Rhine,
When an empress he saw and the robe she was wearing
All over with diamonds did shine.
A goddess in splendor was never yet seen,
To equal this fair one so mild and serene,
In soft murmur she says, "My sweet linnet so green,
Are you gone, will I never see you more?

"The cold, lofty Alps you freely went over,
Which Nature had placed in your way,
That Maringo, Saloney, around you did hover,
And Paris did rejoice the next day,
It grieves me the hardships you did undergo,
Over mountains you travelled all covered with snow
The balance of power your courage laid low,
Are you gone, will I never see you more?

"The crowned heads of Europe when you were in splendor
Fair they would have you submit,
But the Goddess of freedom soon bid them surrender
And lowered the standard to your wit,
Old Frederick's colours in France you did bring,
Yet his offspring found shelter under your wing,
That year in Vienna you sweetly did sing,
Are you gone, will I never see you more?

"That numbers of men are eager to slay you,
Their malice you viewed with a smile,
Their gold thro' all Europe they sowed to betray you,
And they joined the Mamelukes on the Nile,
Like Ravens for blood their vile passion did burn,
The orphans they slew and caused their widows to mourn.
They say my green linnet's gone and ne'er will return,
Is he gone will I never see him more?

"In great Waterloo, where numbers lay sprawling,
In every field high and low,
Fame on her trumpets thro' Frenchmen were calling,
Fresh laurels to place on her brow.
Usurpers did tremble to hear the loud call,
The third old Babe's new building did fall,
The Spaniards their fleet in the harbour did call,
Are you gone, I will never see you more?

"I roam thro' the deserts of wild Abyssinia,
And yet find no cure for my pain.
Will I go and enquire in the Isle of St. Helena,
No, we will whisper in vain.
Tell me you critics, now tell me in time,
The nation I will range, my sweet linnet to find,
Was he slain at Waterloo, at Elba, on the Rhine?
No, he's dead on St. Helena's bleak shore."

Napoleon Bonaparte

I heard this one sung by Patsy Whelan, a fiddler and guitarist,
a few years back up in Boston. It was at a real marathon
event; a Margaret Barry concert preceded by guest spots
from seemingly a thousand singers and musicians, all of
whom pressed or were pressed into service for the occasion.
Patsy was in the latter group and got a really big hand for
this song.

Source: Text from a broadside; tune learned from the singing of Patsy Whelan.

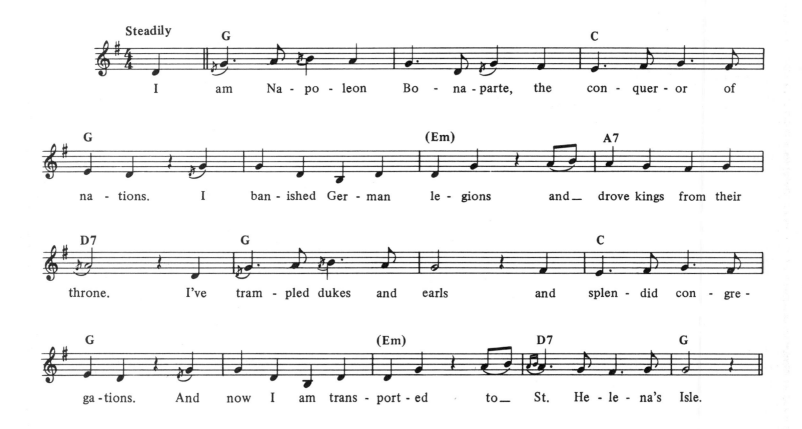

I am Na-po-leon Bo-na-parte, the con-quer-or of na-tions. I ban-ished Ger-man le-gions and drove kings from their throne. I've tram-pled dukes and earls and splen-did con-gre-ga-tions. And now I am trans-port-ed to St. He-le-na's Isle.

I am Napoleon Bonaparte the conquerer of nations
I banished German legions and drove kings from their throne.
I've trampled dukes and earls and splendid congregations.
And now I am transported to St. Helena's Isle.

Like a Hannibal I crossed the Alps o'er burning sands and rocky
    cliffs,
O'er Russian hills, through frost and snow and still the laurel bore.
Now I'm on a desert isle, the very devil it would fright.
I thought to shine in armour bright through Europe once more.

My spread eagles were pulled down by Wellington's bold army.
My troops, in disorder, could no longer stand the field.
It was said that afternoon on the eighteenth day of June;
My reinforcements proved traitors which forced me for to yield.

Ah! though I'm in the allied yoke with fire and sword I'd make the
    smoke,
For I conquered Dutch and Danes and surprised the Grand Signor.
I beat the Russians, Austrians, the Portuguese and Prussians
As Joshua Alexander and the great Ceasars of yore.

Some say it was my first downfall, the parting of my consort
And to wed the German's daughter, which grieved my heart full sore.
The female train I do not blame, they never yet did me defame.
They saw my sword in battle flame and then did me adore.

Sincerely I do feel the rod for meddling with the house of God.
In coining golden images, some thousands away I bore.
The sacrilege grieves me much for robbing of the Christian Church,
But had they gave me time and place I would it all restore.

Unto the south of Africa, unto the Atlantic Ocean,
To view the wild emotion and flowing of the tide,
I was banished from my royal throne of imperial promotion,
From the French throne of glory to see the billows glide.

Libert's cause I did maintain for full three days on Waterloo's plain,
Many thousand troops I left slain and Wellington did annoy.
I did not fly without revenge nor from their allied army cringe,
But now my sword is full sheathed and Bony is no more.

The Grand Conversation on Napoleon

Napoleon's popularity in Ireland and Britain came not so much from his military success but from his legitimizing the dream of ambition. He was sensational! As the song says, "He caused the money for to fly wherever he did go."

Source: Text from a broadside by Disley; tune from Mick Moloney.

Recording: Tony Rose, *Under the Greenwood Tree*, Trailer LER 2024.

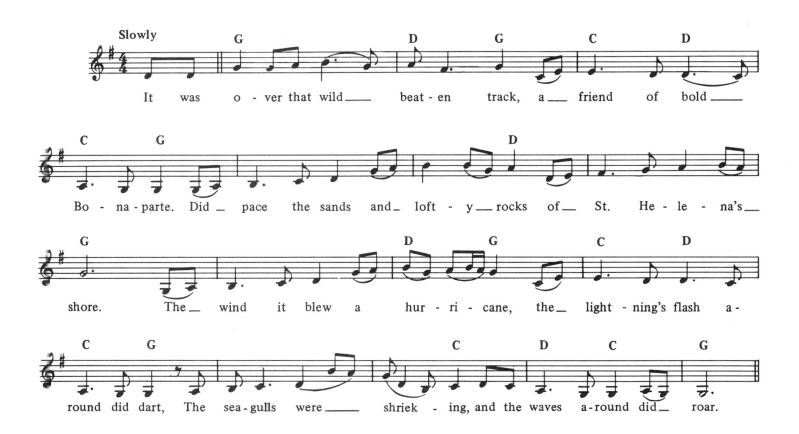

It was over that wild beaten track, a friend of bold Bonaparte,
Did pace the sands and lofty rocks of St. Helena's shore.
The wind it blew a hurricane, the lightning's flash around did dart,
The sea-gulls were shreiking, and the waves around did roar.

Ah! hush, rude winds the stranger cried awhile I range the dreary spot,
Where last a gallant hero his envied eyes did close.
But while his valued limbs do rot, his name will never be forgot,
This grand conversation on Napoleon arose.

Ah England! he cried, you did persecute that hero bold,
Much better had you slain him on the plains of Waterloo;
Napoleon he was a friend to heros all, both young and old,
He caused the money for to fly wherever he did go.

When plans were ranging night and day, the bold commander to betray,
He cried, I'll go to Moscow, and then 'twill ease my woes,
If fortune shines without delay, then all the world shall me obey;
This grand conversation on Napoleon arose.

Mick Moloney Photo by David Gahr

Thousands of men he then did rise, to conquer Moscow by surprise,
He led his men across the Alps, oppressed by frost and snow,
But being near the Russian land, he then began to open his eyes,
For Moscow was a burning and the men drove to and fro.

Napoleon dauntless viewed the flame, and wept in anguish for the
  same,
He cried, retreat my gallant men, for time so swiftly goes;
What thousands died on that retreat, some forced their horses for to
  eat;
This grand conversation on Napoleon arose.

At Waterloo his men they fought, commanded by great Bonaparte,
Attended by field-marshall Ney, and he was bribed with gold;
When Blueher led the Prussians in, it nearly broke Napoleon's heart,
He cried, my thirty thousand men are killed, and I am sold.

He viewed the plain, and cried it's lost, he then his favorite charger
  crossed,
The plain was in confusion with blood and dying woes.
The bunch of roses did advance, and boldly entered into France—
This grand conversation on Napoleon arose.

But Bonaparte was planned to be a prisoner across the sea
The rocks of St. Helena, it was the fatal spot,
And as a prisoner there to be, till death did end his misery.
His son soon followed to the tomb, it was an awful plot.

And long enough they have been dead, the blast of war is round us
  spread,
And may our shipping floar again, to face the daring foe;
And now my boys when honour calls, we'll boldly mount the
  wooden walls;
This grand conversation on Napoleon did close.

The Bonnie Bunch of Roses

*"I urge my son never to forget that he was born a French
prince, and never to lend himself to the triumvirate which
oppresses the people of Europe. In no way is he to fight or
harm France. He is to adopt my own device: Everything
for the French people.*

*I die before my time, murdered by the English oligarchy
. . . . The people of England will avenge me all too soon."*
—Napoleon. April 15, 1821. St. Helena.

Source: Dáithí Sproule.

Recording: Seamus Ennis, *The Bonny Bunch of Roses*,
Tradition TLP 1013.

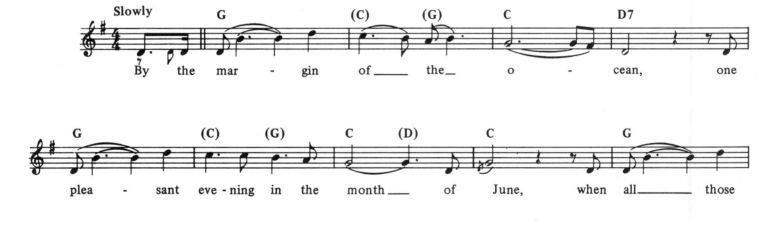

By the mar - gin of the o - cean, one

plea - sant eve - ning in the month of June, when all those

plea - sant song - sters their li - quid notes did

By the margin of the ocean, one pleasant evening in the month of June,
When all those pleasant songsters their liquid notes did sweetly tune,
'Twas there I met with a female, who seemed to be in grief or woe,
Conversing with young Bonaparte, concerning the Bonnie Bunch of Roses O.

Then up spake young Napoleon, and took his mother by the hand,
Saying, "Mother dear, be patient until I'm able for to take command;
And I'll build a mighty army, and through tremendous dangers go.
And I never will return again until I've conquered the Bonnie Bunch of Roses, O."

"When first you saw great Bonaparte, you knelt upon your bended knee,
And asked your father's life of him and he granted it right manfully.
'Twas then he took his army, and o'er frozen Alps did go,
Saying, "I never will return again until I've conquered the Bonnie Bunch of Roses, O."

"He took ten hundred thousand men, and kings likewise for to bear his train,
He was so well provided for, that he could sweep the world for gain;
But when he came to Moscow, he was overpowered by the sleet and snow,
And with Moscow all a-blazing, sure he lost the Bonnie Bunch of Roses, O."

"Oh son, be not too venturesome, for England is the heart of oak,
And England, Ireland, and Scotland, their unity shall ne'er be broke;
Remember your dear father, in Saint Helena he lies low,
And if ever you follow after, beware the Bonnie Bunch of Roses, O."

"O mother, dearest mother, now I lie on my dying bed,
If I lived I'd have been clever, but now I droop my youthful head;
And when our bones lie mouldering and weeping willows o'er us grow,
The name of young Napoleon shall enshrine the Bonnie Bunch of Roses, O."

163

Love

The Flower of France and England O!

Glascow Police Superindendent John Ord included **The Flower of France and England O!** in his great collection, *Bothy Songs and Ballads*, though inexplicably, in the section of "Songs of the Forsaken and Jilted."

Ord has the following note: "This song from the reference in the third verse to Carlisle being 'full of rebels' evidently dates back to the Rebellion of 1745. I have never heard the song but once, and that was about forty-five years ago [ca. 1885] at a farm-house in Aberdeenshire." Gavig Greig had a text which referred to "revels" rather than "rebels."

Source: Text is a collation; tune learned from the singing of Archie Fisher.

Recording: Archie Fisher, *Will Ye Gang, Love*, Topic 12TS277.

Pentatonic

As I was on my rambles,
I came from Dover to Carlisle.
The town was full of rebels;
You could hear them for a mile.
I called at "The Grapes" to see
What entertainment I could find;
And being brisk, I ran the risk,
And I called for a pint o' wine
And saw a smiling bonny lass,
The flower of France and England O!

As all were in a hurry,
I for a private room did call.
They sent to me the cadie,
The boy that rings the morning bell.
But in there came this brisk young dame,
And said, "Kind sir, please follow me;
It is not fit for you to sit.
Among such roving company.
The hearty, smiling, bonny lass,
The flower of France and England O!

She led me to a private room,
Where everything was neat and clean,
And said, "Young man, it is not fit
You should have something on to dine."
The table soon she covered o'er
And dinner then she did bring in.
She looked not like an idle slut
Nor one that was not taught to spin,
The hearty, smiling, bonny lass,
The flower of France and England O!

166

But I could take no dinner
For thinking on the pretty maid
And, if I could but win her,
I would not care how long I stayed.
I rang the bell, she heard the knell
And soon to me she did repair,
I said, "My dear, the table's drawn,
Sit down by me on this chair;
My hearty, smiling, bonny lass,
The flower of France and England O!

She said, "Young man, you are as bad
As any in the house to-night,
For they are drunk and you are mad
Or else you would not speak the like,
Take up the cup and drink it up
And drive such fancies out by sleep
For if you dream you had me well,
I'm sure you would rise up and weep."
The hearty, smiling, bonny lass,
The flower of France and England O!

I could not fall a-sleeping.
For thinking on the bonny lass,
That spent her name a-scouting
Among the pewter and the brass.
I rang the bell, she heard the knell,
And soon to me she did repair;
Said I, "We'll to St. Mary's Church
And there we will undo our care,
My hearty, smiling, bonny lass,
The flower of France and England O!"

We went unto St. Mary's,
And there the priest the knot did tie:
I brought her home my bonny bride
As fast as ever I could hie.
Through Scotland broad we took the road,
Until we came to Balquhidder braes.
The servants all did skip and dance
To see their Lord and Lady's face.
The hearty, smiling, bonny lass,
The flower of France and England O!

We spent some days a-feasting
Among our friends and neighbours all,
The bride did think't no jesting
When they did on the lady call.
Now she's a lady frank and free,
And needs no more to toil or spin
And all her friends may bless the day
That e'er I came "The Grapes" within,
And met the smiling, bonny lass,
The flower of France and England O!

Matt Hyland

A beautiful Ulster love song I got from Tony Callanan of "Stockton's Wing." Tony was quick to point out that, as lovestruck as Matt was, he still had the presence of mind to collect his pay prior to departure.

Source: Learned from Tony Callanan.

Recording: Frank Harte, *Through Dublin City,* Topic 12T218.

There was a Lord lived in the North, who had a ver-y love-ly daugh-ter. She was court-ed by a hand-some man, who was a serv-ant to her fa-ther, But, when her par-ents came to know, they

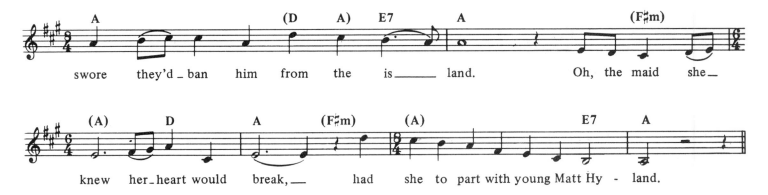

swore they'd ban him from the is____ land. Oh, the maid she__

knew her heart would break,___ had she to part with young Matt Hy - land.

There was a Lord lived in the North, who had a very lovely daughter.
She was courted by a handsome man, who was a servant to her father
But, when her parents came to know, they swore they'd ban him from the island.
Oh, the maid she knew her heart would break, had she to part with young Matt Hyland.

So straightway to her love she went and then into his room to wake him.
Saying, "Rise my love and go away. This very night you will be taken.
I overheard my parents say, in spite of me they would transport you,
So rise, my love, and go away. I wish to God I'd gone before you."

They both sat down upon the bed all for the sight of one another.
And not one word did either speak till down her cheeks the tears did shower.
She lay her head upon his breast, around his neck her arms entwined then.
"Not a Duke nor Lord nor Earl I'll wed. I'll wait for you my own Matt Hyland."

"How can I go away my love? How can I leave without my wages,
Without one penny of my own, just like some low and lonesome vagrant?"
"Here's twenty guineas in bright bold. That's far much more than father owes you,
So take it, love, and go away. You know right well I do adore you."

Oh the Lord conversed with his daughter fair one night above in her bed chamber.
"I'll give you leave to bring him back, since there's no one can win your favour."
She wrote a letter then in haste, for him her heart was still repining.
They brought him back, to the church they went, and made a Lord of young Matt Hyland.

The Blacksmith

A tight folk lyric about love misplaced, in tone not unlike any number of Appalachian banjo songs.

Source: Text from a Henry Parker Such broadside; tune is commonly sung.

Recording: Planxty, *Planxty*, Polydor 2383 186.

Dorian of E

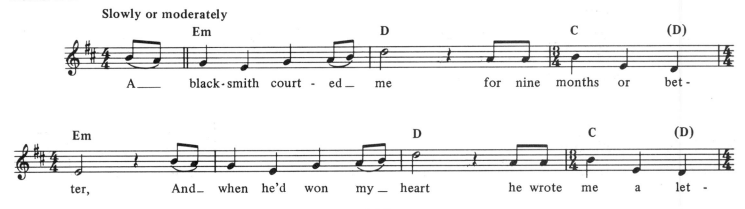

Slowly or moderately

A____ black-smith court - ed__ me for nine months or bet-

ter, And__ when he'd won my__ heart he wrote me a let-

ter, With his ham - mer in his _ hand he _ looks so clev -

er, Was _ I _____ with my _ love I could live _ for - ev - er.

A blacksmith courted me for nine months or better.
And when he'd won my heart he wrote me a letter,
With his hammer in his hand he looks so clever,
Was I with my love I could live forever.

"It's not what you promised when you did lie by me,
You said you'd marry me and never deny me."
"If I said I'd marry you it was only to try you
So bring your witness in and I'll not deny you."

Witness I have none but the Almighty,
And he'll surely punish you for slighting of me.
Looking in the glass makes my poor heart tremble,
To think I loved a man who proved deceitful.

My love's across the fields with cheeks like roses,
My love's across the fields seeking primroses,
I'm afraid the scorching sun will spoil his beauty,
If I was with my love he would do his duty.

Strange news has come to me, strange news is carried,
And now, it's all the talk, my love is married,
I wish them both much joy, though they can't hear me,
I never shall die for love, young men believe me.

The Banks of the Bann (The Brown Girl)

The Bann River rises in the Mourne Mountains no more than ten miles from the Irish Sea, but flows northward over a hundred miles through Lough Neagh and out into the Atlantic Ocean.

The song has been quite a traveler too. It's been collected in England and as far away as the Maritimes of Canada.

Source: Séan Cannon.

Recording. A. L. Lloyd, *The Best of A. L. Lloyd*, Prestige International 13066.

Fairly slowly

When _ first _____ to this coun - try a _ stran - ger I _

came, I _ placed my af - fec - tion with a come - ly young _

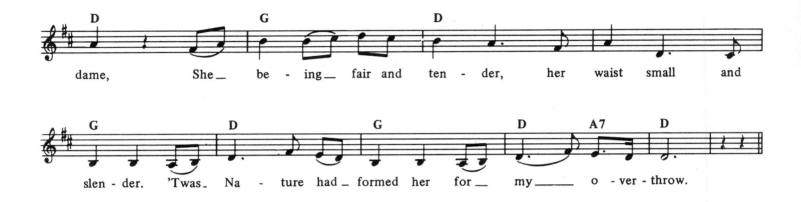

dame, She— be - ing— fair and ten - der, her waist small and

slen - der. 'Twas— Na - ture had— formed her for — my——— o - ver - throw.

m 5

placed my af -

m 10

ten - der her

When first to this country a stranger I came,
I placed my affection with a comely young dame,
She being fair and tender, her waist small and slender.
'Twas Nature had formed her for my overthrow.

On the banks of the Bann, it was there I first met her.
She appeared like an angel or Egypt's fair queen.
Her eyes like the diamonds or stars brightly shining,
She's one of the fairest in the world that I've seen.

Now, it was her cruel parents that first caused our variance
Because they are rich and above my degree,
But I do endeavour to gain my love's favour,
Although she is come from a high family.

Now, my name it is Delaney—it's a name that won't shame me—
And if I'd saved money I'd never have roamed,
But drinking and sporting, night rambling and courting
Are the cause of my ruin and absence from home.

Well, if I had all the riches there are in the Indies,
I'd put rings on her fingers and gold in her ears,
And ever on the banks of that lovely Bann River
In all kinds of splendour I'd live with my dear.

Repeat first verse

Lovely Willie

Dáithí Sproule sang this song for me one cold night in the winter farmland of New Jersey. Dáithí, James Kelly, and Paddy O'Brien spent about six months in the U. S. during 1978 and made a nice record for Shanachie while over.

Lovely Willie was learned from John Healy, who probably got it from Kevin Mitchell, an Ulster singer who now lives in Glasgow.

In the United States, the ballad's been collected in Maine, Michigan, and Missouri.

Source: Dáithí Sproule.

Recordings: Dáithí Sproule, *"Is It Yourself?"* Shanachie 29015. Paddy Tunney, *Singing Men of Ulster,* Green Linnet SIF 1005.

Oh, it happened one evening at the playing of ball
That I first met lovely Willie so proper and tall.
He was neat, fair and handsome and straight in every limb.
There's a heart in this bosom lies breaking for him.

"And will you go with me a short piece of the road
For to view my father's dwelling and place of abode?"
Well he knew by her look and her languishing eye
That he was the young man she valued most high.

"There a house in my father's garden, lovely Willie," said she,
"Where lords, dukes and earls they await upon me
And when they are sleeping in their long silent rest,
It's then I'll go with you. You're the boy I love best."

But her father being listening, in ambush he lay
For to hear the fond words these true lovers did say.
And with a sharp rapier he pierced her love through
And the innocent blood of her Willie he drew.

So, the grave it being dug and lovely Willie laid in,
The mass it was chanted for to cleanse his soul from sin.
And it's "Oh, honoured father, you may speak as you will,
But the innocent blood of my love you did spill."

So, I will go off to some foreign country,
Where I shall know no one and no one knows me,
And there I will wander till I close my eyes in death.
All for you my lovely Willie; you're the boy I love best.

Moorlough Mary

A real Ulster song closely associated with one of its finest singers, Paddy Tunney.

Source: Text from a broadsheet printed by Such; tune learned from the singing of Paddy Tunney.

Recording: Paddy Tunney, *The Man of Songs*, Folk-Legacy FSE-1.

Pentatonic

The first time I saw you, Moor-lough Mar-y, Was in the mar-ket of sweet Stra-bane, Her smil-ing coun-te-nance was so en-gag-ing, The hearts of young men she did tre-pan. Her kill-ing glanc-es be-reaved my sens-es Of peace and com-fort by

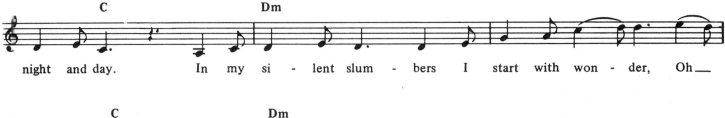

night and day. In my si - lent slum - bers I start with won - der, Oh___

Moor - lough Mar - y, won't you come a - way?

The first time I saw you, Moorlough Mary,
Was in the market of sweet Strabane,
Her smiling countenance was so engaging,
The hearts of young men she did trepan.
Her killing glances bereaved my senses
Of peace and comfort by night and day.
In my silent slumbers I start with wonder,
Oh, Moorlough Mary, won't you come away?

To see my darling on a summer's morning,
When Flora's fragrance bedecks the lawn,
Her neat deportment and manner courteous,
Around her sporting the lamb and fawn.
On her I ponder where'er I wander,
And still grow fonder, dear maid, of thee,
By thy matchless charms I am enamoured,
Oh, Moorlough Mary, won't you come away?

Now, I'll away to my situation
Though recreation is all in vain,
On the river Mourne where lambkins sport,
The rocks re-echoing my plaintive strain.
I'll press my cheese while my wool's a-teasing,
My ewes I'll milk by the peep o'day,
The whirring moorcock and the lark alarms me,
Oh, Moorlough Mary, won't you come away?

On Moorlough's banks I will never wander,
Where heifers graze on a pleasant soil,
Where lambkins sporting, fair maids resorting,
The timorous hare and blue heather bell.
The thrush and blackbird will join harmonious,
Their notes melodious on the river brae,
And the little small birds will join the chorus,
Oh, Moorlough Mary, won't you come away?

Were I a man of great education,
Or Erin's Isle at my own command,
I'd lay me down on her milk-white bosom,
In wedlock's bands, love, we'd join our hands.
I'd entertain thee both night and morning,
With robes I'd deck thee both night and day,
With kisses sweet, love, I would embrace you,
Oh, Moorlough Mary, won't you come away?

Farewell my charming young Moorlough Mary,
Ten thousand times I bid you adieu,
While life remains in my glowing bosom,
I'll never cease, love, to think of you.
Now, I'll away to some lonely valley,
With tears bewailing both night and day,
To some silent arbour where none can hear me,
Oh, Moorlough Mary, won't you come away?

Tibbie Dunbar

Burns wrote the words for **Tibbie Dunbar** in 1789 at the age of thirty. The air is **Johnie McGill**, said to be the composition of a fiddler by the same name from the coastal town of Girvan in Burns's native Ayrshire.

Declan Hunt, who's recorded rebel songs for Outlet and Rounder and who once contested (unsuccessfully) the mayorality of Newburyport, Massachusetts, taught me this song. The second verse isn't in Burns's poem. Decky says, "It's just around, you know."

Source: Declan Hunt.

Recording: Dan Milner, *Traditional Music from Ireland, England and Scotland*, Adelphi AD 1029.

Tibbie Dunbar

Fairly slowly

Oh, will you go with me, sweet Tibbie Dunbar? Oh, will you go with me, sweet Tibbie Dunbar? Will you ride on a horse or be drawn in a car Or walk by my side, sweet Tibbie Dunbar? I care not your daddie his lands or his money. I care not your kin, so high and so lordly, But say you'll go with me for better or worse And come in my coatie, sweet Tibbie Dunbar.

Oh, will you go with me, sweet Tibbie Dunbar?
Oh, will you go with me, sweet Tibbie Dunbar?
Will you ride on a horse or be drawn in a car
Or walk by my side, sweet Tibbie Dunbar?
I care not your daddie, his lands or his money.
I care not your kin, so high and so lordly,
But say you'll go with me for better or worse
And come in my coatie, sweet Tibbie Dunbar.

Oh, will you go with me sweet Tibbie Dunbar?
Oh, will you go with me sweet Tibbie Dunbar?
Will you ride on a horse or be drawn in a car
Or walk by my side, sweet Tibbie Dunbar.
I care not your daddie, his lands or his money.
I care not your kin, so high and so lordly,
But say you'll go with me for better or worse
And come in my coatie, sweet Tibbie Dunbar.

I offer you nothing in silver or land.
What man can determine the price of your hand?
But give your consent you'll be better by far.
Oh, say that you'll have me sweet Tibbie Dunbar!
Oh, will you be known as a poor beggar's lady
And sleep in the heather rolled up in my plaidie,
A sky for your roof and your candle a star,
My love for your fire, sweet Tibbie Dunbar?

The Flower of Magherally

Local songs of this sort, praising women, men horses,
scenery, and the like are quite common all over Ireland,
and to prove it we've included two more.

Source: Cathal McConnell.

Recording: Cathal McConnell, *Live at Passims*, Philo 1026.

175

sum - mer's ___
was a ___

she's the

One pleasant summer's morning when the birds were all a-singing O.
Nature was adorning and the flowers were all a springing O.
I met my girl near Banbridge town, my charming blue-eyed
  Sally O,
She's the queen of the County Down, and my flower of Magherally O.

With admiration I did gaze, all on this fair-eyed maiden O,
Adam was not half so much pleased when he saw Eve in Eden O.
Her skin was like the lily white, that grows in yonder valley O.
And she's the girl that I adore, my flower of Magherally O.

Her bonnet with two ribbons strung, her shoes were Spanish leather
  O.
Her golden hair in ringlets clung, her scarlet cap and feather O.
Like Venus bright she did appear, my charming blue-eyed Sally O.
And she's the girl that I adore, my flower of Magherally O.

I hope the day will surely come when we join hands together O,
And I will wed the girl I love, let there be stormy weather O.
And let them all say what they will, and let them storm or rally O,
For I will wed the girl I love, my flower of Magherally O.

The Flower of Sweet Strabane

Strabane's an old linen town in Co. Tyrone, but the object
of affection in this song could be from anywhere in Ireland
(indeed Co. Kildare as in the next song!). These words are
from Aberdeenshire. The tune is another very pretty one,
the same as **The Banks Of The Nile.**

Source: Text from G. Greig, *Folk Songs of the North-East*;
tune learned from Margaret Barry.

Recordings: Margaret Barry, *Her Mantle So Green*, Topic
12T123. Paddy Tunney, *A Wild Bees' Nest*, Topic 12T139.

Dorian of A

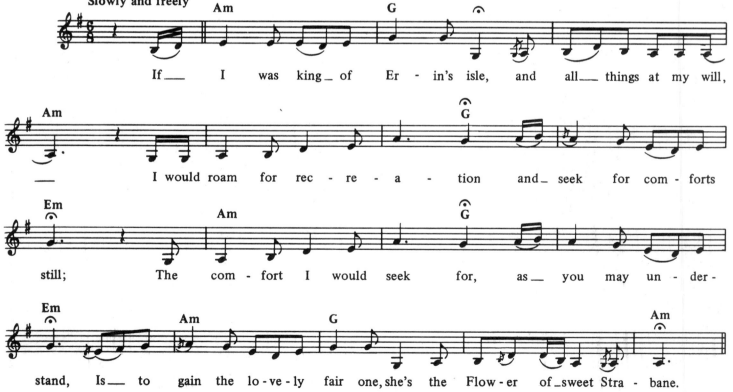

Slowly and freely

If ___ I was king ___ of Er - in's isle, and all ___ things at my will,

___ I would roam for rec - re - a - tion and ___ seek for com - forts

still; The com - fort I would seek for, as ___ you may un - der-

stand, Is ___ to gain the lo - ve - ly fair one, she's the Flow - er of ___ sweet Stra - bane.

176

Margaret Barry

If I was king of Erin's isle, and all things at my will,
I would roam for recreation, and seek for comforts still;
The comfort I would seek for, as you may understand,
Is to gain the lovely fair one, she's the Flower of sweet Strabane.

Her cheeks they are of rosy red, her eyes a lovely brown
And o'er her lily-white shoulders her yellow hair hangs down.
She is one of the rarest creatures, the treasure of her clan,
And my heart is captivated by the Flower of sweet Strabane.

Once I was in the Phoenix Park, the fairest of the fair;
The lonesome braes of Scotland, and the lovely banks of Ayr;
And in all my lonesome travels I never yet met one,
I do declare, whom I could compare to the Flower of sweet Strabane.

I wish I had my darling girl safe down by Ennishown,
Or in some lonesome valley near the green woods of Tyrone;
I would make my whole endeavour, and work the nearest plan,
For to gain that lovely fair one,—She's the Flower of sweet Strabane.

Farewell unto you Liverpool, Newmills, and Waterside;
My mind is on the ocean whatever may betide.
I sailed away from Derry quay, down by the Isle of Man;
And I bid adieu to Molly, she's the Flower of sweet Strabane.

Erin the Green

Seán Cannon, a Galwayman now living in Barnsley, Yorkshire, sang **Erin The Green** for me in London a couple of
years ago. He has a lovely tenor voice. "Like a lark," Mick
Moloney says.

You'll find one more verse in Robin Morton's *Folk Songs
Sung in Ulster*, though these are the best.

Source: Seán Cannon.

Recording: Frank Harte, *And Listen to My Song*, Ram
RMLP 1013.

Slowly and freely

Oh, draw _ near each young_ lov - er, give ear
to my _ dit - ty _ That _ bears _ my _ sad,_
mourn - ful tale. Come _ join me in _ con - sort and

177

Oh, draw near each young lover, give ear to my ditty
That bears my sad, mournful tale.
Come join me in consort and lend me your pity
Whilst I my misfortune bewail.
The grief of my poor heart no tongue can disclose;
My cheeks are now pale that once bloomed like a rose.
And it's all for a young man whom I do suppose
Is now far from sweet Erin the green.

Now, when we were children we walked out together
Along the green meadows so neat
And, although we were childish, we loved one another
While gathering the wild berries sweet.
It was to sweet Garvagh we were sent to school.
He was first in his class and correct in each rule.
And I cheerfully walked home by Kilnacoole,
With the flower of sweet Erin the green.

Ah! His head on my bosom he used to reposed
Each evening in under the shade.
A song in my praises my darling composed
And styled me the cool Derry maid.
At the time I denied him I'd die for his sake.
It was little I thought my denial he'd take.
Ah! But my misfortune, I made a mistake
When he left me in Erin the green.

Oh, come all you young maids of our dear Irish nation,
I pray you be steady and wise.
Likewise, lend an ear to my kind assertation
And never your true love dispise
For such foolish folly distracted I rave
There is no place for me but the dark, silent grave.
And when all hopes deny me I'll then take my leave
Of the flower of sweet Erin the green.

178

The Red-Haired Man's Wife

Also from the singing of Seán Cannon. The song was inspired by an older Gaelic one, **Bean An Fhir Ruaidh**, and it shows strong traces of the Gaelic tradition itself with its intra-line rhyming.

The type of sinful sexuality which would allow one to covet another's wife is more common in Erse than in English-language Irish folk song.

Source: Séan Cannon.

Recording: Cathal McConnell, *Wish You Were Here*, Flying Fish 070.

Combined Mixolydian and Major of D

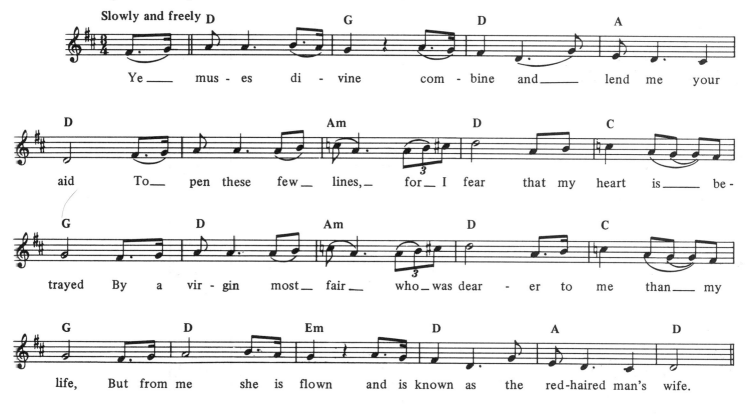

Ye __ mus - es di - vine com - bine and __ lend me your aid To __ pen these few __ lines, __ for __ I fear that my heart is __ be-trayed By a vir - gin most __ fair __ who __ was dear - er to me than __ my life, But from me she is flown and is known as the red-haired man's wife.

ms 1 and 2, 16 and 17

mus - es di - vine com __
me she __ is flown and __ is

ms 9 and 14

heart is __ be-
me than __ my

Séan Cannon

179

Ye muses divine combine and lend me your aid
To pen these few lines, for I fear that my heart is betrayed
By a virgin most fair who was dearer to me than my life,
But from me she is flown and is known as the red-haired man's wife.

A letter I'd send by a friend down to the seashore,
To let her understand I'm the man that does her adore,
And if she would leave that slave I would forfeit my life
And she'd be a lady and ne'er be the red-haired man's wife.

Ah! Remember the day that I gave to you my true heart,
When you solemnly swore that no more we ever would part,
But your mind's like the ocean, each notion has taken her flight
And left me bewailing the red-haired man's wife.

I straight took my way next day through a shady green grove
And crossed purling streams where sweet birds mostly do rove
Thence I was conveyed to where Nature boasts of her pride,
Where I stood all amazed and gazed on the red-haired man's wife.

I offered a favour and sealed it with my own hand.
She thus answered and said, "Would you lead me to break the command?
Therefore, take it easy, since Nature has caused so much strife.
I was given away and will stay as the red-haired man's wife."

My darling sweet Phoenix if now you will be my own,
For the patriarch David had a number of wives 'tis well known,
So yield to my embraces and straight put an end to all my strife.
If not, I'll run in sin or gain the red-haired man's wife.

The Dear Irish Boy

This song is frequently played as a slow air. I've heard it
sung only by Margaret Barry—and then only a fragment.
I couldn't imagine anyone else doing it better, though.

Source: Text is a broadside from Fortey's "Catnach Press"
collated with a text from P. W. Joyce, *Old Irish Folk Music
and Songs*; tune learned from Margaret Barry.

moun - tains we strayed. With each oth - er de - light - ed and fond - ly u -

nit - ed I've__ lis - tened all day to my dear I - rish boy.

My Connor, his cheeks are as ruddy as morning,
The brightest of pearl doth but mimic his teeth,
Whilst nature with ringlets his mild brow adorning,
His hair Cupid's bow-strings, and roses his breath.

Smiling, beguiling, cheering, endearing,
Together oft over the mountains we strayed.
With each other delighted and fondly united
I've listened all day to my dear Irish boy.

No roebuck more swift can fly over the mountain,
No veteran more bold in danger or scars,
He is slightly, is sparingly, and clear as the fountain,
His eyes twinkled love, he is gone to the wars.

Smiling, beguiling, cheering . . .

The soft tuning lark, her sweet notes change mourning.
The dull moping hour shall employ my night's sleep,
While seeking lone walks in the shade of the evening,
Until my Connor returns I will ne'er cease to weep.

The wars are all over, and he is not returning,
I fear that some envious plot has been laid.
Or some cruel maid has him so captivated,
He'll ne'er return to his dear Irish maid.

Alas for the love we so wonderously cherished!
All faded the vision that filled us with joy.
Throughout these deep shadows of hopes that are perished,
I wander alone for my dear Irish boy.

Heather on the Moor

Here's a bouncy song Robin Morton collected from Hugh
Lees of Enniskillen, Co. Fermanagh. Paul Brady was always
being asked to sing this one when he lived in New York.

Source: R. Morton, *Folksongs Sung in Ulster.*
Recording: Paul Brady, *The Gathering*, Green Hays 705.

With spirit

Oh, as I roved out on a bright May morn - ing, calm and clear__

was the wea - ther,_____ I chanced to roam some

miles from home a - mong the beau - ti - ful bloom - ing heath - er, And it's

heath-er on the moor, o - ver the heath-er, O - ver the moor and a - mong the heath - er, _____ I chanced to roam some miles from home a - mong the beau - ti - ful bloom - ing heath-er, And it's heath-er on the moor.

Oh, as I roved out of a bright May morning, calm and clear was the weather,
I chanced to roam some miles from home among the beautiful blooming heather,
And it's heather on the moor, over the heather,
Over the moor and among the heather,
I chanced to roam some miles from home among the beautiful blooming heather,
And it's heather on the moor.

As I roved along with my hunting song my heart as light as any feather,
I met a pretty maid upon the way, she was tripping the dew down from the heather.
And it's heather on the moor, over the heather,
Over the moor and among the heather,
I met a pretty maid upon the way, she was tripping the dew down from the heather,
And it's heather on the moor.

'Where are you going to my pretty fair maid, by hill or dale come tell me whether.'
Right modestly she answered me, 'to the feeding of my lambs together,'
And it's heather on the moor, over the heather,
Over the moor and among the heather,
Right modestly she answered me, 'to the feeding of my lambs together,'
And it's heather on the moor.

We both shook hands and down we sat, it being the longest day in summer,
We sat till the red setting beams of the sun came sparkling down among the heather.
And it's heather on the moor, over the heather,
Over the moor and among the heather,
We sat till the red setting beams of the sun came sparkling down among the heather.
And it's heather on the moor.

'Now,' she says, 'I must away; my lambs and sheep have strayed from other,
For I am loth to part from you as those fond lambs are to part their mother.'
And it's heather on the moor, over the heather,
Over the moor and among the heather,
For I am loth to part from you as those fond lambs are to part their mother.'
And it's heather on the moor.

Up she rose and away she goes, her name or place I know not either,
But if I was king, I'd make her queen, the lass I met among the heather.
And it's heather on the moor, over the heather,
Over the moor and among the heather,
But if I was king, I'd make her queen, the lass I met among the heather.
And it's heather on the moor.

The Rigs O' Barley

Scots love songs are the most physical in the Isles, and there is a special beauty to this forthright admission of sexual, as well as cerebral, joy.

The text is from a broadside. I matched it up with **The Rigs o' Rye**.

Source: Text from a Fortey broadside; tune is common.

It was upon a Lam-mas night When the corn rigs were bon-nie, Be-neath the moon's un-cloud-ed light, I held a-wa to An-nie.

It was upon a Lammas night
When the corn rigs were bonnie,
Beneath the moon's unclouded light,
I held awa to Annie.

The time flew by wi' tentless heed,
Till 'tween the late and early;
Wi' sma' persuasion she agreed,
To see me thro' the barley.

The sky was blue, the wind was still,
The moon was shining clearly;
I set her down wi' right good will,
Amang the rigs o' barley.

I kept her heart, was a' my sin;
I loved her most sincerely,
I kissed her owre and owre again,
Amang the rigs o' barley.

I locked her in my fond embrace,
Her heart was beating rarely;
My blessing on that happy place,
Amang the rigs o' barley.

But by the moon and stars so bright,
That shone that hour so clearly,
She ay shall bless that happy night,
Amang the rigs o' barley.

I hae been blythe wi' comrades dear,
I hae been merry drinkin;
I hae been joyfu' gath'rin gear;
I hae been happy thinkin.

But a, the pleasures e'er I saw,
Tho' three times doubled fairly,
That happy night was worth them a'
Amang the rigs o' barley.

The Lily of the West

This broadside favorite enjoyed popularity again in the 1960s when Joan Baez recorded an American version. The tune is the same as one of John McCormack's best-loved songs, **The Star of the Co. Down.**

Source: Text from a broadside with no imprint; tune is often heard.

Pentatonic

When first I came to Ireland, some pleasure for to find,
It's there I spied a damsel fair, most pleasing to my mind.
Her rosy cheeks and rolling eyes, like arrows pierced my breast.
They call her lovely Molly-O, the Lily of the West.

Her golden hair in ringlets hung and her dress was spangled o'er,
With a ring on every finger brought from a foreign shore.
'Twould entice both kings and princes, so costly was she dressed.
She far excelled Diana bright, the Lily of the West.

I then did court this one a while in hopes her love to gain,
But soon she turned her back on me, which caused me all my pain.
She robbed me of my liberty. She robbed me of my rest.
I roam, forsook by Molly-O, the Lily of the West.

One day as I was walking down by a shady grove,
I espied a lord of high degree conversing with my love.
She sang a song delightful while I was sore oppressed,
Saying, "I bid adieu to Molly-O, the Lily of the West."

I walked up to my rival with a dagger in my hand
And dragged him from my own false love and boldly bid him stand.
Being mad with desperation, I swore I'd pierce his breast.
I was then deceived by Molly-O, the Lily of the West.

I then did stand my trial and nobly made my plea.
A flaw was in my indictment found which quickly set me free.
That beauty bright I did adore, the judge did her address,
Saying, "Go you faithless Molly-O, the Lily of the West."

Now that I've gained my liberty, a roving I will go.
I'll ramble through old Ireland and I'll travel Scotland o'er.
Although she swore my life away, she still disturbs my rest,
I still must style her Molly-O, the Lily of the West.

....and Marriage

The Unfortunate Wife

A clear antecedent of numerous Southern Appalachian
women's songs the like of:

When I was single I wore clothes so fine,
Now I am married, Lord I go ragged all the time.
Wish I was a single girl again.

Source: This text if from a broadside by Wood of New
Meeting Street, Birmingham; the tune is my own.

Pentatonic

A maid was I, and a maid was I, And I lived with my ma-ma at
home, And I ate and I drank in my good clothing, For mon-ey I want-ed none.

A maid was I, and a maid was I,
And I lived with my mama at home,
And I ate and I drank in my good clothing,
For money I wanted none.

My cap was made of finest muslin,
And plaited neat all round,
A maid was I, and a maid was I,
And I lived with my mama at home.

My gown was made of the finest cotton,
My stays they was silk,
My shift was made of the finest of holland,
Washed as white as milk.

A maid was I, and a ...

My stockings was made of the finest cotton,
My garters they was silk,
My shoes was made of the best spanish leather,
My buckles they was gilt.

A maid was I, and a ...

There came a young man to my bedside,
And asked me if I would wed,
I being as willing as him,
He stole my maidenhead.

And a wife was I, and a wife was I,
And trouble and strife came on,
Trouble and strife, all the days of my life,
For money I never have none.

My cap was made of the coarsest cloth,
And never a plait all round,
And a wife was I, a wife I was.
When trouble and strife came on.

My gown was made of the coarsest linfey,
As for stays I went without,
My shift was made of the coarsest of herden,
And ragged all round about.

A wife was I, and a ...

My stockings was made of the coarsest woollen,
As for garters I went without,
My shoes was made of old boot-legs,
And bottoms come tumbling out.

A wife was I, and a ...

How to Cook a Husband

As Mr. Glass said of the hare, you must first catch him. Having done so, the mode of cooking him, so as to make a good dish of him is as follows: Many good husbands are spoiled in the cooking; some women go about it as if their husbands were bladders, and blow them up. Others keep them constantly in hot water, while others freeze them by conjugal coldness. Some smother them with hatred, contention and variance, and some keep them in pickle all their lives.

These women always serve them up with tongue sauce. Now it cannot be supposed that husbands will be tender and good if managed in this way. But they are, on the contrary, very delicious when managed as follows: Get a large jar called the jar of carefulness, (which all good wives have on hand) place your husband in it, and set him near the fire of conjugal love; let the fire be pretty hot, but especially let it be clear—above all let it be constant. Cover him over with affection, kindness and subjection. Garnish him with modest, becoming familiarity, and the spice of pleasantry and if you add kisses and other confectionaries let them be accompanied with a sufficient portion of secrecy; mixed with prudence and moderation. We would advise all good wives to try this receipt and realize how admirable a dish a husband is when properly cooked.

How to Cook a Wife

While men spare no pains in obtaining the best materials for this superlative dish, they are often totally regardless after the first mouthful of the necessary precautions to render it permanently sweet, and if through neglect it turn sour they invariably slander the dish, while the fault is in themselves. It is true the merits of this dish cannot be ascertained at first taste, which is always sweet—the "after" taste is the proper criterion of the merits which depend entirely on the cooking of the dish. Our great objection therefore is not to "make" the wife a sweet companion, but to "keep" her so. This may be accomplished in the following manner: Obtain an adequate supply of pure water of affection, and gently immerse her therein. Should the water during this process become ruffled a little of the original Balm of Courtship will soon restore it to its usual smoothness. The fire should be composed of true love, with a few sighs to increase the flame, which should not be too warm, nor yet suffered to abate entirely, as that would spoil the dish. Coolness is often the rain of the dish, erroneously asserted by some cooks to be necessary, which cooks add also sprigs of indifference, but this is a very dangerous practice, as a good wife is exquisitly delicate and susceptible. A few evergreens such as industry, sobriety, and fondness are necessary and a moderate quantity of the spirit of coaxings, and one of the kisses may be added giving the whole a most delicate flavour. Garnish with flowers of endearment and kindness, and you will then appreciate the delights of a dish compared with which all others sink into insignificance, namely, A GOOD WIFE.

—from an early 19th-century broadside.

Katie Kearney

A précised song of connubial scraping I first heard from Banjo Burke of Johnstown, Co. Kilkenny. Joe, along with singer Tony Callanan and Kerry fiddler Johnny Cronin, formed The Wild Geese in New York during 1974. They were a hard playing, hard drinking and hard singing trio that held court on Friday and Saturday nights at the Bunratty Pub on Kingsbridge Road in the Bronx. They were by no means a fine group, merely a great one, and considerably brightened the local musical scene during their heydey.

Source: Learned from Joe Burke.

Recording: Johnny Moynihan, *De Dannan*, Shanachie 79001.

Pentatonic

"Love, won't you marry me, marry me, marry me?
Love, won't you marry me and keep me out of danger?"
"No, I won't marry you, marry you, marry you.
No, I won't marry you, you dirty, ugly stranger."

My wife she has a hairy thing, a hairy thing, a hairy thing.
My wife she has a hairy thing, she showed it to me Sunday.
Bought it in a furrier's shop, a furrier's shop, a furrier's shop.
Bought it in a furrier's shop, it's going back on Monday.

Some say the Devil's dead, the Devil's dead, the Devil's dead,
Some say the Devil's dead and buried in Killarney.
More say he rose again, rose again, rose again,
More say he rose again and married Katie Kearney.

Poor Man's Labour

This is an English song I first heard from Phil Callery, resident at the Green Linnet Club in Dublin. A Scots version from the James Duncan collection has an additional verse worth repeating:

Kissin' and clappin' [hugging] was my occupation.
Amang the families [females] I did rove,
But now I am married and repent at my leisure,
So the poor man's labour is never o'er.

Source: Learned from the singing of Phil Callery.

Recording: Martin Carthy, *Shearwater*, Mooncrest CREST 25.

Pentatonic

When I was a young man I was a rov-er, noth-ing would sat-is-fy me but a wife.

Soon as I reached the age of twen-ty, wea-ry was I for a sin-gle life.

When I was a young man I was a rover, nothing would satisfy me but a wife.
Soon as I reached the age of twenty, weary was I for a single life.

The very first year my wife I married, out of her company I could not stay.
Her voice was as sweet as the lark and the linnet and the nightingale at the break of day.

The very next year that we were married, scarce could I get one half hour's sleep,
With her two heels she ran on my shins, saying, "Husband dear put down your feet."

The baby cried, she bitterly scolded. Out of the house I was forced to run
Without trousers, a wig or a waistcoat. A poor man's labour is never done.

I ran up to the top of the hill for to view my sheep that I'd thought gone astray,
When I got back she was lying in her bed at twelve o'clock of a winter's day.

When I got back so wet and weary, weary and wet, boys, where could I run,
She was lying in her bed with the fire up beside her, says, "Young man, is the kettle done?"

I'll go home to my agèd mother. She'll be sitting all alone.
There are plenty of young women to be had. Why should I be tied to one?

Come all young men that is for to marry, though it may grieve you for evermore,
Death, oh death, come take my wife and then my sorrows will be o'er.

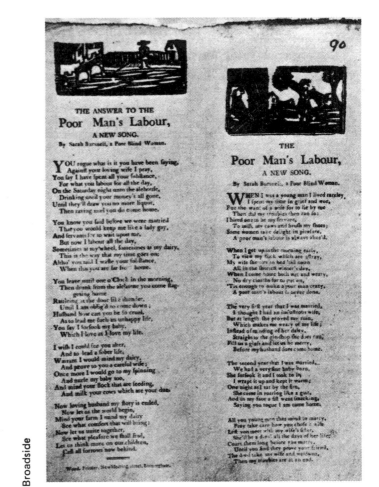

Broadside

189

The Wooden Leg'd Parson

Often associated with the gentry, the English parson was regarded very differently by his parishioners than was the Irish priest, who could be both a religious and political figure such as Father Murphy.

Other songs in this genre are **The Parson and the Maid** and **The Parson and the Clerk**.

John Roberts supplied the chorus and tune, a variant of **The Three Cripples** or **John Brown's Old Mare**.

Source: Text from a Such broadside; chorus and tune from John Roberts.

Possible variant for other verses

A barber there was named Timothy Briggs,
Quite famous he was for making good wigs;
Till with a lass called Becky Bell,
Slap over the ears in love he fell.
  *Sing: Rumble dum dairy rumble dum dey! Mark well the truth
  that I say.*

So they went to the church the knot to tie,
To a wooden leg'd parson named Jonathan Sly,
If you'd seen him you'd have laughed at him plump,
As he mounted the pulpit with a stump.

Sing: Rumble dum dairy . . .

They'd been married a week or two,
When Becky turned out a most terrible shrew,
"No comfort I have with this woman," he said.
"I'll go back to the parson and get unwed."

So he went to the parson, and he said, "Mr. Sly,
If I live with this woman I surely shall die.
You know, sir, you made us two into one,
So I'm come for to know if we can't be undone."

190

The parson said, "That is a thing rather new.
I don't know that I've the power my flock to undo;
But in hopes that you'll lead a more happy life,
I'll call at your house and admonish your wife."

The barber, quite pleased, went taking his glass,
And the parson stumped off to lecture the lass;
When the barber went home, la, what did he see,
But the parson with Becky a top of his knee.

The barber at this bristled up every hair,
Says he, "Mr. Sly, what are you doing there?"
"Why you know that you wanted undoing, my man,
So you see that I'm trying as fast as I can."

"Yes, I think I'm undone as I ne'er was before."
So he kicked Mr. Parson straight out of the door,
Where he lay in the street, and his wooden leg stood
Like a spade sticking up in a cart load of mud.

They lived after this rather more reconciled,
And in nine months from then she brought him a child,
But the barber hung himself up on a peg,
When he found the child born with a new wooden leg.

Rap-A-Tap-Tap

The story of the faithful servant well rewarded. A great bawdy song, not forced, not even vaguely obscene.

Source: Text and tune learned from Dave Surman; words collated with broadside by Henry Disley.

Recording: Frank Purslow, *Rap-A-Tap-Tap*, Folklore F-LET-1

My mas-ter's gone to mar-ket (and mas-ters of-ten roam). He told me to mind his bus-'ness as if he'd been at home. As soon as my mas-ter's back was turned I bun-dled out the barn, I went 'round to the door with my rap-a-tap-tap and nev-er a thought of harm. I went 'round to the door with my rap-a-tap-tap and nev-er a thought of harm.

My master's gone to market (and master's often roam).
He told me to mind his bus'ness as if he'd been at home.
As soon as my master's back was turned I bundled out the barn,
I went 'round to the door with my rap-a-tap-tap and never a thought
   of harm.
I went 'round to the door with my rap-a-tap-tap and never a thought
   of harm.

Soon as my mistress heard the knock, she asked me to come in.
I told her I was thirsty as she gave to me some gin.
She gave to me some gin, my boys, and never a word to say
And as soon as I had finished it upstairs we went straightway.
And as soon as I had finished it upstairs we went straightway.

We hadn't been sporting on the bed for half an hour or more,
My mistress like the game so well she swore she'd never give o'er.
"You've won my heart, young man," she says, "My husband's not
   for me,
For he can't come with his rap-a-tap-tap not half so well as thee.
For he can't come with his rap-a-tap-tap not half so well as thee."

As soon as my master, he came home, he asked me what I'd done.
I told him I'd minded his business as if he'd been at home.
He gave to me some beer, me boys, Indeed he did not know
That I'd been there with my rap-a-tap-tap; if he had he'd not done so.
That I'd been there with my rap-a-tap-tap; if he had he'd not done so.

Come all you young men like me, I'd have you not make bold,
But if you do as I have done I'm sure you'll never catch cold.
When your master's gone a walking to view the fields in May,
I would have you come with your rap-a-tap-tap be it either night or
   day.
I would have you come with your rap-a-tap-tap be it either night or
   day.

Dave Surman Photo by Darlene MacIntosh

The Butcher's Frolic

A butcher who deals in all varieties of meat.

Source: Text from a broadside by Wood, Birmingham.

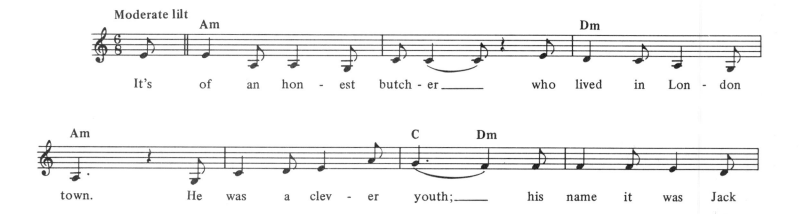

Moderate lilt

It's of an hon - est butch - er who lived in Lon - don town. He was a clev - er youth; his name it was Jack

Brown. The tai-lor's wife went out,___ some mut-ton for___ to buy. "What do you want good wom-an? What would you wish to buy?" ___

It's of an honest butcher who lived in London town.
He was a clever youth; his name it was Jack Brown.
The tailor's wife went out, some mutton for to buy.
"What do you want good woman? What would you wish to buy?"

"I want a loin of mutton, if you don't ask too dear."
"Come hither, honest woman, I'll use you kind and fair.
You are the cleverest woman that I have seen today.
I would have you come and buy my meat before you go away."

She took a loin of mutton and she liked it very well.
She said, "Now honest butcher, the price unto me tell?"
"My dear, it's at your service, or any joint I have
If that you tell me where you live, your company I must have."

"The place where I do live, it's near 'The Blazing Star'.
If you ask for 'The Hand, and Shears', you'll surely find me there."
"Tomorrow night for certainty, I'll come and visit thee."
"With all my heart, kind sir," said she. "You're welcome unto me."

She took the loin of mutton, to refuse it she would not.
Straight home then she did carry it to boil it in the pot.
And when her husband did come home she told him what she had.
Which made the tailor jump for joy, he was so very glad.

She said, "Now loving husband, how must this contrivance be,
Tomorrow night for certainty the butcher comes to me.
You must get underneath the bed and take a sword with you
And if the butcher comes to me, swear you'll run him through."

"I never used a sword, my dear, nor fought in all my life.
And butchers are such terrible men, I fear he'll take my life."
"You must not be faint-hearted, but fight with courage bold,
And if that you should win the day, we'll gain great stores of gold."

The butcher he thought to himself he'd best prepared be,
For fear the tailor and his wife should play a trick on he.
He took a brace of pistols and threw them on the bed,
Which made the tailor quake for fear. He lay like one that's dead.

"What is that smell, good woman?" the butcher he did say.
"It is my husband's little dog that under the bed does lay."
"If that's your husband's little dog, I'll turn him out of the room."
"I beg you would lie still, my dear, and I'll spray a little perfume."

The butcher then arose and there he chanced to spy
One of the tailor's legs that under the bed did lie.
"If that's your husband's little dog, I'll kill him out of spite."
"Oh, spare my life," the tailor cried, "and you may have my wife."

"Oh how," said the butcher, "let you and I agree
That I may come when I please your own good wife to see."
"With all me heart!" the tailor cried. "You're welcome to my wife,
For I never have been so frightened before in all my life!"

There's Nothing Can Equal a Good Woman Still

To the women . . . God bless them! They've carried us all.

Source: Text from a ballad sheet printed by Disley; tune from John Roberts.

You sweet pret - ty las - ses where e'er you may be, Now
just pay at - ten - tion and lis - ten to me. I will not of -
fend you de - pend on my word, I will sing, you a verse or two
such as I've heard. For the men they may both - er and say what they
will, But there's noth - ing can e - qual a good wom - an still.

You sweet pretty lasses where e'er you may be,
Now just pay attention and listen to me.
I will not offend you depend on my word,
I will sing you a verse or two such as I've heard.

The men, they may bother and say what they will,
But there's nothing can equal a good woman still.

I say that a woman is the pride of the land,
We know that they're the joy and the comfort of man.
A man may as well put an end to his life,
As to think to live single without a good wife.

The men, they may bother . . .

There is many a man both in country and town,
That begrudges to see his wife wear a new gown,
Tho' she works like a horse till she's nearly half-dead,
Still he growls like a bear that has got a sore head.

You men that are single just listen to me,
And I'll tell you as plain as a child's A B C,
If you wish to enjoy the comforts of life,
Don't delay, but look out for a good tempered wife.

There is many a man, now it's plain to be seen,
That growls if his wife wears a hoop crinoline;
But why not be happy then things would go right,
And let the dear woman wear just what they like.

There is some men will quarrel and kick up a row,
And serve the poor woman I can't tell you how,
And swear that woman's the plague of their life,
But what would they be now without a good wife?

Some men tell their wives that they wish they were dead,
And that all their troubles would be off their heads,
But still they know it's a comfort in life,
When once a man marries a good tempered wife.

I know an old man keeps a sign of the gate,
And they tell me his age is about ninety-eight,
He says he is ready to lay down his life,
Without he can marry a good tempered wife.

Now, all that's around me, you hear what I say,
You that are single be sure don't delay,
Get married with speed for you'll find that's your plan,
As a woman's the joy and the pride of the land.

Close Encounters

The Little Ball of Yarn

I got the **Little Ball of Yarn** from a cousin's cousin, Patsy Lane of Newmarket, Co. Cork. He also gave me a splendid rendition of **The Grand Coulee Dam** that same night.

This is very much a Munster version, but the song is well known in England and was a pump shanty at sea.

Source: Learned from Patsy Lane.

Recording: Martin Carthy, *Second Album*, Topic 12TS341.

Dorian of A

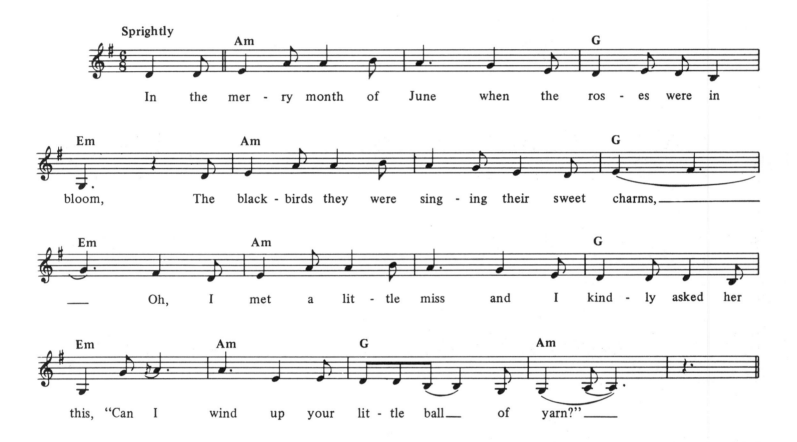

In the merry month of June when the roses were in bloom,
The blackbirds they were singing their sweet charms,
Oh, I met a little miss and I kindly asked her this,
"Can I wind up your little ball of yarn?"

"Yerra no, kind sir," said he, "You're a stranger unto me
And I fear you have some dearly other charmer."
"Oh, well no, me turtle dove! You're the only one I love.
Can I wind up your little ball of yard?"

So I took her to a nook right beside the shady brook,
Not intending for to do her any harm.
Oh, and to me great surprise, when I looked into her eyes,
I was winding up her little ball of yarn.

Now, nine months have passed and gone since I met this fair young one.
She has a little baby in her arms.
I said unto her, "Miss, sure I never dreamed of this
When I was winding up your little ball of yarn."

Come all you maidens young and old, take a warning when you're told.
Never rise up early in the morning.
Be like the blackbird and the thrush, keep one hand upon your bush
And the other on your little ball of yarn.

The Banks of the Bann (Willie Archer)

One of a half-dozen songs with the same title. I first hear Seán Cannon sing it at the Green Linnet Folk Club in Dublin. Antoinette McKenna has much the same version.

Sean O'Boyle dates the song to the early days of power-loom weaving in Ulster.

Such printed a broadsheet, **The Banks of the Band,** which starts:

> *By yon noisy harbour near sweet Milltown,*
> *Where fountains, clear fountains did me surround,*
> *I spied a fair maid, as you may understand,*
> *She was watching fine fishes on the Banks of the Band.*

Source: Learned from Seán Cannon.

Recording: Antoinette McKenna, *At Home*, Shanachie 29016.

Oh, as I was a-walking all down by the town,
Those lovely green mountains they did me surround,
'Twas there I spied a female and to me she looked grand.
She was plucking wild roses by the banks of the Bann.

I quickly approached her and to her I did say,
"Since Nature has ordained we should meet in this way,
Since Nature has ordained it, come give me your hand
And we will walk together by the banks of the Bann."

It was into a corner where the changes took place.
I knew by the blood that beat on her face.
Her feet they fell from her on a neat bed of sand
And she fell into my arms by the banks oft the Bann.

"Oh, young man, now that you've wronged me come give me your name,
So that when the child is born I might call him the same."
"My name is Willie Archer as you may understand
And my home and habitation lie close to the Bann.

"But I cannot marry you, I'm apprenticed and bound
To the spinning and the weaving in Rathfriland town,
But when my time is over I will give you my hand
And we will walk together by the banks of the Bann."

Come all you fair maidens and take warning by me—
Well don't go out a-courting by one, two or three,
No don't go out a-courting by three, two or one
For you might meet Willie Archer by the banks of the Bann.

The Buxom Lass

I found **The Buxom Lass** on a broadside and composed this melody for it right in the Birmingham Library. There's a traditional tune in *The Wanton Seed*, where Frank Purslow writes: "[it is] of nineteenth century broadside origin and would have been sung to any tune which the ballad-singers knew which happened to fit. This one is unmistakably Irish as, in fact most tunes of broadside songs of this period are; an indication of the country of origin of the majority of ballads-singers of the time...."

Source: Text from a broadside with no imprint; the tune is my own.

Recording: Chris Foster, *Layers*, Topic 12TS329

Mixolydian of A

As I roved out one morning I met a buxom lass.
She was going to the dairy and she kept a field of grass.
It grew below two mountains and down by a rising spring.
She hired me to cut it down while the birds did sweetly sing.

I said, "My pretty fair maid, what wages do you give?
Mowing is hard labor and it's far from here I live."
She said, "If you do please me, I solemnly do swear,
I'll give you a crown an acre and plenty of strong beer."

I said, "My pretty fair maid, I like your wages well.
And if I mow your meadow down, you shall say it is done well.
My scythe is in good order and lately has been honed.
My buxom lass, I'll cut your grass close unto the ground."

With courage like a lion, I entered in the field.
I'll mow the meadow down now before that I do yield.
But before I'd mowed a rood of ground my scythe it bent and broke.
She said, "my man, you must give in. You're tired of your work."

I said, "My handsome fair maid do not on me frown,
For, if I stay the summer through, I still can't mow it down.
Since it is such pleasant weather there bears such crops of grass
And it's watered by a spring below which makes it grow so fast.

She said, "My man, you must give in for energy you lack.
For mowing is hard labor and weakening to the back.
Yes, mowing is hard labor and you must it forsake.
But round my little meadow you may use your rake."

Maggie Lauder

A paradox of the folk-song revival is that lovers of old songs constantly demand to hear "new" ones. I haven't heard **Maggie Lauder** much lately—except from Cilla Fisher and Artie Trezise—but it's had a good deal of popularity over the years, perhaps, as Burns said, because it's "so pregnant with Scottish naivete and energy."

Source: Text from a broadside by E. Hodges of Seven Dials, London; tune first heard from the singing of Ewan MacColl.
Recording: Ewan MacColl, *Scots Folk Songs*, Washington WLP 733.

Wha wad-na be in love, wi' bon-ny Mag-gie Lau-der, A pip-er met her gaun to Fife, And spiered what was't they ca'd her. Right scorn-ful-ly she an-swered him. "Be gone you hal-lan-shak-er, Jog an your gate you bal-der-skate My name is Mag-gie Lau-der."

Wha wadna be in love,
Wi' bonny Maggie Lauder,
A piper met her gaun to Fife,
And spiered what was't they ca'd her.
Right scornfully she answered him.
"Begone you hallanshaker,
Jog an your gate you balderskate
My name is Maggie Lauder."

"Maggie," quoth he, "and by my ba
I'm fidging fain to see thee,
Sit down by me my bonny bird,
In truth I winna steer thee.
For I'm a piper by my trade,
My name is Rob the ranter,
The lasses loup as they were daft
When I blaw up my chanter."

"Piper," quoth Meg, "hae you your bags,
Or is your drone in order,
If you be Rob I've heard of you,
Live you upon the border,
The lasses all both far and near,
Hae heard of Rob the ranter.
I'll shake my foot wi' right good will
If you'll blaw up your chanter."

Then to his bags he flew w' speed
About the drone he twisted,
Meg up and wallop'd o'er the green
For brawly could she frisk it.
"Weel done," quoth he. "Play up," quoth she.
"Well bob'd," quoth Rob the ranter,
" 'Tis worth my while to play indeed
When I had sic a dancer."

"Well hae you play'd your part," quoth Meg,
Your cheeks are like the crimson,
There's nane in Scotland plays so weel
Since we lost Habby Simpson.
I've liy'd at Fife baith maid and wife,
These ten year and a quarter,
Gin you shall come to Anster fair
Spier you for Maggie Lauder."

Fire! Down Below

An old music hall song that'll still get a low laugh. Best
known as a pumping shanty.

Source: Text is a broadside from Such; tune is an adaptation of one found in S. Hugill, *Shanties from the Seven Seas.*

Oh, I am a simple country lad, From London just come down, To tell you the scrapes and narrow escapes, I had when last in town; 'Twas market day, I'd sold my hay, And stood things to admire, When all at once a chap bawled out, "Hey Master, mind the fire." Fire, fire, fire! Fire down below, Let us hope that we shall never see, A fire down below.

Oh, I am a simple country lad,
From London just come down,
To tell you the scrapes and narrow escapes,
I had when last in town;
'Twas market day, I'd sold my hat,
And stood things to admire,
When all at once a chap bawled out.
"Hey Master, mind the fire."

Fire, fire, fire!
Fire down below,
Let us hope that we shall never see,
A fire down below.

I turned me round to ask a lass,
The cause of all this stir,
And if she'd mind to be so kind,
As to tell me where it were;
Says she, "Young man, yes that I can,
Do all that you require,
Just come with me and you shall see,
I'll take you where there's fire."

Fire, fire, fire . . .

200

With that she linked her arm in mine,
And down the street we steered
To some back slum she called her home,
But still no fire appeared.
For a house we peeped, upstairs we creeped,
Three stories high or higher,
In a room we popped, all night we stopped
But I couldn't find the fire.

In the morning when I wakened up,
My lady-bird had flown,
Not only lass, but all my brass
And watch and clothes were gone;
Bare legged and feet, I ran in street,
My shirt my sole attire.
The women laughed, and the men they chaffed
While I kept bawling, "Fire!"

By some good chance I reached my home,
Half-dead with shame and fright,
And all that saw me and all that know me,
Said, "Spoony, served him right."
But the worst wasn't past, oh, it came at last,
I thought I should expire,
Say what you will, I was very ill
And the doctor said 'twas fire!

So all you good gentlemen,
Who a-courting have not been,
Be advised by me, don't foolish be,
By all I have done and seen.
Don't miss your ways on market days,
Or stand things to admire,
But avoid back slums, and female chums,
And don't go catching fire.

The Gay Old Man

My mother was apprenticed to a dressmaker in Abbeyfeale,
Co. Limerick, about 1930. She received food, lodgings, and
sewing lessons—but no pay—for housework. She didn't stay
long, moving on to England, didn't get to be much with
needle and thread, and never had any trouble like this.

Source: Text from a broadside with no imprint; tune heard
from the singing of Frankie Armstrong and Martin Carthy.

Recordings: Frankie Armstrong, *Out of Love, Hope and
Suffering*, Bay 206. Martin Carthy, *Crown of Horn*, Topic
12TS300.

Combined Mixolydian and Major of D

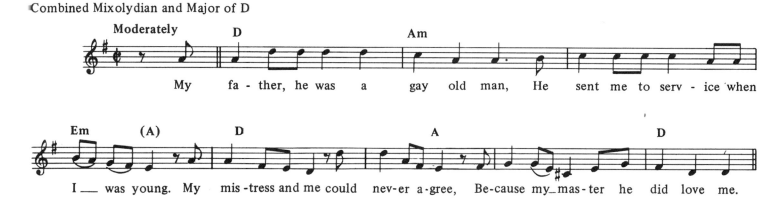

My father, he was a gay old man,
He sent me to service when I was young.
My mistress and me could never agree,
Because my master he did love me.

My mistress sent me up aloft,
To make her bed both nice and soft,
My master followed after and gave me a ring,
Saying "Take this Betty, for your bed making."

My mistress coming up in great haste,
She caught my master's arms around my waist,
From the top to the bottom she did me fling,
Saying, "Take this for your bed making."

First in the kitchen, then in the hall,
Then in the parlor amongst them all,
They asked where I had been.
I told them aloft at bed making.

My mistress turned me out of doors,
She called me a nasty, dirty little whore,
She bade me walk till my shoes grew thin,
And then I should remember the bed making.

When six long weeks were gone and past,
Then this young maid grew thick at last.
She longed for mutton, veal and pig,
Her stomach was little, her body was big.

When nine months were gone and past,
She brought forth a son at last.
And then she had him christened John,
And sent it home to the gay old man.

Come all you maids where'er you be,
Make your bed while you can see,
For I made mine by the candle light,
Which caused me to rue all the days of my life.

Brave Old Donnelly

John Beggan, a singer and mandolin player from Dublin, taught me this great version of **The Jolly Tinker.** I once recorded it with Declan Hunt in Boston, but mercifully, our rendition was never issued. The song goes well in either jig or polka time.

Source: Learned from Johnny Beggan and Declan Hunt.

Recording: The Flying Cloud, *Traditional Music from Ireland, Scotland and England*, Adelphi AD 1029.

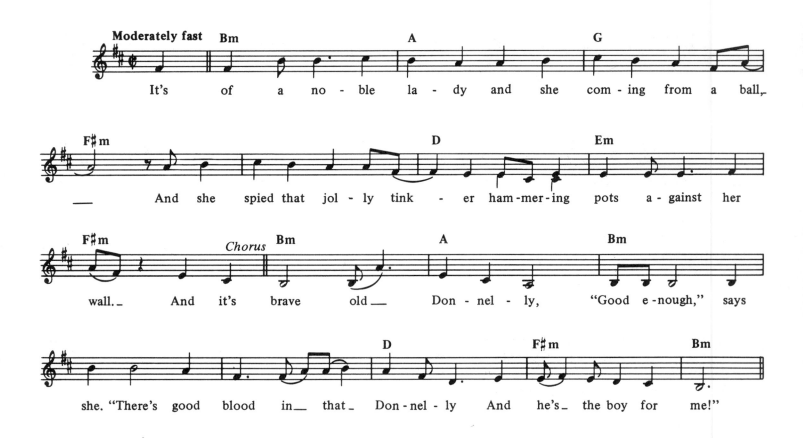

It's of a noble lady and she coming from a ball,
And she spied that jolly tinker hammering pots against her wall.

   And it's brave old Donnelly,
   "Good enough," says she.
   "There's good blood in that Donnelly
   And he's the boy for me!"

He sauntered through the kitchen and he sauntered through the hall.
And he sauntered through the parlour over nobles great and small.

   And it's brave . . .

She then went up the stairs all for to make the bed,
But in two steps he was after her and he tapped her on the bed.

She then went down the stairs for to bolt and bar the door
And in two steps he was after her and he tapped her on the floor.

She then took our her whistle and she blew it loud and shrill
And twenty fat policemen came a-running down the hill.

She then had him arrested and he got six months in jail
Then she went in behind his back, let another man out on bail.

It's of a noble lady and she coming from a ball,
She spied that jolly tinker hammering pots against her wall.

Ramble Away

A strange, demonic creature is Ramble Away; he seems to be the essential Everyrake.

Source: Text from broadsides by Wood of Birmingham and Fortey of London; tune first heard some time ago, possibly from Andy O'Brien or Tony Callanan.

Recording: Cyril Tawney, *Down Among the Barley Straw*, Trailer LER 2095.

As I was a-going to Birmingham fair
With my scarlet coat and everything rare,
Enough to entice girls buxom and gay
Who are willing to go with young Ramble Away, Ramble Away.

When first I set my foot at the fair
I saw pretty Nancy a-combing her hair.
I gave her a wink. She rolled her black eye.
Thinks I to myself, "I'll be there bye and bye."

As I was a-walking one night in the dark,
I took pretty Nancy to be my sweetheart.
She smiled in my face and this she did say,
"Are you the young man they call Ramble Away?"

I said, "Pretty Nancy, don't smile in my face,
For I do not intend to stop long in this place."
So I tipped her the double to fair Lincolnshire
And I swore I would ramble, the devil knows where.

When twenty-four weeks they were over and past,
This pretty fair maid she fell sick at last.
Her gown would not meet nor her apron strings tie
And she longed for the sight of young Ramble Away.

My dad and my mam they are both gone from home
And when they return I will sing them a song;
I will sing them a song and leave them to say,
"No doubt you've been playing with Ramble Away."

Come all pretty fair maids whoever you be,
With those jolly lads I'd have you go free;
Hat, cap and feather you'll have to wear
And a bunch of blue ribbons to tie up your hair.

Rosemary Lane

This is the forerunner of the more jocular **Home, Dearie, Home** group of songs.

Source: Text from a broadside by Disley; tune learned from Brian Brooks.

Recording: Bert Jansch, *Rosemary Lane*, Reprise: RF 6455

Dorian of A

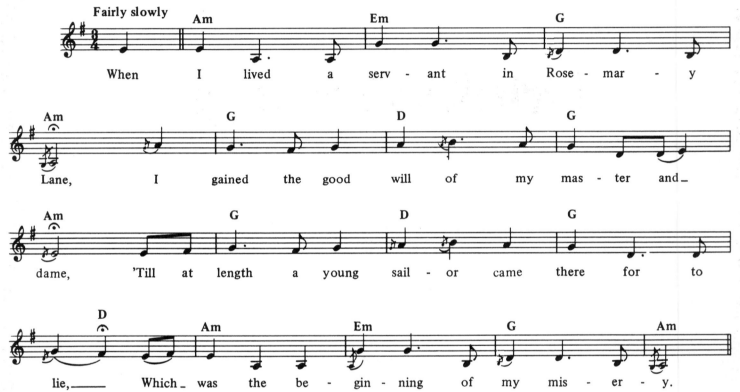

When I lived a servant in Rosemary Lane,
I gained the good will of my master and dame,
'Till at length a young sailor came there for to lie,
Which was the beginning of my misery.

He called for a candle to light him to bed,
He called for a napkin to tie up his head,
To tie 'round his head as sailors all do,
And he vowed and he swore I should come to bed too.

I crept into bed to keep myself warm,
He vowed and he swore he would do me no harm;
What he did to me I ne'er will declare,
But I wish that short night had been seven long years.

In the middle of the night this young man grew bold
And in my smock tail he threw handfuls of gold,
Saying, take this my dear, and more you shall have.
I'll be a friend to you, as long as I live.

So, we tumbled and tossed by the light of the moon.
We rose the next morning all in the same tune;
The very next morning this young man arose,
And dresses himself out in his tarpauling clothes.

"Alas!" then I cried, "O! I am undone,
He has left me with child, a daughter or son;
And it 'tis girl, she shall stay home with me,
And if 'tis a boy he shall plough on the sea.

"With his long quartered shoes, check shirt, and blue gear,
On the quarter-deck standing like a bold British tar,
I'll dry up my milk and you shally plainly see
And I'll pass for a maid in my own country."

Drinking Songs

The Punch Ladle

To make a hot punch:

Roast 6 crab apples stuck with 4 cloves each. Set aside and keep warm.

Heat 2 quarts of a good flavorful ale and 1 bottle of white wine with 3 sticks of cinnamon bark till quite hot.

Add 1 ground nutmeg, ½ teaspoon of ginger, the juice and pulp of 1 orange, the juice and some rind of 1 lemon and enough brown sugar to please your taste.

Stir over heat until all sugar dissolved.

Add rum or brandy to taste.

Place in punch bowl and put in apples.

Ladle away.

Source: Text from a broadside by Fortey; tune learned from the singing of The Watersons.

Recording: The Watersons, *The Watersons*, Topic 12T142.

m 15

fath - om   the —

m 19

fath - om   the —

Come all you bold heroes, give ear to my song,
I'll sing in the praise of good brandy and rum.
There's clear crystal fountain, near England shall flow;
Give me the punch ladle, I'll fathom the bowl.

I'll fathom the bowl, I'll fathom the bowl.
Give me the punch ladle, I'll fathom the bowl.

From France we get brandy, from Jamaica comes rum,
Sweet oranges and lemons, from Portugal come;
Strong beer and good cider, o'er England shall flow;
Give me the punch ladle, I'll fathom the bowl.

I'll fathom the bowl . . .

My wife she comes in, when I sit at my ease,
She scolds and she grumbles, and does as she please;
She may scold and she may grumble 'till she's black in the face as a
   coal;
Give me the punch ladle, I'll fathom the bowl.

My father, he lies in the depth of the sea,
With stones at his feet, what matters for he;
There's a clear crystal fountain near him it doth roll;
Give me the punch ladle, I'll fathom the bowl.

When Jones's Ale Was New

When Jones's Ale Was New comes from the "calling on" tradition of the English mumming plays, whereby individual, costumed members of the cast or "jovial crew" are introduced to the audience by means of song. **Jones's Ale** was used by Lancashire "pace-eggers" (from Pasch, after the Hebrew *pesah*, i.e., Easter, Passover) as they made their door-to-door rounds.

In 1941, Sailor Dad Hunt of Marion, Virginia, sang the song at a White House gathering attended by F. D. R.:

Now the next come in was a sailor, with his marlinspike
and his sheaver,

For none could be more clever among this jovial crew;
He called the landlord into the place, and said it was time
to splice the main brace,
And if he didn't he'd wreck the place . . .

Source: Text is a collation made over a few years; tune is very common.

Recording: A. L. Lloyd, *English Drinking Songs*, Riverside RLP 12-618.

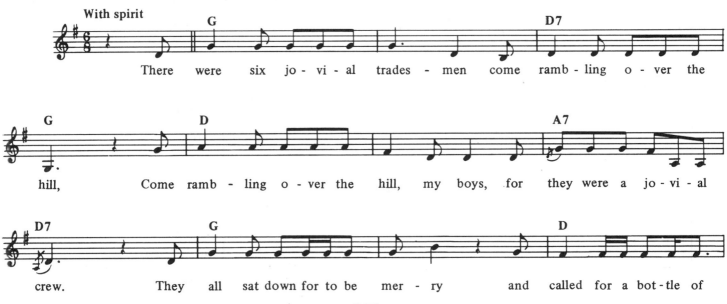

There were six jo-vi-al trades-men come ramb-ling o-ver the hill, Come ramb-ling o-ver the hill, my boys, for they were a jo-vi-al crew. They all sat down for to be mer-ry and called for a bot-tle of

sher - ry   "You're   wel - come o - ver the hills," says   Nel - lie.   When_ Jones - 's ale was

new,   my boys   When   Jones - 's   ale   was   new.   And   they   or - dered their

pints   of beer   and bot - tles of   sher - ry   To   help   them o - ver the hill   so

mer - ry,   To   help   them o - ver   the hills   so   mer - ry,   When_

Jones - 's   ale   was   new,   my boys,   When   Jones - 's   ale   was   new.

There were six jovial tradesmen come rambling over the hill,
Come rambling over the hill, my boys, for they were a jovial crew.
They all sat down for to be merry and called for a bottle of sherry.
"You're welcome over the hills," says Nellie.

*When Jones's ale was new, my boys. When Jones's ale was new**
And they ordered their pints of beer and bottles of sherry
To help them over the hills so merry,
To help them over the hills so merry,
When Jones's ale was new, my boys,
When Jones's ale was new.

The first come in was a soldier with a flintlock over his shoulder,
Sure no Captain ever looked bolder and a long broadsword he drew.
He swore he would fight for England's ground before the nation
  should be run down
And he boldly drank their healths all round.

When Jones's ale was new . . .

The next come in was a hatter, sure no one could be blacker,
And he began to chatter among the jovial crew.
He threw his hat upon the ground and tossed the landlord half a
  crown
And the company drank his health all round.

The next come in was a dyer and he sat himself down by the fire
For it was his heart's desire to drink with the jovial crew.
And he told the landlord to his face that the chimney corner should
  be his place
And there he sat and dyed his face.

The next come in was a mason, his hammer needed refacing
And no man could be more boasting among the jovial crew.
Then he dashed his trowel against the wall and wished every church
  and steeple would fall
So there would be work for masons all.

The next come in was a tailor with his bodkin, shears and thimble.
He swore he would be nimble among the jovial crew.
They sat and they called for ale and stout until the poor tailor was
  spent out
And the landlord forced him to go without.

The last come in was a ragman wary and his rag bag he did carry
And he was already merry among the jovial crew.
And while he was kissing and squeezing the lasses, they burnt his
  rag bag all to ashes
And gave the ragman fifty lashes.

The ale was always improving, so nobody thought of moving.
And the longer they sat boozing, the greater friends they grew.
So rowdily they drank about, until the ale had all ran out
And they asked old Jones to give them a shout.

When he had brewed anew, my boys. When he had brewed anew.

208

The Derby Ram

Here's a well-traveled song! Richard Chase, in *American Folk Tales and Songs*, writes of meeting a man whose great-uncle was often taken on the knee of George Washington, who, despite his almost being the first king of the United States, took great delight in singing all the "naughty" verses of this song! In sea-going versions of **The Derby Ram**, the ram and a sailor get drunk and ship out together, the beast proving as ready a hand as man on board.

Roy Harris has a particularly nice version of this song, one he learned in childhood in the midlands.

Source: Text and tune originally learned from the singing of A. L. Lloyd.

Recordings: The Watersons, *A Yorkshire Garland*, Topic 12T167. John Roberts and Tony Barrand, *Dark Ships in the Forest*, Folk-Legacy FSI-65.

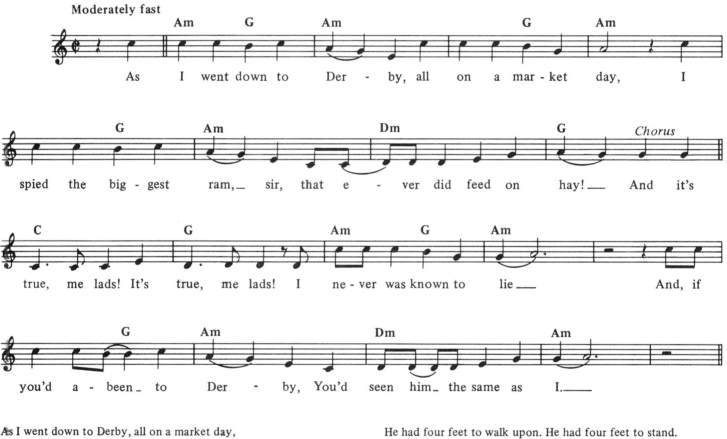

Moderately fast

As I went down to Der- by, all on a mar- ket day, I spied the big- gest ram,— sir, that e - ver did feed on hay!— And it's true, me lads! It's true, me lads! I ne - ver was known to lie — And, if you'd a- been— to Der - by, You'd seen him— the same as I.—

As I went down to Derby, all on a market day,
I spied the biggest ram, sir, that ever did feed on hay!

And it's true, me lads! It's true, me lads!
I never was known to lie.
And, if you'd a-been to Derby,
You'd seen him the same as I.

Oh, the wool upon this ram, sir, it reached up to the sky.
The eagles built their nests up there. You could hear the young 'uns cry!

And it's true . . .

Oh, the horns on this ram's head, sir, they reached up to the moon!
A little boy went up in January and he never got back till June!

He had four feet to walk upon. He had four feet to stand.
And every foot that he put down it covered an acre of land!

Well, the tail upon this ram, sir, it reached on down to hell!
The devil grabbed a hank of it and he rang the fire bell!

Oh, the man that killed this ram, sir, was up to his knees in blood
And the little boy that held the bowl was carried away in the flood!

This flood became a river, sir, and flowed down Derby Moor.
It turned the biggest water wheel that ever was turned before!

Took all the men in Derby to carry away his bones.
Took all the women in Derby to roll away his stones.

Oh, the man that fed this ram, sir, he must have been very rich.
And the singer of this song, sir, is a lying son of a _____!

209

John Barleycorn

Like **The Derby Ram, John Barleycorn** is ritualistic in nature, giving the life cycle of the barley grain from seed to ale and a few versions continuing the metamorphosis even farther with the ale being returned to Mother Earth in the form of urine. It is a very old song, likely pre-Christian, and has been often collected in England, Ireland, and Scotland. The early *Roxburghe Collection* contains a verse well worth repeating:

> *It is the cunningist Alchimist,*
> * that ere was in the land:*
> *Twill change your mettle when it list,*
> * in the turning of a hand,*
> *Your blushing gold to silver wan,*
> * Your silver into brasse:*
> *Twill turn a Taylor to a man,*
> * and a man into an asse.*

as is the next, collected from the Haxey, Lincolnshire, "boggens" chorus by Jean Ritchie and George Pickow:

> *He'll make a maid dance around this room*
> *Stark naked as ever she was born.*
> *He'll make a parson pawn his books*
> *And a farmer burn his corn.*

Source: Learned from the singing of Fred Jordan.

Recordings: Vic Gammon, *The Tale of Ale*, Freed Reed FRRD 023/024. Fred Jordan, *Songs of a Shropshire Farm Worker*, Topic 12T150. Haxey "Boggens," *Field Trip/England*, Folkways FW 8871.

right fol - air - y - Oh!

Oh, there came three men out of Kent, me boys,
For to plough for wheat and rye
And they made a vow and a solemn vow;
John Barleycorn must die.
So, they ploughed him deep in the furrow
And they sowed rye o'er his head
And these three men home rejoicing went;
John Barleycorn was dead!

To-me-right-fol-airy, fol-de-diddle-day
To-me-right-fol-airy-Oh!
To-me-right-fol-airy, fol-de-diddle-day,
To-me-right-fol-airy-Oh!

But, the sun shone warm and the wind blew soft
And it rained in a day or so.
John Barleycorn felt the sun and rain
And he soon began to grow.
But the rye began to grow as well,
The rye grew slow but tall.
John Barleycorn he grew short and quick
And he proved them liars all.

To-me-right-fol-airy . . .

Then they hired men with sickles
To cut him off at the Knee.
And, worst of all, poor Barleycorn,
They served him barbarously.
They they hired men with pitchforks
To toss him on to a load
And when they'd tossed John Barleycorn
They tied him down with cord.

Then they hired men with threshels
To beat him high and low.
They come smick-smack on poor Jack's back
Till the flesh began to flow.
Then they put him into the kiln, me boys,
Thinking to dry his bones,
And, worst of all, poor Barleycorn,
They crushed him between two stones.

Then they put him into the mashing tub,
Thinking to burn his tail,
And when he came out, poor Barleycorn,
They called him home-brewed ale.
So, come put your wine into glasses
And your cider in pewter cans.
Put John Barleycorn in the old brown jug
For he's proved the strongest man!

The Card Song

Frank Kidson, a Yorkshire collector who printed **The Card Song** in his book *Traditional Tunes* wrote of the piece as "being an extemporaneous drinking song, each member of the company contributing a rhyme as he drains off his glass." For this reason or another, Kidson did not give all the words he had obtained (from an old soldier who had learned it in India, a Mr. Washington Teasdale) but left their composition to the man of the moment. You might like to keep that tradition going.

The words printed here are Ewan MacColl's, the tune being Ewan's adaption of the setting in Kidson.

Source: Ewan MacColl.

Recording: Ewan MacColl, *The Best of Ewan MacColl*, Prestige International 13004.

The Card Song

The king will take the queen, but the queen will take the knave
And since we're in good company, more liquor let us have.

Here's to you, Tom Brown!
And to you, me jolly soul.
And to you with all me heart,
And with you I'll take a quart,
With you I'll drink a drop or two before that we do part.
Here's to you, Tom Brown!
Here's to you, Tom Brown!

The queen will take the knave, but the knave will take the ten
And now we're all together, boys, we'll deal 'em out again.

The knave will take the ten, but the ten will take the nine
And now we're all together, boys, we'll deal 'em out again.

The ten will take the nine, but the nine will take the eight
And now we're all together, boys, make sure you play it straight.

The nine will take the eight, but the eight will take the seven
And now we're all together, boys, we're artful as the devil.

The eight will take the seven, but the seven will take the six
And now we're all together, boys, we're watching out for tricks.

The seven will take the six, but the six it takes the five
And now we're all together, boys, I'll skin yez all alive.

The six, it takes the five, but the five it takes the four
And now we're all together, boys, I'll put yez on the floor.

The five, it takes the four, but the four it takes the tray
And now we're all together, boys, we won't go home till day.

The four, it takes the tray, but the tray it takes the deuce
And now we're all together, boys, we'll never cry a truce.

The tray, it takes the deuce, but the ace it takes 'em all
And now we're all together, boys, we'll never go home at all.

Lanigan's Ball

Like the better known **Finnegan's Wake**, Lanigan's Ball tells of a social affair gone awry. In this instance, the function was a "hooley" (or house party) called to celebrate an inheritance. In *Ballads from the Pubs of Ireland*, Healy indicates that, while this party probably did occur, in reality the night was more cordial than described and that the ballad was designed as a type of "pleasant joke—a way of saying 'thanks.' " A good thing too or pity the poor piper!

The tune has a distinct second part courtesy of Jean Ritchie and George Pickow, who recorded it from the famed Cork singer Mrs. Elizabeth Cronin in the early 1950s.

Source: Text from Liam Milner; tune from recordings of Patrick Galvin and Elizabeth Cronin.

Recording: Christy Moore, *Christy Moore*, Polydor 2383 426.

In the town of Athy one Jeremy Lanigan
Battered away till he hadn't a pound.
His father he died and made him a man again,
Left him a farm and ten acres of ground.
He gave a grand ball to his friends and relations,
Who hadn't forgot him went sent to the wall.
If you'll only listen, I'll make your eyes glisten
At the row and the ruction at Lanigan's Ball.

Myself, to be sure, got free invitations
For all the nice girls and boys I might ask.
In less than a minute, both friends and relations
Were dancing as merry as bees round a cask.
Miss Julie McManus, the nice little milliner,
Tipped me a wink for to give her a call
And soon we arrived with Timothy Galligan,
Just in time for Lanigan's Ball.

213

There was lashings of punch and wine for the ladies,
Potatoes and cakes; there was bacon and tea.
There were the Nolans, Dolans, O'Gradys
Courting the girls and dancing away.
The songs they went round as plenty as water,
From "The Harp That Once Sounded in Tara's Old Hall,"
To "Sweet Nelly Gray" and "The Ratcatcher's Daughter,"
All singing together at Lanigan's Ball.

They were doing all kinds of nonsensical polkas
All round the room in a neat whirligig,
But Julie and I soon banished their nonsense
And tipped them a twist of the real Irish jig.
Mavourneen, how the girls got mad on me
And danced till you'd think the old ceiling would fall,
For I'd just spent a fortnight at Brooke's Academy,
Learning the steps for Lanigan's Ball.

The boys were all merry, the girls were all hearty,
Dancing away in couples and groups
Till an accident happened, young Terence McCarthy,
He put his right leg through Miss Flaherty's hoops.
This creature created and roared "Holy Murder!"
Called for her friends and gathered them all.
Ned Carmody swore that he'd go no further
Till he had satisfaction at Lanigan's Ball.

In the midst of the row Miss Kerrigan fainted,
Her cheeks at the same time as red as a rose.
Some of the ladies declared she was painted,
She took a small drop; too much, I suppose.
Her sweetheart, Ned Morgan, so powerful and able,
When he saw his fair colleen stretched out by the wall,
Tore the left leg from under the table
And smashed all the chinery at Lanigan's Ball.

Boys, oh boys, 'tis them there was ructions,
Myself got a lick from big Phelim McHugh,
But soon I replied to his kind introduction
And kicked up a terrible hullabaloo.
Old Casey the piper was near being strangled.
They squeezed up his pipes—bellows, chanters and all.
The girls in their ribbons, they all were entangled,
And that put an end to Lanigan's Ball!

Preab San Ól

Preab San Ól (Drinking with Spirit) is the work of another eighteenth-century Irish poet, Richard Barrett, a Co. Mayo schoolmaster. Like **An Bunnán Buí** (following), the song was composed in Gaelic, as evidenced not only by the title, but the distinctively Irish rhyming pattern.

Source: Learned from D. O'Sullivan, *Songs of the Irish*, and the singing of the Dubliners.

Recording: Luke Kelly and Ciaron Bourke, *The Dubliners in Session*, Hallmark SHM 652.

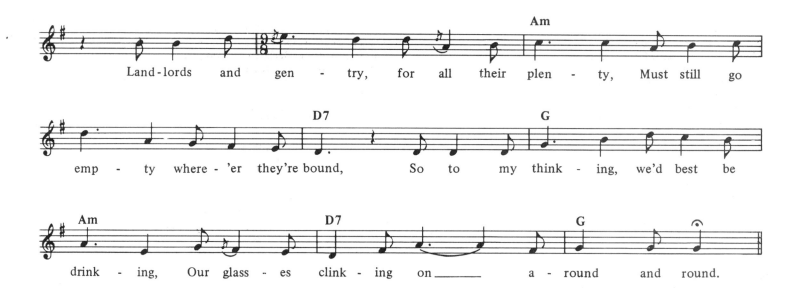

Land-lords and gen - try, for all their plen - ty, Must still go

emp - ty where - 'er they're bound, So to my think - ing, we'd best be

drink - ing, Our glass - es clink - ing on_____ a - round and round.

Why spend your leisure bereft of pleasure,
Amassing treasure; why scrimp and save?
Why look so canny at every penny,
You'll take no money down within your grave.
Landlords and gentry, for all their plenty,
Must still go empty where'er they're bound,
So, to my thinking, we'd best be drinking,
Our glasses clinking on around and round.

The huxter greedy will grind the needy,
Their straits unheeding, shouts, "Money down!"
His special vice is his fancy prices,
For a florin's value he'll charge a crown.
With hump for trammel, the scripture's camel
Missed the needle's eye and so came to ground.
Why pine for riches while still you've stiches
To hold your britches up another round.

The shipmen trading in Spain and Aden
Return well laden with corn and oil.
And from Gibraltar their course they'll alter
And steer for Malta and the Golden Horn.
With easy motion, they sail life's ocean
And ne'er a notion they'll soon run aground,
So, lads and lasses for another round.

King Solomon's glory, so famed in story,
Was far outshone by the lily's guise,
But hard winds harden both field and garden,
Pleading for pardon, the lily dies.
Life's but a bubble of toil and trouble,
A feathered arrow once shot, ne'er found.
It's nought but miming, so ends my rhyming
And still we've time in for another round.

An Bunnán Buí

Both this and the previous song convey a very Irish feeling towards drink—that it can only be enjoyed while one is alive. Donal O'Sullivan ascribes **An Bunnán Buí** to the eighteenth-century Co. Cavan poet Cathal Buí Mac Giolla Gunna, who composed the words after finding a bittern, dead from thirst, by the shore of a hard-frozen lake.

I got this song from my friend Johnny Beggan, a fine singer and mandolin player who's as well known for his exploits as for his musical performances. On the night he recorded **An Bunnán Buí** for me, he was recovering from a lamp post-to-Earth flight.

The title, by the way, translates as **The Yellow Bittern** and is pronounced ON BUN-NON BWEE.

Source: Verses 1, 3, and 4 and tune from Johnny Beggan; verse 2 from Mick Moloney.

Recordings: Tim Lyons, *The Green Linnet*, Trailer LER 3036. Joe Heaney, *Joe Heaney*, Philo 2004.

bones   are   thrown   on_   a

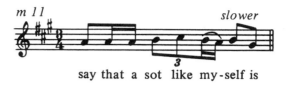

say that a sot like my-self is

fear   I might die   in_   the

An *bunnan buí*, that never broke out
On a drinking bout, might as well have drunk.
His bones are thrown on a naked stone
Where he lived all alone like a hermit monk.
An *bunnán buí*, I pity your plight,
Though they say that a sot like myself is cursed.
I was sober awhile, but I'll drink and be wise
For fear I might die in the end of thirst.

'Tis not for the common bird that I do mourn
For the blackbird, the corncrake or the crane,
But for the *bunnán buí* who is shy and apart
And who lives in the marsh and the lone bog drain.
If I had known that you were near your death,
While my breath held out, I would have run to you,
Till a splash from the lake of the son of the bird
Would have lifted your soul to a life anew.

My darling once told me to drink no more
Or my life would be o'er in a little short while.
I said it's the drink gives me health and strength
And lengthens my road by many a mile.
You can see how the bird of the long smooth neck
Will find his death from the thirst at last.
Oh son of my soul come fill up your cup
For you'll get no sup when your life is passed.

On a wintering island near Constantine's hall,
A bittern cries from a windless place.
And tells me that hither he cannot come,
Till Summer is here and the sunny days.
As he crosses the lake and wings o'er the sea,
A thought comes to me he may fail in his flight.
Oh the wine and the ale, they are drunk every drop,
But a dram won't cure our thirst this night.

Going Home with the Milk in the Morning

Certainly not a traditional song, more likely a once popular music hall ditty, I found **Going Home with the Milk in the Morning** on a broadside. The inscription on that pennysheet gives an interesting insight into earlier music marketing:

Printed by T. King, Birmingham, and sold by Mr. Green, at his Music Stall, near the Turnpike, City-road, and at 27 Featherstone-street, City-road, where an extensive collection of old and new songs, harp and violin strings, fancy stationery, etc. may be had. Tamborines, bows, screws, bridges, rosin, music paper. Fancy walking sticks. Written music for the violin, flute, accordian, cornopeon.

Source: Text adapted from a King broadsheet; tune adapted from the common *Sweet Betsy from Pike* melody.

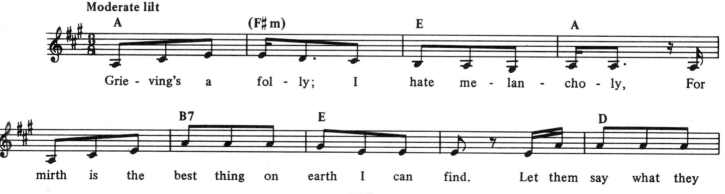

Moderate lilt

A   (F♯m)   E   A

Grie - ving's   a   fol - ly;   I   hate   me - lan - cho - ly,   For

              B7   E   D

mirth   is   the   best   thing   on   earth   I   can   find.   Let   them   say   what   they

will, still my gob-let I'll fill, And water as drink will be

scorn-ing. The headache and pains I all do de-

fy. It is bet-ter, be-lieve me, to laugh than to

cry. "Stop out on the spree," that's the mot-to for

me, And come home with the milk in the mor-ning.

m 3
hate me lan-

m 6
best thing on

m 27
mot-to for

Grieving's a folly; I hate melancholy,
For mirth is the best thing on earth I can find.
Let them say what they will, still my goblet I'll fill,
And water as drink will be scorning.
The headache and pains I all do defy.
It is better, believe me, to laugh than to cry.
"Stop out on the spree," that's the motto for me,
And come home with the milk in the morning.

Some people say, "From the glass keep away."
But they're not to be thought of, the ignorant elves.
I like to go out and to wander about
And stop out with my friends till the dawning.
Sometimes I get more than my head can well bear
With a kind friend, enjoyment to share.
I don't care a pin for the rows I get in
But reel home with the milk in the morning.

To see the sun rising is a sight most surprising,
As it's tipping with gold every red chimney top
Just like the fair cheek of the maiden we seek
And the light of your eyes on it dawning.
To see the small sparrows in quiet paths meet,
Hopping hither and thither their breakfasts in beak,
It's a beautiful sight which your eyes must delight—
To come home with the milk in the morning.

But I hope you don't think I am given to drink,
For that on my part a folly would be.
Mind my example and on it don't trample
But take from my moral a warning—
There's no harm in your grog with a beer with a friend,
But shun dissipation and look to the end.
For would be sad to tell that a black workhouse shell
Took you home with the milk in the morning.

Fare Ye Weel Whiskey

Scots collector Gavin Greig thought enough of this one's moralizing to doubt "any appeal from the pulpit would have any more affect...."

Source: Text from G. Greig, *Folk Songs of the North-East*; tune learned from the singing of Dick Gaughan.

Recording: Dick Gaughan, *The Boys of the Lough*, Trailer LER 2086.

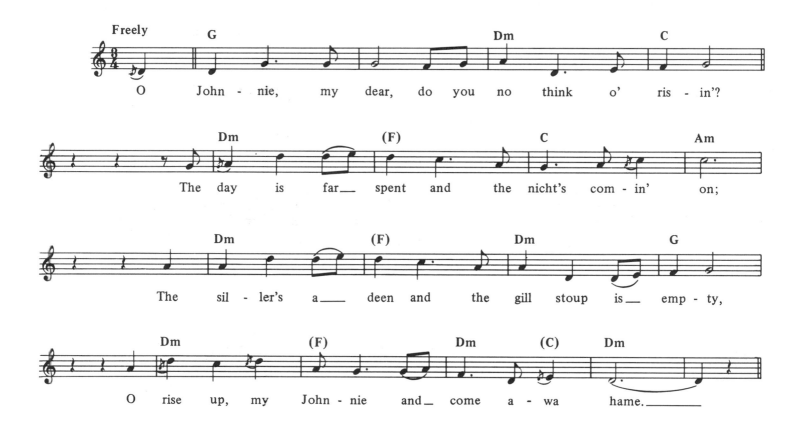

O Johnnie, my dear, do you no think o' risin'?
The day is far spent and the nicht's comin'on;
The siller's a deen and the gill stoup is empty,
O rise up, my Johnnie and come awa hame.

Wha's that at the door that is speaking sae canty?
'Tis the voice o' my wee wifie Maggie by name;
Come in my dear lassie and sit doon beside me,
"O rise up, my Johnnie and come awa hame."

The bairnies at home, they're a roarin' and greetin',
Nae meal in the barrel to fill their wee wame,
While ye sit here drinkin' ye leave us lamentin';
O rise up, my Johnnie and come awa hame.

"O Johnnie my dear, when we were first acquanited,
Nae ale house nor tavern e'er ran in our minds,
But we spent the lang day mang the sweet scented roses
And ne'er took a thought upon gaun awa hame."

"O weel do I mind on the time that ye speak o';
Those days are awa and will ne'er come again;
But as for the present we will try for to mend it;
Sae gie's yer hand Maggie and I'll come awa hame."

Then Johnnie got up and he banged the door open;
Says, "Woe to the day to this tavern I came;
And fare ye weel whiskey that mak's me aye tipsy;
Sae gie's yer hand Maggie and come awa hame."

Noo Johnnie gaes oot on a fine simmer's evenjng
Wi' his wife and his bairnies fu' trig and fu' bien;
But a short time before in rags they were rinnin',
While Johnnie sat drinkin' in the ale-hoose at e'en.

When Fortune Turns Her Wheel

This last song in the book is as close to my favorite as any. The words are from *Folk Songs of the North-East*, where Greig notes: "This is a popular ditty, having considerable circulation as a broadside. The tune which I have got for it seems to have affinity with the tune to which *The Plains of Waterloo* is sung."

Source: Text from G. Greig, *Folk Songs of the North-East*; tune from the singing of Lou Killen (collected from Alan Rogerson in 1958 by Killen and Brian Ballinger).

Recording: Lou Killen, *Old Songs, Old Friends,* Front Hall FHR-012.

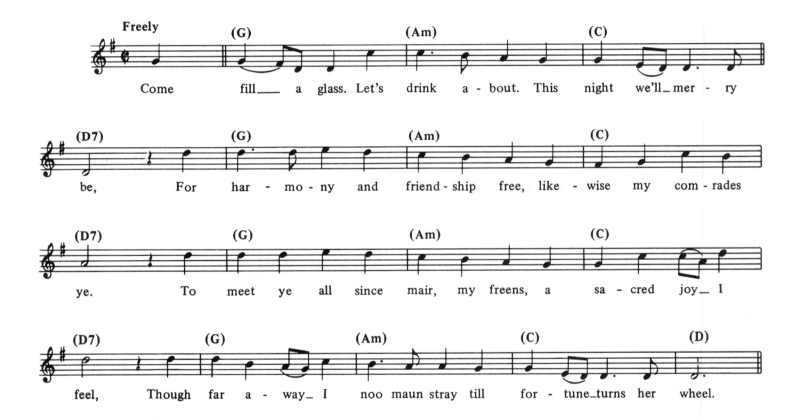

Come fill a glass. Let's drink about. This night we'll merry be,
For harmony and friendship free, likewise my comrades ye.
To meet ye all since mair, my freens, a sacred joy I feel,
Though far away I noo maun stray till fortune turns her wheel.

'Tis not vain clothes nor bold, he says, that's the estimate of man;
For when we meet a man in straits, we shake a friendly hand;
With them we'll sit, with them we'll drink, and to them our minds reveal,
And friends we'll be whatever way Blind Fortune turns her wheel.

But, oh, I loved a bonnie lass, and her I'll justly blame;
For when hard fortune frowned on me, she denied she knew my name;
But falsehood by remorse is paid, and to her I'll never kneel,
I'll sweethearts find baith fair and kind when Fortune turns her wheel.

It's mony the time my heart's been sair and like to brak' in twa;
Mony's the time my feet's been cauld, comin' in frae the frost and snaw;
Wi' nae one to pity me, not yet to wish me weel;
But maybe I'll repay them back when Fortune turns her wheel.

Some of my once pretendin' freen, if freens I may them call,
Proved false and turned their backs on me, when mine was at the wall.
But in this glass I'll let it pass, I'm sure I wish them weel,
If my hard fate on them await, may Fortune turn her wheel.

Adieu, ye hills of Caledon, likewise sweet Avondale,
For friendship binds the strongest ties, love tells the softest tale.
Adieu, my freens and comrades here, I ken ye wish me weel;
And I maybe yet can pay my debt, when Fortune turns her wheel.

Bibliography

This is a short list of books, fifty in all. They are the works of ministers, musicians, factory workers, journalists, innkeepers, tax men, schoolteachers, and policemen, to name a few, and they span a hundred and forty years or so. There's quite a variety here. Included is the grand ballad scholarship of Professors Child and Bronson, reprints from the country newspaper columns of Henry and Greig and the sweeping volume of mid-twentieth century field collection edited by Peter Kennedy. Some focus on specific areas—geographic, occupational or social in nature; some are quite general; one is a close look at a single man.

In the hope that, once you've read and used this book, you'll try to acquire some of these volumes. I've cited the most recent printings rather than the originals. I hope that you'll use their bibliographies in turn. There are many more fine books than these.

Baring-Gould, Sabine. *Folk Songs of the West Country.* London: Keith Prowse, 1974.
Songs from the Baring-Gould (1834-1924) collection, of West-of-England folksongs, edited by Gordon Hitchcock.

Broadwood, Lucy. *English Traditional Songs and Carols.* Totowa, N. J.: Rowman and Littlefield, 1974.
Reprint of a fine turn-of-the-century collection of songs mainly from the South of England. Notes.

Broadwood, Lucy, and Maitland, J. A. F. *English Country Songs.* London: Cramer, 1893.
Folk songs from all parts of England. 92 songs.

Bronson, Bertrand. *The Traditional Tunes of the Child Ballads,* Vols. 1-4. Princeton, N.J.: Princeton University, 1959-1972.
The collection of ballad texts and tunes. Contains North American as well as British and Irish versions.

Bronson, Bertrand. *The Singing Tradition of Child's Popular Ballads.* Princeton, N.J.: Princeton University, 1976.
Affordable abridgement of Bronson's major collection of ballad tunes and texts.

Bruce, J. Collingwood, and Stokoe, John. *Northumbriam Minstrelsey.* Hatboro, Pennsylvania: Folklore Associates, 1965.
Songs and small-pipe tunes.

Buchan, Norman, and Hall, Peter. *The Scottish Folksinger.* London: Collins, 1973.
118 traditional and modern songs drawn, as in this book, from varied sources.

Campbell, J. L., and Collinson, Francis. *Hebridean Folksongs.* London: Oxford University, 1969.
Collection of Gaelic waulking songs (songs sung during the processing of home-made cloth) from the Outer Hebrides.

Chappell, William. *Popular Music of the Olden Time.* New York: Dover, 1965.
Variety of English non-folk and folk songs, some reprinted from the earliest collections.

Child, Francis James. *The English and Scottish Popular Ballads,* 5 vols., New York: Dover, 1965.
Exhaustive collection of 1882-1894, mostly from printed sources. Rich in background and scholarship relating these ballads to songs and tales of Europe. Virtually no tunes (Volume 5). See also Bronson.

Copper, Bob. *A Song for Every Season.* St. Albans, Hertfordshire: Padadin, 1975.
Songs of the Copper family of Sussex, prefaced by recollections of English village life.

Dallas, Karl. *The Cruel Wars.* London: Wolfe, 1972.
Dallas, Karl. *100 Songs of Toil.* London: Wolfe, 1974.
Occupational folksongs, mainly industrial.

Davison, Peter. *The British Music Hall.* New York: Oak Publications, 1971.
Songs of (and information about) the popular music institution which influenced and was influenced by traditional song.

Dearmer, Percy; Williams, Ralph Vaughan; Shaw, Martin. *The Oxford Book of Carols.* London: Oxford University, 1928.
Includes quite a few traditional songs.

Galvin, Patrick. *Irish Songs of Resistance.* London: Oak Publications, 1962.
Folk and national songs with history. Quite good.

Greig, Gavin. *Folk-Song in Buchan and Folk-Song of the North-East.* Hatboro, Pennsylvania: Folklore Associates, 1963.

Reprints from *Transactions of the Buchan Field Club* (1906-1907 and articles contributed to the "Buchan Observer" (1907-1911). Words only.

Greig, Gavin, and Keith, Alexander. *Last Leaves of Traditional Ballads and Ballad Airs.* Aberdeen: The Buchan Club, 1925.
Great ballad collection.

Hamer, Fred. *Garners Gay.* London: E. F. D. S. Publications, 1967.
50 folksongs, mainly from Bedfordshire.

Healy, James N. *Ballads from the Pubs of Ireland.* Cork: Mercier, 1965.
Paperback collection of 64 Irish drinking songs with a nice, chatty text.

Healy, James N. *Irish Ballads and Songs of the Sea.* Cork: Mercier, 1967.
83 songs.

Hugill, Stan. *Shanties from the Seven Seas.* London: Routledge and Kegan Paul, 1961.
An excellent and long book on sailors' songs from a former seaman and eternal character. Often gives many variants.

Hugill, Stan. *Shanties and Sailors' Songs.* New York: Praeger, 1969.
Background and songs. Fine and concise.

Joyce, P. Weston. *Old Irish Folk Music and Songs.* Dublin: University Press, 1909.
Classic early collection of Irish songs.

Kennedy, Peter. *Folksongs of Britain and Ireland.* New York: Schirmer Books, 1975.
360 songs (many in national languages with translations) from traditional sources. By far the broadest collection.

Kidson, Frank. *Traditional Tunes.* Wakefield, Yorkshire: S. R. Publishers, 1970.
Fine late 19th-century collection (83 titles, 111 total versions) from North-East England.

MacColl, Ewan. *Folk Songs and Ballads of Scotland.* New York: Oak Publications, 1965.
Handy book of many fine Scots songs.

MacColl, Ewan, and Seeger, Peggy. *Travellers' Songs from England and Scotland.* London: Routledge and Kegan Paul, 1977.
Gypsy and tinker songs collected by MacColl and Seeger.

Morton, Robin. *Folksongs Sung in Ulster.* Cork: Mercier, 1970.
50 songs, with background, collected by Robin Morton from The Boys of the Lough.

Morton, Robin. *Come Day, Go Day, God Send Sunday.* London: Routledge and Kegan Paul, 1973.
Songs and story of John Maguire, Co. Fermanagh farmer.

Moulden, John. *Songs of the People.* Belfast: Blackstaff, 1979.
Part one of a projected series, reprinting songs collected by Sam Henry and contributed by him to the Ulster newspaper "Northern Constitution" (1923-1939). A totally fine work.

O'Boyle, Sean. *The Irish Song Tradition.* Dublin: Gilbert Dalton, 1977.
Songs with music plus invaluable discussion of Irish folksong style.

O Lochlainn, Colm. *Irish Street Ballads.* New York: Corinth, 1960.
A great general collection of English language Irish folksongs, well known and used by many singers. Recently republished by Pan in England.

O Lochlainn, Colm. *More Irish Street Ballads.* London: Pan, 1978.
Another 100 songs (plus appendix giving additional words). Well selected and used.

Ord, John. *Bothy Songs and Ballads.* Edinburgh: John Donald, no date.
Classic collection of Scots farm laborers' songs. Newly reprinted. Many texts, few tunes.

O'Shaughnessy, Patrick. *Yellowbelly Ballads.* Lincoln: Lincolnshire and Humberside Arts, 1975.
30 Lincolnshire folksongs, mainly from the collection of Percy Grainger.

O'Sullivan, Donal Joseph. *Songs of the Irish.* New York: Crown Publishers, 1960.
An anthology of Irish language folksongs with translations.

Palmer, Roy. *Songs of the Midlands.* Wakefield: E. P. Publishing, 1972.
Newly collected songs (including some from the fine Birmingham singer Cecilia Costello) together with some pieces from early 20th century collectors. Notes.

Palmer, Roy. *A Touch On the Times.* Hammondsworth: Penguin, 1974.
Social history and songs, 1770 to 1914.

Polwarth, Gwen, and Polwarth, Mary. *Folk Songs from the North.* Newcastle: Frank Graham, 1970.
. . . of England, plus a number of instrumental tunes.

Purslow, Frank. *Marrowbones.* London: E. F. D. S. Publications, 1965.
A fine, inexpensive collection of mainly Hampshire and Dorset folksongs culled from the manuscripts of the Hammond brothers and George Gardiner, occasionally filled in from other sources. Originals at Cecil Sharp House, London. See also *The Wanton Seed, The Constant Lovers,* and *The Foggy Dew.*

Ranson, Joseph. *Songs of the Wexford Coast.* Enniscorthy: Redmond, 1948.
Sea songs from Southeastern Ireland. Interesting book.

Raven, Jon. *Victoria's Inferno.* Wolverhampton: Broadside, 1978.
British industrial songs from the 18th and 19th centuries. Includes background.

Robertson, T. A. *Da Sangs At A'll Sing Ta Dee.* Shetland Islands: Shetland Folk Society, 1973.
"National" and traditional songs of this Norse-Scots area.

Sedley, Stephen. *The Seeds of Love.* London: Essex Music, 1967.
Nice book of very singable songs. Love, in one meaning or another, is the central theme.

Sharp, Cecil. *Cecil Sharp's Collection of English Folk Songs,* 2 Vols. London: Oxford University Press, 1974.
Extensive and expensive. A great collection.

Sharp, Cecil. *The Crystal Spring,* 2 Vols. London: Oxford University Press, 1975.
Two fairly inexpensive spiral bound books of 72 songs each

collected in the early 20th century. Quite varied, but with only collection data notes.

Stubbs, Ken. *The Life of a Man*. London; E. F. D. S. Publications, 1970.
50 songs collected in the counties surrounding London. Background on informants.

Vaughan Williams, Ralph, and Lloyd, A. L. *The Penguin Book of English Folk Songs*. Hammondsworth, Middlesex: Penguin, 1959.
Selections from the "Journal of the English Folk Dance and Song Society," with notes on songs.

Williams, Alfred. *Folk-Songs of the Upper Thames*. London: Duckworth, 1923.
Unfortunately, no tunes. Over 300 song texts.

ABOUT DAN MILNER AND PAUL KAPLAN

Dan Milner was born in Birmingham, England of mixed Irish and British parentage. He was raised partly there and partly in Ireland, Canada, and America, emigrating about the Cunard liner *Aquatania,* sister ship to the famed *Lusitania.* In New York he has co-founded two ethnic cultural organizations, formed three music groups: The Flying Cloud, The Derby Ram, and The New York Packet, and has presented hundreds of concerts at the Eagle Tavern, perhaps the permier traditional music venue in the United States.

He says of himself and his relationship with folk music, "I've become a complicated man, I suppose, though I am by nature both basic and direct. The complexity comes from the sort of restlessness that causes a person to walk to the tip of the next hill and from the experience that a different view brings. I'm an emotional man too—Kerry fire and English sentimentality! For me, the beauty of folk song comes from its odd coupling of great musical sophistication and true simplicity, and its natural use of strong human emotion, for the music of the people chronicles the heights and depths of common man and woman."

Dan's other interests are geography, cooking, nature, photography, and lately, the mandolin. In 1979 and 1980 he was first prize winner for traditional singing at the New York Fleadh Cheoil.

Paul Kaplan is the composer of finely crafted songs; first and foremost, that is what he does. His love for folk music stems from early family involvement in the great American labor-political movement and his own interest in the folk revival of the 1960s. Although one of New York's busiest guitar teachers, Paul has still found time to earn a degree in music theory, prodice five Phil Ochs albums for Folkways using extant tapes of the late polemicist/balladeer, perform regularly with Dan Milner and piper Larry Cole in The Derby Ram, and pursue an independent contemporary song career.

A Philadelphian by both birth and nature, Paul has a number of other interests which include baseball, the Phillies, and Pete Rose. He is currently recording his first album of original songs.

223